Buddhism and Displacement

This book analyzes Buddhist perspectives on the human experience of displacement and on the ethics of resettlement, humanitarian aid, and protection for displaced communities. Bringing to light both ancient and modern insights from Buddhist traditions across cultures, *Buddhism and Displacement* provides a robust account of Buddhism's contributions to an urgent, global humanitarian challenge.

As a religion that begins with an act of taking refuge, Buddhism has much to offer our contemporary displacement crisis: not only insights into the psychological and existential dimensions of displacement, but also compelling visions of human security and political ethics. This book offers a critical perspective on a wide range of sources in order to illuminate humanitarian ideals that are distinctively Buddhist, yet relevant for non-Buddhist social and political actors. *Buddhism and Displacement* integrates Buddhist scriptural interpretation, ethnographic interviews, ethical argumentation, and legal analysis to build a conceptual as well as practical guide to understanding displacement—rethinking Buddhism in the process.

Buddhism and Displacement is well suited for undergraduate and graduate students in Buddhist studies, humanitarian studies, anthropology, ethics, and political science. Audiences who will benefit from this book's practical recommendations include international aid workers, policymakers, community leaders, and government leaders in whose hands the well-being of today's displaced people rests.

Christina A. Kilby, Ph.D., is Associate Professor of Religion and Executive Director of the Center for International Stabilization and Recovery at James Madison University.

Buddhism and Displacement

An Analysis at the Intersection of Religion, Humanitarianism, and Law

Christina A. Kilby

Routledge
Taylor & Francis Group
LONDON AND NEW YORK

First published 2027
by Routledge
4 Park Square, Milton Park, Abingdon, Oxon OX14 4RN

and by Routledge
605 Third Avenue, New York, NY 10158

Routledge is an imprint of the Taylor & Francis Group, an informa business

British Library Cataloguing-in-Publication Data
A catalogue record for this book is available from the British Library

Library of Congress Cataloging-in-Publication Data
Names: Kilby, Christina A. author
Title: Buddhism and displacement : an analysis at the intersection of religion, humanitarianism, and law / Christina A. Kilby.
Description: New York : Routledge, 2026. |
Includes bibliographical references and index.
Identifiers: LCCN 2026016908 (print) | LCCN 2026016909 (ebook) |
ISBN 9781032330877 hardback | ISBN 9781032330907 paperback |
ISBN 9781003318149 ebook
Subjects: LCSH: Human ecology–Religious aspects–Buddhism |
Humanitarian intervention–Moral and ethical aspects |
Emigration and immigration–Religious aspects–Buddhism | Spiritual life–Buddhism
Classification: LCC BQ4570.E23 K55 2026 (print) |
LCC BQ4570.E23 (ebook) | DDC 294.3/377–dc23/eng/20260702
LC record available at https://lccn.loc.gov/2026016908
LC ebook record available at https://lccn.loc.gov/2026016909

ISBN: 9781032330877 (hbk)
ISBN: 9781032330907 (pbk)
ISBN: 9781003318149 (ebk)

DOI: 10.4324/9781003318149

Typeset in Sabon
by Newgen Publishing UK

To my family, with gratitude

Contents

Foreword

This work is indebted to the wisdom and generosity of many people, some of whom I have been fortunate enough to meet.

The International Committee of the Red Cross project on Religion and Humanitarian Principles introduced me to international humanitarian law (IHL) and to how Buddhist traditions can inform contemporary humanitarian action. To Andrew Bartles-Smith and his former team at the International Committee of the Red Cross (ICRC) Global Affairs regional office in Bangkok, I will always admire your visionary leadership. Our conferences on the interface between Buddhism and IHL showed me what is possible when military, religious, humanitarian, and civic actors share dialogue on critical humanitarian issues. Thanks especially to Venerable Dr. Mahinda Deegalle, Dr. Diane Denis, and Dr. Stefania Travagnin as well as our Internal Displacement Working Group for their ongoing collaboration and hospitality. Working with the ICRC changed the trajectory of my academic career and made this book possible.

The Buddhist Critical-Constructive Working Group steering committee at the American Academy of Religion first encouraged my work on Buddhism and displacement and offered me a platform to share my burgeoning research in this area, for which I remain grateful.

For their insights into the themes I grapple with in this book, my special thanks go to Andrew Bartles-Smith, Dr. Elizabeth Harris, and the Venerable Dr. Pinnawala Sangasumana. My many teachers and colleagues at Davidson College, Harvard Divinity School, the University of Virginia, Rangjung Yeshé Institute, and Qinghai Nationalities University all helped form the questions and humanistic values that I bring to my work. James Madison University's College of Arts and Letters generously supported me with the Edna T. Shaeffer Humanist Award in 2022 to advance this manuscript. My colleagues at the Center for International Stabilization and Recovery, as well as my students, inspire me to embody the ethical ideals I study and motivate me to serve.

Finally, to all those in the Tibetan community who have shown me hospitality and grace over these twenty years: your stories first drew me to Buddhism and to refugee studies. Thank you.

Acronyms

ICRC	International Committee of the Red Cross
IHL	International Humanitarian Law
IHRL	International Human Rights Law
IRL	International Refugee Law
PTSD	post-traumatic stress disorder
UN	United Nations
UNHCR	United Nations High Commissioner for Refugees
USAID	United States Agency for International Development

1 Introduction

"The world is without shelter, without protector."

(Raṭṭhapālasutta[1])

The Contemporary Displacement Landscape

Displacement, although an age-old part of human experience, has become a defining feature of our twenty-first-century world. By May 2022, for the first time on record there were more than 100 million displaced people, constituting over one percent of the global population; by 2025, more than 1 in 67 people globally were displaced.[2] Over three-quarters of the world's displaced people are in countries facing food crises, and forty percent of the world's displaced are children—an increasing number of them unaccompanied.[3] These millions are fleeing their homes due to imminent threats to their lives or their livelihoods, propelled by causes that range from violent conflict or persecution to natural disasters, ecological degradation, and state development projects. Although individual reasons for flight vary, and often overlap or intersect, the underlying cause of displacement is always the same: insecurity. As poet Warsan Shire writes, "no one leaves home unless/ home is the mouth of a shark [...] you have to understand, / that no one puts their children in a boat/ unless the water is safer than the land."[4]

Flight is not only a response to insecurity at home, but also a cause for a further cascade of insecurities. Inadequate food and shelter, family separation, exploitation by strangers, vulnerability to sexual violence, loss of property, and inability to access personal legal documents and essential government services are hardships that displaced people frequently face on the road. The prevalence of psychological trauma among displaced populations has been well documented, as have the long-term economic consequences of displacement for communities, such as loss of the annual harvest and loss of education. Because only a small fraction of displaced people each year are safely returned to their homes or permanently resettled, the insecurities of displacement may loom for a lifetime or even for generations. Preventing and reducing displacement, as well as providing protection and durable solutions

DOI: 10.4324/9781003318149-1

for displaced people and their host communities, are vital for the sake of human security, state security, and global security.

Why Religion?

Why should religion be part of the contemporary conversation on displacement, which is a humanitarian and political problem rather than a religious one? In some cases, religious identity plays a visible (though never isolated) role in the social divisions that either drive displacement or that emerge in its aftermath. In other cases, when religious identity does not appear to be a major factor in a displacement situation, I argue that religion still matters. Displacement can be understood as a "cosmology episode," an experience where a person's foundational understanding of the world or of themselves is fractured and needs to be mended. Organizational scientist Karl Weick coined the term "cosmology episode" to describe the debilitating loss of meaning that can occur when events shatter our assumptions about the orderliness of the universe and our place in it. According to Weick,

> Cosmology is the ultimate macro perspective, directed at issues of time, space, change, and contingency as they relate to the origin and structure of the universe. Integrations of these issues, however, are not just the handiwork of philosophers. Others also must make their peace with these issues, as reflected in what they take for granted. People [...] act as if events cohere in time and space and that change unfolds in an orderly manner. These everyday cosmologies are subject to disruption. And when they are severely disrupted, I call this a cosmology episode [...]. A cosmology episode occurs when people suddenly and deeply feel that the universe is no longer a rational, orderly system.[5]

Displacement can rupture the anchor in space and time that a person or a community has cultivated over months or years of storytelling, meaning making, and social cohesion. Displacement is existentially as well as geographically disorienting. The experience requires new forms of meaning, new autobiographical narratives, new skills and social roles, new visions of the future, and new beliefs about destiny, redemption, or justice. Religion, broadly defined, is the realm of human life where we can best assign the work of cosmological repair; wherever displaced people or their hosts are undertaking various practices of cosmological repair, I argue that religion is at work.

Finally, religion has for much of the twentieth century been somewhat marginalized by secular humanitarian organizations, both as a lasting effect of the "Westphalian synthesis" and in an effort to transcend the colonial legacy of Christianity.[6] Despite the strong Protestant commitments of its founders, the International Committee of the Red Cross (ICRC) has minimized the role of religion in its impact over the years. An ICRC historian argues:

> While Christian beliefs played a role in triggering and inspiring the inception of the ICRC, the Red Cross and Red Crescent Movement, and the Geneva Conventions, their actual realization was nevertheless secular and non-denominational. The 1864 Geneva Convention enshrined the protection of all wounded and medical personnel, no matter their affiliation, and the concepts of impartiality and neutrality continue to define the Movement, and it may not take sides in hostilities at any time.[7]

Similarly, the English text of the 1945 *Charter of the United Nations* only mentions "religion" as a protected characteristic ("for all without distinction as to race, sex, language, or religion"), but does not acknowledge religious traditions as sources of humanitarian ethics or religious groups as partners for achieving humanitarian goals.[8] Yet attempts to ignore religion in favor of a secular humanitarian regime did not make religion or its colonial legacies disappear, and the power of religious actors to effect sociopolitical change has grown only more apparent in the wake of terrorist attacks by religious extremists, most notably the Al Qaeda attacks of September 11, 2001.

In response, international organizations like the United Nations (UN) and the ICRC began to engage more directly with religious groups in order to accomplish their humanitarian goals. In 2011–2012, the Office of the UN High Commissioner for Human Rights led a series of expert workshops on prohibitions against the incitement of "racial and religious hatred," culminating in the signing of the *Rabat Plan of Action* in Morocco in 2012. The *Rabat Plan of Action* was formed "with a view to creating and strengthening a culture of peace, tolerance and mutual respect among individuals, public officials and members of the judiciary, as well as rendering media organizations and religious/community leaders more ethically aware and socially responsible"; five years later, the Office of the UN High Commissioner for Human Rights took a significant next step in religious engagement when it launched its "Faith for Rights" initiative with the adoption of the *Beirut Declaration* and eighteen commitments to human rights.[9]

The ICRC, which had long distanced itself from religion, now calls faith-based organizations and religious leaders "essential partners in humanitarian action":[10]

> The principles of IHL are based on humanitarian principles that are ultimately rooted in the world's religious traditions, and the role of religious leaders and institutions in promoting common humanitarian principles is therefore crucial. In times of war and crisis, religious networks play a vital role in carrying out and facilitating humanitarian action, and it is imperative that humanitarian actors strengthen their religious and cultural literacy in order to effectively engage and cooperate with them, developing the mutual trust required to sustain humanitarian action.[11]

In 2014 and again in 2020, ICRC President Peter Maurer met with Pope Francis, and in 2015, the ICRC adviser for global affairs Ronald Ofteringer cited not only the long-standing traditions of ethics and justice developed through religion, but also the effectiveness of religious networks and the trust that many communities place in the guidance of their religious leaders, as reasons why the ICRC should engage in collaboration with religious groups.[12]

The ICRC's more concerted re-engagement with religious circles, documented on the ICRC blog *Religion and Humanitarian Principles*,[13] began with Islam: the ICRC has "a long-standing academic dialogue with Muslim scholars in Iran. It has also taken part in conferences and roundtables on Sharia and IHL in Pakistan, Africa and across the Middle East."[14] More than 100 articles, translations, and podcasts now populate the "Islamic Circles" tab on the ICRC's *Religion and Humanitarian Principles* website. Similar engagements gradually followed with Jewish, Christian, Hindu, and indigenous traditions across a variety of national contexts.

As of 2019, the ICRC extended its work into Buddhist circles. At an international conference in Dambulla, Sri Lanka, Andrew Bartles-Smith (the then Regional Manager for Humanitarian Affairs, Asia) convened a cohort of Buddhist monks and nuns, Buddhist Studies academics, international humanitarian law (IHL) legal advisers, and military and government officials to debate the implications of Buddhist texts, teachings, and traditions for IHL and *vice versa*. A selection of conference papers was published as a special double-issue of *Contemporary Buddhism* in 2021,[15] which was republished in 2023 as an edited volume entitled *Buddhism and International Humanitarian Law*.[16] In 2022, a second conference in Chiang Mai, Thailand expanded the network of participants involved in the project, and at this time of writing, the number of publications and posts on the "Buddhist Circles" tab of the *Religion and Humanitarian Principles* site has grown to sixty. My personal involvement with these two conferences and the ongoing publication efforts they catalyzed have inspired my commitment to serving the humanitarian sector with my academic research. The people I met, from generals to monastics, from traditionalists to progressives, from many countries in Asia as well as Europe and the UK, have deeply shaped my perspectives on Buddhism and my intention to write this book.

Aims, Scope, and Audiences of this Book

The aim of this book is to analyze resources from Buddhist traditions for understanding and addressing human displacement. *Buddhism and Displacement* integrates scriptural interpretation, ethnography, ethical argumentation, and legal analysis to provide a robust account of Buddhism's contributions to an enduring global humanitarian challenge. As a religion that begins with an act of taking refuge, Buddhism has much to offer our contemporary displacement regime: not only insights into the psychological, ethical, and political dimensions of the sufferings that accompany displacement, but also compelling visions of human security and state responsibility. This book offers a critical perspective on a wide range of sources, both textual and ethnographic, in order to illuminate humanitarian ideals that are distinctively Buddhist, yet relevant for non-Buddhist academic, religious, social, and political actors who influence the discourse and practice around displacement today.

Addressing a Critical Gap in Religious Studies

In this book, I seek to fill a critical research gap in the academic field of religious studies. Scholarship on religion and displacement—still a relatively new area of study, and centered in the Anglosphere—focuses largely on Christianity and Islam, with Buddhism almost absent from the literature. For example, in *Refugees and Religion: Ethnographic Studies of Global Trajectories* (2021),[17] only one of thirteen chapters addresses Buddhism[18]; in *The Refugee Crisis and Religion* (2017),[19] none of the sixteen chapters addresses Buddhism (neither "Buddhism" nor "Buddhist" even appears in the index); in the hefty two-volume collection *Migration and Religion* (2016),[20] only one of sixty-six chapters addresses Buddhism;[21] and in *Building Noah's Ark for Migrants, Refugees, and Religious Communities* (2015),[22] only two of the sixteen chapters address Buddhism.[23]

The disproportionate emphasis on Christianity and Islam in the English-language scholarship directly reflects concerns about an Islamic-western "clash of civilizations"[24] as well as scholarly responses to the Islamophobia that has become more visible in the west since the 9/11 terrorist attacks. The scholarship has also disproportionately focused on global south-to-north migration trajectories, even though the majority of contemporary migration occurs on south-to-south trajectories. Moreover, Buddhist immigrants to western countries have often been viewed as "model minorities" as they assimilate in ways that pose less existential unease for their host societies.[25] For these various reasons, the societies producing Anglophone scholarship have not been as anxious about Buddhist immigrants and refugees as they have been about Muslim immigrants and refugees, which plays a significant role in academic production.

Despite their underrepresentation in scholarship on religion and displacement, Buddhist-majority groups have figured prominently among displaced peoples in the modern era.[26] Nearly 172,000 Koreans were deported to Central Asia under Stalin and Molotov in 1937; 120,000 Japanese Americans were forcibly displaced and interned in the United States during World War II; 150,000 Tibetan refugees fled the People's Liberation Army after 1959; and more than one million refugees fled Southeast Asia after 1975 (two million more in the following decades). Large proportions of these displaced populations practiced Buddhist traditions.

The two most famous Buddhist teachers in modern history—teachers who globalized Buddhism like no one before them—were refugees.[27] The fourteenth Dalai Lama of Tibet, Tenzin Gyatso (bstan 'dzin rgya mtsho, 1935–) and the Venerable Thich Nhat Hanh of Vietnam (1926–2022) both fled their homelands in the mid-twentieth century due to violent conflict. For both, returning to their homelands was either impossible or dangerous for most of their lives. The Dalai Lama took refuge in India in 1959 and Ven. Thich Nhat Hanh lived primarily in France after his 1966 exile; in 2018, he returned to Vietnam to live out his final years. These two teachers' presentations of Buddhism to the world are infused with their experiences of displacement. This is in part why Ven. Thich Nhat Hanh composed works of calligraphy that read "I have arrived, I am home" and "at home in the present moment." For these teachers, the Buddhist teachings paved the way to a spiritual home, security, and refuge in a world that is unstable. Their experiences as refugees have also empowered the cross-cultural reach of Buddhism as they have endeavored to open the dharma to new audiences in their new homelands. They have contributed just as much to Buddhism's emplacement in the west as to Buddhism's universalizing or "placeless" appeal.

While the fourteenth Dalai Lama and Ven. Thich Nhat Hanh have played outsized roles in Buddhism's refugee presence, many other Buddhist refugee leaders and activists across the globe continue to work for healing, recognition, and progress for their communities, even several generations after displacement. This book addresses some of these Buddhists' strategies for making sense of their displacement and remaking their lives; where this book inevitably falls short, an open invitation awaits for more robust research in the future.

Buddhist-majority societies have also been sites of displacement. Recall the flight of more than 700,000 Rohingya people from Myanmar since 2017; the displacement of more than 300,000 (largely non-Buddhist) civilians during the Sri Lankan civil war of 1983–2009; and the expulsion of almost 100,000 Lhotsampa people from Bhutan since the late 1980s.[28] Just like people of other religions, Buddhists have struggled to reconcile treasured notions of identity, sovereignty, and security with the ethical obligations and humanitarian principles that are central to their tradition. Buddhist communities and governments have grappled with significant decisions about whom to include and exclude, what kind of support to offer displaced people living in limbo, and for how long.

There are also reasons for Buddhism's absence from the scholarship on religion and displacement that are related to Buddhism itself as a tradition. As a religion that prizes non-attachment, reverences a monastic ideal of homelessness, and understands cosmic time in cycles of inevitable decline, Buddhism may appear to have nothing significant to say about the undeniably this-worldly concerns of home, place, and security.[29] I aim to deconstruct this assumption in this book. Scholars and practitioners alike are not wrong in identifying strong currents of transcendence in Buddhist tradition—those currents that exemplify what Thomas Tweed calls the "crossing" function of religion,[30] currents that carry us "from place to placelessness"[31] and situate human experience within cosmic rather than mundane scale of time. These "crossing" currents serve as critical resources for Buddhists experiencing displacement who are seeking in Buddhism a more coherent way to experience disruptive change, loss, and disorientation. Yet if these currents of crossing and transcendence were all that Buddhism had to offer, then Buddhism's contributions to resolving the humanitarian and political urgencies of the displacement crisis would be few.

As I argue in this book, Buddhism also offers generous currents of what Thomas Tweed calls "dwelling"—those currents that situate, embed, embody, anchor, and emplace.[32] From the *jātaka* narratives to the monastic *vinayas* and from site consecration rituals to ideas about righteous kingship, Buddhism across its various schools and lineages is rich with teachings on the vulnerabilities of displacement, the critical importance of home, the politicization of space, and the relevance of secure places to Buddhist practice—and of Buddhist practice to securing places. Buddhism as a tradition is robustly equipped to inform the wider scholarly conversation about religion and displacement, as well as the global humanitarian response to the displacement crisis.

Displacement has formatively shaped contemporary Buddhism; Buddhists have shaped displacement as we know it today. For these reasons, Buddhist experiences with displacement not only serve as important elements of historical memory but also introduce relevant new conceptual frameworks into the field of religious studies. One major aim of this book is to illuminate these unique contributions so that religious studies may become a more balanced and globally informed field for the study of displacement.

Contributing to a Placemaking Emphasis in Buddhist Studies

A second scholarly contribution this book aims to make is to the field of Buddhist studies: joining with other recent studies of Buddhist refugees' emplacement strategies,[33] this book affirms the central role of placemaking and homemaking in Buddhist traditions. While the values of renunciation and detachment are highly prized in Buddhism, particularly in the ideals of the monastic discipline, Buddhism is not only a religion of "placelessness."[34] I argue that throughout time and across the textual traditions, Buddhists have consistently acknowledged their tradition's emphasis on cultivating both other-worldly and this-worldly forms of security. The sources that I explore in this book reveal a picture of Buddhism that is colored more by "dwelling" than by "crossing," which may be surprising for a book on displacement.[35] The "dwelling" dimension of Buddhism—while far from new to Asian Buddhist communities, who are more likely to ask for monks' blessings on their homes or to center their daily movements around Buddhist monuments—is less emphasized in the western convert Buddhism that has strongly shaped Anglophone Buddhist studies scholarship.

Informing the Humanitarian Sector

My third and final aim is for this book to inform humanitarian and political actors who are working to relieve the sufferings of displacement in Buddhist contexts, whether on behalf of displaced people or on behalf of the reception communities who make room for them. Buddhist voices are integral to understanding the contemporary displacement landscape and to achieving durable solutions to its manifold challenges. For the benefit of this latter audience—those working in the humanitarian space, whether as government agencies, non-governmental organizations, monastics, engaged Buddhists, or others—I offer a conclusion with recommendations on how my findings could be explored in practical application. I hope that this work can inspire a more informed understanding of the communities they serve and lead to more effective approaches to security, healing, cooperation, and flourishing.

In this book, I take a critical-constructive approach to Buddhism and displacement. My approach is critical because I bring a range of humanistic methods of interpretation and analysis to bear on my source material. I do not assume that Buddhist perspectives on displacement are inherently good or effective; instead, I analyze these perspectives in light of humanitarian norms and probe how they can inform various communities of research or practice. My approach is constructive because I encourage applications that can mitigate the sufferings of displacement, and to that end, I take ethical positions in this book on issues of state responsibility. I do some deconstructive work in this book, but I spend more time constructing possibilities that I hope will support the work many others are doing to assist and advocate for displaced people and their hosts.

Buddhism and Migration in Historical Perspective

Buddhists have always been on the move. At the tradition's founding, the call to monastic ordination involved physically leaving one's household to join an itinerant community of renunciants; "going forth from home to homelessness" remains central to Buddhist monastic identity today. Buddhism's gradual spread across Asia followed in the footsteps of the traveling merchants and missionaries who navigated the Silk Road network and maritime routes to further their respective enterprises. Pilgrimage has long been a popular practice in Buddhist communities, and with the advent of modern travel technologies, millions of people each year now make pilgrimages to holy sites connected to the Buddha or to local saints.

While the term "migration" refers more generally to human movement, whether for work, education, pleasure, conquest, or asylum, "displacement" refers specifically to human movement that is compelled by insecurity. Displacement may be caused by natural disasters, drought, famine, war, violence, political oppression, state development projects, poverty, or fear. Displacement necessarily entails suffering. Displacement means the loss of home, community, personal property, social identity, and sometimes, exclusion from education, employment, or political participation. These losses may be temporary or enduring.

Where there is suffering, Buddhism makes itself relevant. Displacement is a human experience not limited to those of any particular tradition or region; most of its sufferings are recognizable to anyone who has experienced it. But even against the universality of the sufferings of displacement, Buddhists have their own stories to tell that are shaped by their cosmologies, their ritual practices, their ethical and doctrinal systems, and their shared histories. Buddhists have developed some distinctive ways of responding to displacement that can enhance the global community's understanding of and compassionate response to the contemporary displacement crisis.

Buddhists in Displacement Contexts

The story of modern displacement is a human story, but it is also a Buddhist story. Buddhists are present across all the dimensions of our contemporary displacement crisis: they have displaced others and have been displaced, they have offered refuge to others and have been offered refuge. They have supported policies that drive displacement as well as policies preventing displacement. They have interpreted their experiences of displacement in light of Buddhist doctrines, narratives, and traditions (as well as non-religious frameworks); they have grappled with these experiences and sought healing and renewal by relying on Buddhist practices and institutions (as well as non-religious ones). Their experiences within the larger human story of displacement matter. Understanding how Buddhist lives and traditions intersect with displacement can help Buddhist communities and governments meet the challenges of displacement, but Buddhist lives and traditions also have something to offer the rest of the world: ethical insights, ritual practices, and visions of security that can bolster our global implementation of an informed and effective protection agenda for displaced people across religions and contexts.

Speaking of "Buddhism"

Some readers new to the field of religious studies may benefit from a brief working definition of Buddhism. A common tendency within the Protestant-influenced west has been to look for a tradition within its corpus of scriptures. While the textual tradition is highly revered within most Buddhist communities, there are limitations to defining Buddhism textually. To start, there are several scriptural canons in the Buddhist world recognized as authoritative by different groups, so searching for "Buddhism" in a single agreed-upon corpus of sacred texts is untenable. Even for Buddhists who share the same scriptural canon, such as Theravāda Buddhists holding authoritative the Pāli canon with its forty or so volumes (the smallest of the Buddhist canons), the texts are so voluminous that relatively few people read the canon in its entirety, much less master it. Finally, even a single verse of scripture may be interpreted and engaged with in many differing ways.

Defining Buddhism is a much more welcome task than defining religion, but even so, the traditions deriving from the ancient sage Gotama are many and varied, and they continue to evolve in distinct lineages and cultural contexts (some of them Hindu or Christian rather than Buddhist). In this book, by "Buddhism," I mean the collection not only of scriptural texts, but also of practices, institutions, discourses, and material artifacts that link back to—or are perceived to link back to—the Buddha of our age, Siddhattha Gotama (Sanskrit Siddhārtha Gautama). For this reason, in this book I have engaged texts, ritual practices, historical experiences, legal traditions, ethical systems, artistic traditions, and contemporary discourse. I hope the twofold point is clear, that there are many lived forms of Buddhism and that "Buddhism" cannot merely be extracted from texts.

Scholars today sometimes speak of "many Buddhisms" in order to emphasize Buddhism's diversity across cultures and lineages and to resist essentializing the tradition. This plural noun can be instructive for humanitarian professionals, aid workers, and clinicians, in order to acknowledge Buddhism's diversity of forms and to motivate the kind of research needed to provide culturally appropriate assistance to people. As I will discuss in this book, providing mental health care to refugees from Cambodia and from Tibet could each involve Buddhist ideas or practices, but the Buddhist traditions of those two places are quite different from one another, as are the ways Buddhism tends to influence clinical responses to post-traumatic stress disorder in those communities.

While pluralizing "Buddhism" makes a certain rhetorical point, it is also useful to treat the varied Buddhist traditions together as a group, knowing that within this group there are some areas of strong consensus and other areas of divergence. Buddhist civic organizations and aid organizations are most impactful when they are larger and able to integrate members across the spectrum of Buddhist expressions and affiliations. From a practical or constructive perspective, resisting the scholarly temptation to differentiate *ad infinitum* will make our research findings more legible and actionable to those outside our fields; generalizing can tap into the power of a shared identity that emboldens shared perspectives with a stronger voice.

For the purposes of the present work, I emphasize several dimensions of Buddhist tradition across its cultural and denominational forms: its cosmological dimensions (How can humans be rightly oriented and secure in the world? How can they make sense of displacement?); its therapeutic dimensions (How can humans be well in body and mind, especially when faced with the stresses and losses of displacement?); its ethical dimensions (What duties are at stake in contexts of displacement and emplacement? How are moral possibilities made legible in these contexts?); its legal dimensions (How do Buddhist monastic law and other forms of law approach the politicization, contestation, and sharing of space?); and its political dimensions (What Buddhist discourses and frameworks can best articulate the needs of displaced people and our shared global responsibility for addressing displacement?).

Notes

1 "Ratthapala Sutta: About Ratthapala" (MN 82), translated from the Pāli by Thanissaro Bhikkhu. *Access to Insight (BCBS Edition)*, 30 November 2013. Accessed on 20 May 2026. www.accesstoinsight.org/tipitaka/mn/mn.082.than.html.

2 United Nations High Commissioner for Refugees. "Figures at a Glance." Accessed on 29 August 2025. www.unhcr.org/us/about-unhcr/overview/figures-glance.

3 United Nations High Commissioner for Refugees. "Figures at a Glance." Accessed on 29 August 2025. www.unhcr.org/us/about-unhcr/overview/figures-glance; United Nations High Commissioner for Refugees. "Acute Food Insecurity and Malnutrition Rise for Sixth Consecutive Year in World's Most Fragile Regions – New Report." 16 May 2025. Accessed on 29 August 2025. www.unhcr.org/news/announcements/acute-food-insecurity-and-malnutrition-rise-sixth-consecutive-year-world-s-most.

4 Shire, Warsan. "'No One Puts their Children in a Boat Unless the Water is Safer than the Land': A Poem about Seeking Asylum." Republished by *Global Citizen* on 7 September 2015. Accessed on 29 August 2025. www.globalcitizen.org/en/content/no-one-puts-their-children-in-a-boat-unless-the-wa/.

5 Weick, Karl E. "The Collapse of Sensemaking in Organizations: The Mann Gulch Disaster." *Administrative Science Quarterly* 38 (1993): 628–652. I was introduced to Weick's theory and its usefulness for the study of religion and displacement by Naidu, Maheshvari. "Displaced Sense: Displacement, Religion and Sense-Making," *Journal for the Study of Religion* 29, no. 1 (2016): 104–126.

6 Philpott, Daniel. "The Challenge of September 11 to Secularism in International Relations." *World Politics* 55 (October 2002): 66–95.

7 Cotter, Cédric. "The Religious Convictions of Henri Dunant, Founder of the ICRC." August 11, 2021. Accessed on 29 August 2025. https://blogs.icrc.org/religion-humanitarianprinciples/the-religious-convictions-of-henri-dunant-founder-of-the-icrc/.

8 United Nations. *United Nations Charter (full text)*. [26 June 1945]. Accessed on 12 September 2025. www.un.org/en/about-us/un-charter/full-text.

9 United Nations Office of the High Commissioner for Human Rights. "Faith for Rights." Accessed on 12 September 2025. www.ohchr.org/en/faith-for-rights.

10 International Committee of the Red Cross. "Faith-Based Organizations and Religious Leaders: Essential Partners in Humanitarian Action." Last modified 22 July 2015. Accessed on 12 September 2025. www.icrc.org/en/document/faith-based-organizations-and-religious-leaders-essential-partners-humanitarian-action.

11 International Committee of the Red Cross. "Religion and Humanitarian Principles—About." Accessed on 12 September 2025. https://blogs.icrc.org/religion-humanitarianprinciples/about/.

12 International Committee of the Red Cross. "Faith-Based Organizations and Religious Leaders: Essential Partners in Humanitarian Action." Last modified

22 July 2015. Accessed on 12 September 2025. www.icrc.org/en/document/faith-based-organizations-and-religious-leaders-essential-partners-humanitarian-action.

13 International Committee of the Red Cross. "Religion and Humanitarian Principles —About." Accessed on 12 September 2025. https://blogs.icrc.org/religion-humanitarianprinciples/about/.

14 International Committee of the Red Cross. "Faith-Based Organizations and Religious Leaders: Essential Partners in Humanitarian Action." Last modified 22 July 2015. Accessed on 12 September 2025. https://www.icrc.org/en/document/faith-based-organizations-and-religious-leaders-essential-partners-humanitarian-action.

15 Bartles-Smith, Andrew, Kate Crosby, Peter Harvey, Asanga Tilakaratne, Daniel Ratheiser, Noel Maurer Trew, Stefania Travagnin, Elizabeth J. Harris, Mahinda Deegalle, and Christina A. Kilby, eds. *Buddhism and International Humanitarian Law.* Special issue of *Contemporary Buddhism* 22, no. 1–2 (2021).

16 Bartles-Smith, Andrew, Kate Crosby, Peter Harvey, Asanga Tilakaratne, Daniel Ratheiser, Noel Maurer Trew, Stefania Travagnin, Elizabeth J. Harris, Venerable Mahinda Deegalle, and Christina A. Kilby, eds. *Buddhism and International Humanitarian Law.* New York: Routledge, 2023.

17 Meyer, Birgit and Peter van der Veer, eds. *Refugees and Religion: Ethnographic Studies of Global Trajectories.* London: Bloomsbury Academic, 2021.

18 Ngo, Tam T.T., and Nga T. Mai. "In Search of a Vietnamese Buddhist Space in Germany." In Birgit Meyer and Peter van der Veer, eds., *Refugees and Religion: Ethnographic Studies of Global Trajectories*, pp. 105–122. London: Bloomsbury Academic, 2021.

19 Mavelli, Luca, and Erin K. Wilson, eds. *The Refugee Crisis and Religion: Secularism, Security and Hospitality in Question.* New York: Rowman and Littlefield, 2017.

20 Beckford, James A., ed. *Migration and Religion.* London: Edward Elgar Publishing, 2016.

21 Usarski, Frank. " 'The Last Missionary to Leave the Temple Should Turn Off the Light': Sociological Remarks on the Decline of Japanese 'Immigrant' Buddhism in Brazil." *Japanese Journal of Religious Studies* 35, no. 1 (2008): 39–59.

22 Horstmann, Alexander, and Jin-Heon Jung, eds. *Building Noah's Ark for Migrants, Refugees, and Religious Communities.* New York: Palgrave Macmillan, 2015.

23 Gravers, Mikael. "Religious Imaginary as an Alternative Social and Moral Order—Karen Buddhism Across the Thai-Burma Border." In Alexander Horstmann and Jin-Heon Jung, eds., *Building Noah's Ark for Migrants, Refugees, and Religious Communities*, pp. 45–76. New York: Palgrave Macmillan, 2015; Horstmann, Alexander. "Secular and Religious Sanctuaries: Interfaces of Humanitarianism and Self-Government of Karen Refugee-Migrants in Thai-Burmese Border Spaces." In Alexander Horstmann and Jin-Heon Jung, eds., *Building Noah's Ark for Migrants, Refugees, and Religious Communities*, pp. 129–156. New York: Palgrave Macmillan, 2015.

24 Huntington, Samuel. "The Clash of Civilizations." *Foreign Affairs* 72, no. 3 (1993): 22–49.

25 For a discussion of how the model minority myth has affected Buddhist immigrants in the United States, refer to "The Assimilationist Paradigm and Burmese Americans," pp. 80-92 in Cheah, Joseph. *Race and Religion in American*

Buddhism: White Supremacy and Immigrant Adaptation. Oxford: Oxford University Press, 2011.

26 For a detailed bibliographical article pointing to sources that investigate these historical experiences, refer to Kilby, Christina. "Buddhism, Immigrants and Refugees." In Courtney Bruntz, ed., *Oxford Bibliographies in Buddhism.* New York: Oxford University Press, 2022.

27 For a detailed discussion of how Buddhism and the contemporary refugee experience are intertwined, refer to Kilby, Christina. "Buddhism and Migration." In Anna Rowlands and Elena Fiddian-Qasmiyeh, eds., *Oxford Handbook of Religion and Contemporary Migration.* New York: Oxford University Press, 2027 (forthcoming).

28 One news analyst calls Bhutan "the world's biggest creator of refugees per capita." Refer to Mørch, Maximillian. "Bhutan's Dark Secret: The Lhotsampa Expulsion: The Mass Deportation of Bhutanese-Nepalis in the 1990s Remains Unresolved 20 Years Later," *The Diplomat,* 21 September 2016. Accessed on 12 September 2025. https://thediplomat.com/2016/09/bhutans-dark-secret-the-lhotshampa-expulsion/.

29 Critics of socially engaged Buddhism may argue that these concerns are distractions from the core work of Buddhism. Donald Lopez, Jr. skillfully outlines this position in "Buddhism in the Real World." *Tricycle: The Buddhist Review.* Summer 2021. Accessed on 25 November 2025. https://tricycle.org/magazine/history-of-buddhism-and-activism/.

30 Tweed, Thomas. *Crossing and Dwelling: A Theory of Religion.* Cambridge, MA: Harvard University Press, 2006.

31 Tuan, Yi-fu, with Martha A. Strawn, Ed. *Religion: From Place to Placelessness.* Chicago, IL: University of Chicago Press, 2009.

32 Tweed, Thomas. *Crossing and Dwelling: A Theory of Religion.* Cambridge, MA: Harvard University Press, 2006.

33 Lopes, Ana C. *Tibetan Buddhism in Diaspora: Cultural Re-signification in Practice and Institutions.* London: Routledge, 2015; Rangkla, Prasert. "Refuge and Emplacement through Buddhism: Karen Refugees and Religious Practices in a Northwestern Border Town of Thailand," *Asia Pacific Journal of Anthropology* 14, no. 1 (2013): 8–22; Sangasumana, Ven. Pinnawala. "Mapping Inbetweenness: A Conceptual Model for War-Induced Resettlement in Sri Lanka." *Social Science Research Network*, 26 November 2012. http://doi.org/10.2139/ssrn.3455629.

34 Tuan, Yi-fu, with Martha A. Strawn, Ed. *Religion: From Place to Placelessness.* Chicago, IL: University of Chicago Press, 2009.

35 Tweed, Thomas. *Crossing and Dwelling: A Theory of Religion.* Cambridge, MA: Harvard University Press, 2006.

2 Place and Displacement in Buddhist Text Worlds

Introduction

In this chapter, I read across a variety of textual sources from Buddhist traditions to understand how displacement has been imagined in scripture, both as a metaphor for the existential condition and as a literal experience of human (and animal) insecurity. I analyze several narratives that offer complex perspectives on displacement, its causes, and its ethical valences. I likewise probe the reception of some of these stories in Buddhist communities, engaging both "authoritative" and "oppositional" readings: in other words, readings that go with and against the grain of institutionally authorized doctrine.[1] In Buddhist texts, as in Buddhist communities, we meet a polyphony of voices, even within a single lineage or locale. My aim here is to introduce a wide horizon of exploration that includes the expected as well as the provocative, the playful as well as the devout, so that the full range of human emotions these texts evoke can inform our study of displacement in Buddhist text worlds.

I use the term "text worlds" in this chapter to emphasize that texts are not mere latent materiality.[2] They are embodied and generative—most tangibly, as oral texts that are memorized and recited according to particular rhythms of physical discipline and social practice. Across Asian Buddhisms, orality continues to be a primary mode in which the Buddhist canon is present in the world. Orality entails performance, shared and unshared worlds of reference, and audience response and reinvention. Yet even in print form, texts are far from inert. They act in the lives of those who relate to them; they inform the interpretation of events and are changed in the process of their use. Scriptural texts are active interlocutors within Buddhist communities.

Reading Metaphors of Displacement and Refuge

"I take refuge in the Buddha, I take refuge in the dharma, I take refuge in the sangha." This phrase is repeated day after day, in many languages and melodies, by Buddhists across the world. Many consider this verbal act, called taking "refuge" (Sanskrit *śaraṇa*; Pāli *saraṇa*), to serve as the key identity

DOI: 10.4324/9781003318149-2

marker or conversion requirement of a Buddhist. Speaking from a Theravāda perspective, Thānissaro Bhikkhu writes that

> In pre-Buddhist India, going for refuge meant proclaiming one's allegiance to a patron—a powerful person or god—submitting to the patron's directives in hopes of receiving protection from danger in return. In the early years of the Buddha's teaching career, his new followers adopted this custom to express their allegiance to the Buddha, Dhamma, and Sangha, but in the Buddhist context this custom took on a new meaning. Buddhism is not a theistic religion—the Buddha is not a god—and so a person taking refuge in the Buddhist sense is not asking for the Buddha personally to intervene to provide protection. Still, one of the Buddha's central teachings is that human life is fraught with dangers—from greed, anger, and delusion—and so the concept of refuge is central to the path of practice, in that the practice is aimed at gaining release from those dangers.[3]

In the framework of Buddhist cosmology, all beings are refugees. From what do we flee? From the sufferings of cyclic existence, likened to a stormy sea that tosses us hither and thither and offers no stable ground on which to stand. This is *dukkha,* the first of the noble truths: not only pain and loss, but flux, instability, and insecurity. The term "samsara" (Sanskrit/Pāli *saṃsāra*), the cycle of rebirth that constitutes the realm of conditioned existence, refers to the experience of "wandering through" or "transmigration."[4] According to the Buddhist teachings, nothing in this world of conditioned and compounded things ultimately lasts, ultimately fulfills us, ultimately relieves our restlessness. We are constantly on the move, from desire to desire and from birth to birth, seeking safety but unable to find it anywhere in this ocean of changes. The dharma is often described as an island in this sea, or nirvana as the far shore, a place of safe haven; and the Buddha is likened to a great protector in whose care we cosmic wanderers can place our trust, the one who grants refuge.

In another extended metaphor of displacement from the *Anusota Sutta* in the Pāli canon, the cravings of the senses are depicted as the flow of a dangerous river.[5] There are four types of people, the Buddha explains: those who go with the flow of their sense impressions and allow themselves to be swept away; those who struggle against the flow, exerting strong effort but failing to find peace; those who stand fast in the flow, weathering its pummels yet achieving a state of equanimity; and those who successfully navigate the current and finally reach firm ground. Nirvana (Pāli *nibbāna,* Sanskrit *nirvāṇa*) is the solid ground on which we find relief from the dangers of our own sense cravings. Today, these water-soaked metaphors evoke news images of migrants battling dangerous waters, whether in the South China Sea, the Mediterranean, or the Rio Grande. The human search for protection and security is so frequently, in metaphor and in life, the search for solid ground amidst the flood and for shelter amidst the storm.

The foundational metaphors in which the Buddhist tradition casts itself, then, are metaphors of displacement and refuge. How do these metaphors work in Buddhist texts and teachings? We understand what they seek to communicate about the human condition, the path of practice, and the goal of liberation, but what do they communicate about displacement and protection? Do such metaphors trivialize the experiences of displaced people by subsuming all living beings within a paradigm of spiritualized displacement? If "we are all refugees" in samsara, does the plight of our displaced neighbors on this planet today become more urgent, or less so?

These questions join a larger debate about the relevance of social justice for Buddhism, given that samsara is inherently unstable. Donald Lopez, Jr. provides an incisive entrée into this debate with his article "Buddhism in the Real World," published in *Tricycle* magazine.[6] In terms of cosmology, Lopez argues that Buddhism's focus on the renunciation of this world, coupled with theories about the world entering an irreversible age of decline, has dampened Buddhist motivation toward political and social reform for much of the religion's history. Why spend time attempting to fix this "disintegrating foundation" (Tibetan *'jigs rten*) of a world rather than seeking escape from it, as one would escape a burning house? In terms of economics, Lopez argues that the sangha's reliance on the lay community and the state has typically placed them in a poor position to effect meaningful structural change, even if their cosmology had sufficiently motivated them to do so. In short, while Buddhists across the world today broadly agree on the centrality of ethics and compassionate action to their tradition, the debate on exactly how much emphasis should be placed on social justice and political reform is far from settled. One could reasonably ask, then, whether Buddhism's metaphors of displacement are only meant to motivate spiritual practice, or whether they also have implications for social and political action.

The Buddha has been traditionally esteemed as a teacher so wise that his words could penetrate the ignorance of each disciple; his words are described as both "oceanic" (full of meaning)[7] and skillful in method (Sanskrit *upāyakauśalya*)—effective in creating the intended realization in his pupils within the limits of their capacities. Some scriptures claim that the Buddha's listeners could understand his words in each of their own languages at the same time. Even without attributing miraculous powers to the Buddha, let us entertain the premise that the Buddha was a skilled rhetorician and teacher, able to use words in a persuasive and illuminating way. When evaluating the Buddha's pedagogical choice to employ metaphors of displacement and refuge to describe samsara and nirvana, we arrive at a paradox. Metaphors only function when the secondary subject or vehicle (displacement, in this case) is familiar to the audience, and metaphors work best when the vehicle is strongly evocative.[8] It is likely from the Buddha's choice of metaphors that physical danger and flight were experiences not only familiar to his audiences, but evocative of a strong sense of desperation and urgency. The urgency that the Buddha wished his listeners to feel toward the spiritual path is achieved only if the Buddha and his audiences acknowledged the extreme sufferings of displacement in a this-worldly sense. This means that the more seriously one takes the Buddha's capacities in wisdom and skillful methods, the more seriously one must also take the sufferings of displacement and the urgent response they warrant.

I argue that the foundational Buddhist language of refuge and protection opens the door into a serious theological engagement with the political and material realities of human displacement in the here-and-now, without compromising the transcendent aims of Buddhism. In the work of metaphor, spiritualized displacement and literal displacement are not opposing themes competing for priority, but are imbued with the same persuasive call to urgent action.

A Buddhist Mandate to Migrate[9]

Migration is often characterized in contemporary political discourse as inherently unethical or even criminal. Sometimes migration is criminalized through legislation, and sometimes when migrants are fully within the bounds of the law (for example, asylum seekers crossing the United States–Mexico border), they are popularly, though incorrectly, believed to be migrating illegally. Crossing an international border—even in cases when one's life is in danger, and even with the legal status of an asylum seeker—has been frequently cited in the United States as an affront to the rule of law.[10] Yet in several of the world's religious traditions, there is a precedent, and in some cases even an ethical mandate, to migrate when life conditions become oppressive or dangerous.

In the Hebrew scriptures, God commands Abraham to "Go from your country and your kindred and your father's house to the land that I will show you."[11] Abraham's obedience to God's command to migrate is reckoned as a sign of his righteousness. In the story of the Hebrews' exodus from Egypt, where they had originally sought relief from famine but later been oppressed as slaves, God directs Moses and Aaron to lead the Hebrews out of the land. God insists that they flee, despite the protests of the Hebrews that they would rather serve the Egyptians as slaves than die in the wilderness.[12] In a midrashic commentary on the exodus story, Avivah Zornberg observes that God works to force the Hebrews out of Egypt the way a midwife uses forceps to assist a birth, so important is it to God that they begin a new life for themselves by fleeing slavery.[13]

In Islamic tradition, God enjoins Muhammad and his followers to migrate when they face worsening persecution from the Quraysh tribe in Makkah. Sura 4:97 from the *Quran* reads (in translation),

> When the angels take the souls of those who have wronged themselves, they ask them, "What circumstances were you in?" They reply, "We were

> oppressed in this land," and the angels say, "But was God's earth not spacious enough for you to migrate to some other place?"[14]

To fail to migrate when one is "oppressed in this land" is to wrong oneself and to deny the gracious capacity of God's wide earth. As one scholar has noted, "The prophet's *hijra* [flight] provided a framework through which trauma and defeat could be made legible,"[15] as well as emphasizing the wide capacity of the earth to support refuge. For many Muslims who feel their insecure life circumstances echoed in the flight of the prophet, the life of piety is characterized as a life on the move.

Buddhist tradition has a similar mandate to migrate: to "go where there is life." In the Pāli scriptures, there is a *jātaka* (a tale of one of the Buddha's previous lifetimes) when he was born as a potter who lived near the river Benares.[16] When there was plentiful rain, the river would swell and fill a nearby lake, but during years of drought the adjacent lake would dry up. The story goes that the fish and tortoises who lived in the river knew which years would see abundant rainfall and which years would see drought, and when drought was coming, they would swim from the lake back into the river. This tortoise, however, loved his lake and didn't want to leave. " 'Here I was born, and here I have grown up, and here is my parents' home. Leave it I cannot!' "[17] He buried himself deep in the clay as the waters dried up around him.

One day, a young potter (the future Buddha) came to the dried-up lake to dig for clay for his workshop. He struck the poor tortoise with his spade, cracked his shell, and turned him up like a lump of clay.

> In his agony the creature thought, "Here I am, dying, all because I was too fond of my home to leave it!" And in the words of these following verses, he made his moan:
>
> "Here was I born, and here I lived; my refuge was the clay;
> And now the clay has played me false in a most grievous way;
> Thee, thee I call, oh Bhaggava (Blessed One); hear what I have to say!
> Go where thou canst find happiness, where'er the place may be;
> Forest or village, there the wise both home and birthplace see;
> Go where there's life; nor stay at home for death to master thee."[18]

Then the tortoise died. The Buddha, as narrator of the story, gave a teaching about this poor tortoise's fate:

> "So you see, he came to his end because he was too fond of his home. Take care not to be like this tortoise. Don't say to yourselves, 'I have sight, I have hearing, I have smell, I have taste, I have touch, I have a son, I have a daughter, I have numbers of men and maids for my service, I have precious gold.' Do not cleave to these things with craving and desire."[19]

This narrative includes its own commentary, where the Buddha makes clear that "Go where there is life" is the tortoise's exhortation to abandon all attachments, to give up home and family as well as one's sense cravings in the pursuit of the (monastic) path toward liberation. Yet this story only makes sense if we also take seriously the literal and immediate sense of the narrative. To stay in a place where there is only danger and death is foolishness; unnecessary tragedy surely follows. This story offers a compelling dimension to the subject of displacement in the Buddhist scriptures because here, those who migrate are characterized by detachment, one of the supreme Buddhist virtues. Their willingness to abandon their homes, possessions, and communities is admired, a mark of their wisdom and discipline to let go of what they must in order to "go where there is life." Through the lens of this *jātaka* narrative, displaced people can be spiritual exemplars who model a similar kind of renunciation to that embraced by the monastic community. This Buddhist tale joins the narratives of other religious traditions in prizing the preservation of life and the opportunity for spiritual development above attachments to property, prosperity, or kinship.

Once the Buddha Was Displaced

Academic literature on religion and migration sometimes points to the presence of divine flight narratives in several of the world's religions. There is an echo among these traditions: the flight of the infant Krishna, the Hebrews' exodus, the escape of the infant Jesus and his family to Egypt, and the *hijra* of the early Muslim community to Medina. These flight narratives embed the liminal experience of displacement into narrative and ritual traditions that continue to hold power for so many across the world. They introduce an element of precarity and vulnerability into the core of what religions hold as stable and sure; they also model the suffering of the innocent, because even the holiest of gods and saints can experience the particular form of suffering that is displacement.

When Buddhism enters the catalog of divine flight narratives, some have cited the young Siddhattha's journey beyond the palace walls when he encounters the four sights (old age, sickness, death, and an ascetic) as a "flight from home" similar to the displacement stories from other traditions mentioned above.[20] Yet I argue that Siddhattha's decision to leave his comfortable home and embark on a spiritual quest—with the option to return safely home at any time—is not an accurate example of displacement, which is compelled by external forces that render home itself unsafe. Citing Siddhattha's journey beyond the palace as Buddhism's primordial flight narrative is not only unconvincing, but may reinforce an assumption that the sufferings displaced people experience today are distant from the merit-charmed life of the Buddha. Indeed, because of the great stores of merit from his previous lifetimes of practice, the Buddha seems impervious to any form of suffering that he does not willingly embrace as part of his spiritual discipline (for example, his extreme fasting).

Instead, I argue that another story provides a more compelling example of displacement at the heart of Buddhist tradition. The *jātaka* of Prince Vessantara continues to be told and retold across Asian Buddhist communities. In the Chinese canon, Vessantara's name is Sudāna (須大拏), and in the Tibetan canon, he is Drimé Künden (*dri med kun ldan*). In Theravāda contexts, where he is most popular, his story tends to be at least as well known as the life story of Siddhattha himself. Extant in a rich variety of textual, oral, and artistic witnesses, this *jātaka* is a dynamic text that evolves and shifts with each performance or recitation.[21] Sometimes it is a tale full of celebration or humor, and sometimes it is an uncanny and unsettling narrative, or one that provokes anguish and even protest. The differences in the story, sometimes regionally based, sometimes idiosyncratic, play on a wide range of emotions as the story's audiences simultaneously admire the Prince's generosity and shudder at its horrific consequences. This story of displacement is important, I argue, because it brings critical questions about justice straight to the heart of Buddhism.

Prince Vessantara's Tale

In the version of the *jātaka* preserved in the Pāli canon,[22] Vessantara is born to a royal family while his queen mother is on a trip to the city. He is born on Vessa Street, and his name "Vessantara" derives "not from the mother's side nor from the father's," but from this in-between place, this no-place of his birth.[23] (Similarly, Siddhattha is born while his mother is on the road). In a Tibetan version of the story, the prince's capital city is called "Town of All" (*thams cad kyi grong rdal*) and his given name is "Liberator of All" (*thams cad sgrol*).[24] With Vessantara's birthplace and name rendered placeless in one tradition and vaguely universalized in another, the audience intuits that this prince does not fully belong to our world with its reliance upon geopolitical identities.

Vessantara's destiny in this particular lifetime along his path toward Buddhahood is to perfect the virtue of generosity. In a previous lifetime, Vessantara's mother had been granted a series of wishes, including a wish that she would someday give birth to a son who excelled in generosity. At the time of Vessantara's conception, his mother is inexplicably filled with the desire to give alms and she constructs six alms-halls around her palace. She builds one alms-hall at each of the four gates of the city, one in the center, and one by her own residence, effectively creating a mandala city whose limits are circumscribed by generosity. This is an important point: generosity defines the limits of a polity. How many people does the state include, and whom does it exclude? What support can it offer to outsiders, and what must it withhold for its own?

When the young prince is born on Vessa Street, he stretches out his hand and asks his mother for something to give away. She gives him a thousand coins. That same day, a flying elephant magically appears and delivers its baby to Prince Vessanatara in order to fulfill his insatiable need to give. The baby is a white wish-fulfilling elephant that brings rain and all manner of treasures to Vessantara's kingdom. Buddhist audiences usually view the elephant as state property; in a Lao telling of the story, the elephant is considered to be the soul-object (*ming khwan*) of the kingdom, vital to its life and well-being.[25]

At age eight, Vessantara strengthens his desire to give, deciding that he would even give away his own eyes, heart, or flesh if someone should ask him (and in fact, he has given his body away to others in previous lifetimes). In response to this unshakable commitment, the earth quakes and Mt. Meru bows and dances. These omens are confirmations of Vessantara's extraordinary merit, but they are also unsettling omens; his great virtue will necessarily disturb the natural order of things.

At age sixteen, Vessantara marries the princess Maddī. In time, she bears a son and later a daughter. All is well until a great drought strikes the neighboring kingdom of Kāliṅga. Their crops fail and the people resort to stealing to feed themselves. They beg their own king for help. Their king undertakes a seven-day vow, but is unable to summon the rain. His people then ask him to beg the white elephant from Prince Vessantara, the elephant that brings blessings of rain wherever it goes.

The king of Kāliṅga sends a delegation of brahmins to Prince Vessantara, who gladly gifts them the white elephant. The earth again trembles at his generosity, but this time Vessantara's people tremble as well: they tremble with fear. They see the brahmins of Kāliṅga riding their precious elephant out of the city gates and desperately ask the king, Vessantara's father, to do something. At first the king refuses, insisting that he would rather lose his kingdom than punish his blameless son for a virtuous gift. The people raise their voice: " 'Not chastisement doth he deserve, nor sword, nor prison cell,/ But from the kingdom banish him, on Vaṁka's mount to dwell.' "[26] In this appeal, the people seem to acknowledge that Vessantara is not exactly guilty of a moral failing, but at the same time, they insist that his generosity is incompatible with the duties of governance. Thus, they propose banishing him to Mt. Vaṁka, the wilderness mountain where ascetics go to renounce the world, but also where criminals and lawbreakers seek refuge from state punishment.[27] The ambiguity and lawlessness of this wilderness at Mt. Vaṁka is critical. Is Vessantara a criminal, or is he a saint? Is he both? Without resolving this multivalence, Vessantara's banishment signals that extreme generosity does not belong in the realm of state power.

Vessantara's mother, the Queen Phusanti, is devastated to hear the news of her son's banishment. "Like mangoes fallen to the ground, like money waste and spent, / So falls thy kingdom, if they will banish the innocent," she cries to her husband.[28] Yet the verdict stands. The night before he departs his home, Vessantara urges his wife Maddī to hide her wealth so that she can stay and take care of their children and parents without him. Maddī declares that she loves him too much to let him go alone, reminding many audiences of Sītā's loyalty to Rāma when he was banished in the *Rāmāyaṇa* epic.

Maddī knows the dangers of the wilderness—stinging insects and snakes, bears and jackals, even plagues from the other side of the river—and her willingness to risk these dangers may be interpreted as loyalty to her husband. But if she remains behind, she knows that widowhood will be a worse danger than these. According to the story in the Pāli canon, in her mind's eye she sees men pulling her down into the dust by the hair, sees them beating her children without a father to protect them. She knows there is no safety at home for her anymore.

On the road out of the city, the royal family encounters brahmins who ask for the family's possessions, their horses, and their chariot. True to his virtue, Vessantara happily gives each away in turn. The princes of a neighboring land hear of Vessantara's plight and offer him lordship over their realm, but Vessantara refuses. The family journeys on, through mountain forests and across shaded rivers, eventually finding shelter in an abandoned hermitage. Living as quasi-monastics, they don robes, assume celibacy, and forage for food in the verdant wood.

One day, while Maddī is away collecting fruit, an old brahmin named Jūjaka comes to ask for Vessantara's two children to serve as slaves for his wife. Vessantara agrees, and the children are bound and taken screaming from their father, who is at once delighted to have the chance to give such a gift and tormented by the pain of losing them. When Maddī returns to discover what has happened, she is crazed with grief, like so many of the first Buddhist women whose poetry comprises the *Therīgāthā*.[29] But when Vessantara describes how he gave the children away (and "a greater gift than children none can be"), Maddī accepts what has come to pass, and even praises Vessantara's virtue.

In other *jātakas* from Buddhist tradition, children and wives are considered the personal property of the patriarch. Even an elephant gives his child away as a gift in the *Alīnacitta-Jātaka*, "The Elephant Who Saved a Kingdom."[30] Yet even with the caveats of historical or cultural perspective, no one who hears this story feels unequivocally that Vessantara's "virtue" is purely virtuous. The Pāli word used for Vessantara's great generosity is *atidāna*, which can mean "great giving" but also "excessive giving."[31] The ambivalence of this term captures the moral ambivalence that the story, with its heart-wrenching description of the children's capture, is designed to cultivate in its audience.

The gods, like the story's human audiences, are rightfully ambivalent about Vessantara's extreme gift. On the one hand, they praise his superhuman selflessness, yet on the other hand, the god Sakka worries that Vessantara may next give away his incomparable wife Maddī. So Sakka descends to Mt. Vaṁka disguised as a brahmin. He approaches Vessantara to ask for

Maddī, and Vessantara gives her away. After praising Vessantara's generosity, Sakka immediately returns Maddī, who can never be given away again because it is wrong to give away a gift one has received from another. Thus, Sakka ensures that the perfect bond between Vessantara and Maddī is made secure. Eventually, the children are ransomed by their grandfather, the king, and Vessantara and Maddī are invited back to the kingdom; the family is reunited and Vessantara is welcomed by his people as king. Despite the horrific sacrifices that his generosity required, everything turns out alright in the end for Vessantara and his family, even if the looming questions their story poses about governance and the limits of generosity are not sufficiently resolved.

This story is emotionally and ethically perplexing. There are many divergent tellings and interpretations of this story, some of which are detailed in the collection edited by Steven Collins, entitled *Readings of the Vessantara Jātaka*.[32] The interpretative angle I invite for consideration in this book is a humanitarian one, focused on the causes and consequences of displacement.

A Humanitarian Reading of Vessantara's Tale

The difficulty of reading or hearing Vessantara's story lies in its portrayal of the worst imaginable—losing one's children, wife, parents, country, security—as the result of an intentional ethical choice. If we read the story of Vessantara a different way, if Vessantara hadn't had a choice, the story might go something like this:[33]

> Vessantara, Maddī, and the children left the next morning. They left by horse and chariot. All their other possessions had been taken. Early on their journey, they were plundered of their horses. Soon after, their chariot was stolen. Vessantara and Maddī each took a child upon their hip and kept moving. The earth under their feet didn't know that their fates hung in the balance. The grass bent toward the morning sun. The breeze ruffled the leaves with a gentleness like a child's touch.
>
> Although the journey to Mount Vaṁka was long, no one sent humanitarian aid. Vessantara and Maddī had to be resourceful. They foraged for food. Their children's small hands were perfect for plucking fruit from the trees on the roadside. But still, the children were hungry and cold. The family found an abandoned hermitage for shelter, hoping that the owner would not return.
>
> Then one day the trafficker came. He took the children while Maddī was gone looking for food, and Vessantara could do nothing. The daughter tried once to escape, but the trafficker beat her cruelly while Vessantara watched. He could call no one for help. Vessantara couldn't feel his heart beating anymore.
>
> When Maddī returned to find out that their children were gone, she was crazed with grief. She returned again and again to the places where

> the children had just been playing and picking fruit. She could almost feel the touch of their tender hands on the leaves. It was only a matter of time before Maddī herself was abducted.

Although Vessantara's story ends well enough in the Pāli version, if we remove the factor of intentional choice from the story, the tragic crescendo of his narrative looks like the narratives of too many displaced people today. A family find themselves no longer safe in their home. They have no choice but to flee, although the road is just as dangerous as home is. They lose their possessions, struggle to find food and shelter, and are exploited by strangers. The children are trafficked and the family is separated. Maddī is abducted. Vessantara is helpless, stripped of the social and economic security he enjoyed before. They have no political protection, no physical assistance, no means to find their missing family members.

Reading the Vessantara story in this "oppositional" way illuminates a profound connection between the Buddha and the more than 100 million people suffering the consequences of displacement today. Just as displaced people are often villainized despite having broken no law, so was Vessantara punished for committing no crime other than the crime of generosity. The Vessantara tradition offers its audiences a productive kind of doubt: whenever displacement happens in our world, Vessantara's narrative begs the question of whether the people being driven out are really the problem, or whether those forced to flee might in fact be more virtuous than their pursuers. This lingering doubt, instilled by the image of Vessantara on the road, could weaken the impulse to vilify and scapegoat displaced people. Just as Vessantara's subjects ultimately decided that the horrors of his sacrifices were less tolerable than losing their elephant was, the tale may spur reflection on whether human brutalization can be tolerated for the sake of economic advantage.

Another important contribution that the Vessantara story makes to Buddhist grapplings with the displacement regime is a structural insight into the sufferings of displacement. First, there is the reality of the family structure: when Vessantara first prepares to flee his kingdom, he urges Maddī to hide their wealth so that she can continue to care for their children and parents in his absence, yet it soon becomes clear that her association with Vessantara is too great a liability for her to stay. She foresees that she and her children will be abused for their connections to him, not to mention that they will be left protectorless in a society that requires a male protector. Although it appears that the king intends to exile only Vessantara, and the queen herself pleads for Maddī and the children to stay, Vessantara's entire family is implicated in the verdict of exile. Like many other displaced families, in the end, Maddī and the children must leave while Vessantara's parents remain behind. Displacement inevitably affects a larger family network, resulting in painful choices.

Furthermore, it is significant that only after being banished do the circumstances arise in which Vessantara can be asked to give away his children and wife. Within the orbit of his kingdom, Vessantara is never compelled to be so shockingly "generous." On the road, however, beyond the circle of protection and righteousness that a *dhammic* monarch ideally provides, he and his family become objects of predation. Only when outside the mandala of state protection do Vessantara and family fall victim to the greedy gaze of Jūjaka. Similarly, humanitarian practitioners emphasize that displacement is not only a form of suffering in its own right, but also a cause for further types of suffering. Being displaced makes a person significantly more vulnerable to violations of their rights, including violence, theft, trafficking, child marriage, labor exploitation, and statelessness.

Without the protection of a state in a state-centric world, displaced people are highly vulnerable. Refugees are displaced people who have crossed international borders and therefore are relying on foreign governments for mercy; internally displaced people remain within the borders of the country where they live, but often face a government that is either unwilling or unable to assist them; and asylum seekers seek refuge after arrival at a port of entry. In each of these cases, good governance can both prevent displacement and greatly alleviate its sufferings by offering the recognition of rights. While no telling or interpretation of Vessantara's story is ever final, my reading of the story here hinges on the critical role of good governance and, in the absence of good governance at the domestic level, of international humanitarian protection and assistance for displaced people.

Paṭācārā and the Limits of Karma[34]

In Buddhist traditions, reflection on karma is often used as a method for processing and accepting the realities of misfortune. The experiences of one's present are taught to be the fruition of seeds planted through one's own intentional actions in the past. We each live in worlds at least partially of our own making, even if we cannot trace the intricate threads that tie our actions and consequences together across time and lifetimes. The Buddhist doctrine of karma can be a helpful discourse for situating one's own suffering within a larger cosmic history that transcends our current circumstances, ideally leading to a more robust sense of personal responsibility and non-hatred that will build a better future. Yet as Charles Hallisey and Anne Hansen have articulated, the "opacity of karma"—the inability of ordinary people to identify the karmic cause of a particular experience, or to predict the karmic results of a particular action to be undertaken—renders karmic reflection a complex undertaking.[35] Such reflection is particularly complex in the context of mass tragedies or humanitarian crises, where many innocents suffer.

A key narrative from Buddhist tradition that deserves a central place beside Vessantara in discussions of displacement is the story of Paṭācārā. The narrative describes how one woman experienced the greatest of tragedies, losing her home twice and losing all her family members. I was introduced to the story of Paṭācārā through Hallisey and Hansen's provocative article on "Narrative, Sub-Ethics, and the Moral Life."[36] Anne Hansen interviewed a group of Cambodian refugees, who had suffered unspeakably under the Khmer Rouge and seen many of their loved ones perish. She asked them, "how could this have happened (—the deaths of two million people)?" They responded through the medium of Buddhist narratives, and many of them appealed in particular to the story of Paṭācārā. I quote here from Hallisey and Hansen's re-telling:

> Paṭācārā was the beautiful daughter of a wealthy man who built a seven-story tower in which she was to live. She fell in love with her servant, and when her parents betrothed her to a man of the same social standing as herself, she ran away with the servant to a remote village. She subsequently gave birth to two sons, each of whom was born on the road as she attempted to return to her parents' home for the deliveries. While she was in labor with the second child, her husband was bitten by a snake and died. She decided to take her sons to her parents. On her way, she needed to cross a river but was unable to carry both sons at the same time. Having set the baby down on the far bank, she was in the middle of the river, returning for the second child, when a hawk suddenly swooped down and carried off the infant. As she made an attempt to frighten off the bird, the toddler fell into the water and was drowned. Filled with grief, Paṭācārā returned to her parental home only to learn that her parents and brother had all been killed when the tower collapsed on them. On hearing this news, she lost her mind, her clothes fell off, and she wandered naked and crazy.[37]

Karma is opaque in several ways in Paṭācārā's story. First, we encounter an opacity of *cause*: where did her karma come from? Running away from home to marry a man from the wrong class is not an adequate sin to account for the sufferings Paṭācārā endured. And there is no way of knowing what other causes from her past, or her past lives, could have merited such tragic outcomes. Second, we encounter in this story an opacity of *agent*: embedded in multigenerational relationships, Paṭācārā's suffering is intertwined with the suffering of her husband, her parents, and her children. Whose karma is at work in each of the tragedies that unfold for Paṭācārā? Hers or theirs? In what proportions? We cannot know. And third, we encounter an opacity of *result*: after Paṭācārā loses everything and goes mad, she is ordained by the Buddha and undertakes years of training and healing until she reaches liberation. One of Hansen's Cambodian informants offered this perspective on Paṭācārā's narrative: "Who can say whether she was bad or good? The consequences of her *dukkha* led her to the dharma which resulted in enlightenment [...]."[38] When life continues after tragedy, leading to new experiences, many of which are positive, we might not be able to determine whether the suffering that we are experiencing, and the karma that led to it, is ultimately bad.

Buddhist refugees in the modern era have appealed to these various modes of karmic opacity to make some sense of their expulsion from their homelands. They may reflect that they cannot know what harmful actions they have perpetrated upon their displacers in the past, which is one approach that Tibetans have often taken to explain their exile and to mitigate feelings of contempt toward the Chinese people.[39] Buddhists may even project optimism about their future by musing that exile is the fruition of good karma because it results, for example, in the chance to spread Buddhism to new parts of the world. They may also retain a healthy agnosticism about whose karma was really at work in the tragedy, particularly when suffering involves such a large number of people: is it personal karma or societal karma?[40]

> American Buddhist laywoman Melody Ermachild Chavis works as a mitigation lawyer for felons facing a possible death sentence. [...] For Chavis, the law of karma is true, but interdependence is true, too. It's not accurate to treat karma as a single line of individual responsibility, divorced from everything else; this is not reality. Interdependence is reality. Both individual responsibility and social responsibility are realities, and they are both integral parts of karma playing out in an ocean of causes and conditions.[41]

Still, these various modes of karmic reflection are not sufficient for everyone who suffers. I would argue that neither are they sufficient for the Buddha. In the Pāli canon, the Buddha teaches that karma is not to be taken as the cause for everything that happens. While karma certainly plays a role in the world's unfolding, the Buddha cautions against three deterministic theories of causation: attributing everything to karma, attributing everything to the creation of a god, and attributing everything to chance.[42] While he sees each of these three totalizing views as dangerous, in this text the Buddha is particularly concerned that attributing all experiences to karma may weaken resolve and lead to inaction. Sallie King has argued that "To the Buddha this view—[attributing everything that happens to karma]—is one of the most destructive views one could hold" because it leads to "fatalism and passivity."[43]

If definitively attributing misfortune to karma is misguided, even potentially destructive, what good is karmic reflection for Paṭācārā? For displaced people? Hansen's Cambodian colleague Bounthay Phath suggests,

> Cambodians are used to the law of karma, but it doesn't always make sense. [...] In my opinion, if people emphasize loving-kindness and think less about the law of karma, there will be a reduction in suffering because people acting out of loving-kindness will create social justice in their community.[44]

Karma cannot make sense of the unthinkable, so think less about karma, Phath suggests: act with loving kindness instead. King observes that

> Engaged Buddhists often argue that traditional, popular understandings of karma are incorrect. In particular they insist that in thinking about karma it is important to turn away from a focus on the past and focus instead on the present and the future; they emphasize that karma means action, coupled with a belief in the openness of the future, and the determination to act.[45]

Like many Engaged Buddhists, Phath emphasizes that actions based on compassion and loving-kindness plant the seeds for positive outcomes in the future. Actively committing to that positive future by performing good deeds is one way that displaced Buddhists have coped with their displacement experiences. I will expand further on the importance of merit-making in addressing the sufferings of displacement in Chapter 3.

Where karmic reflection might play the strongest role in addressing tragedy is not for those in deep suffering, but for those in positions of power to relieve it. Buddhist scriptures teem with advice for rulers to heed the teachings on karma. In the Mahāyāna tradition, Nāgārjuna's *Letter to a Friend* urges a king to reflect on his karma in this way:

> "I have not gone beyond sickness, old age, or death,
> Or being parted from those I hold dear,
> Or beyond what my karma will do to me."
> Contemplating this, again and again,
> As a corrective measure, you avoid becoming full of yourself.[46]

"Contemplating this, again and again"—sustained reflection on karmic consequences—is a task for the potential victimizer even moreso than for the victim. Karmic reflection ideally serves to mitigate the abuse of power by inculcating restraint and ethical deliberation in those who have the authority to affect the well-being of others. As Tibetan scholastic Sumpa Khenpo noted, when writing in his autobiography about a time of war and upheaval in the eighteenth century,

> In any and every world system, the good and evil that befall people, both collectively and individually, is indeed the fruition of their karma that is shared or unshared; but, conventionally speaking, in any place, the waxing and waning of the Buddha's teachings, and the respective happiness or misery of beings, all follow as a consequence of the words and actions of the kings and ministers of that land. [...] Therefore, [...] merit and non-merit and happiness and misery, whatever befalls [the people], follow as a consequence of the powerful rulers of that place—and there is no place where that isn't the case.[47]

If anyone should be engaging in karmic reflection, it is kings and rulers because their actions directly affect the fortunes of those under their care, for good or for ill. Sumpa Khenpo's use of the phrase "conventionally speaking" brings the conversation down from the plane of ultimate reality, which is opaque to unenlightened beings, to the plane of conventional truth where karma is indeed knowable: it is action and power and their effects upon others.

Paṭācārā does find her way to karmic reflection in the end. After many years of distance from her tragedy, after time to practice calming her mind, one day she pours water over her feet and notices how three rivulets form: one short, one middle-length, and one long. In this moment, she is able to reflect on how our lives and our karma are exhausted in different measures. Some die young, like her children; some die in middle age, like her husband and her brother; some die in old age, like her parents. Our life-streams and our karma are unknowable, and Paṭācārā finally makes peace with that truth. She attains awakening and goes on to teach many other nuns in the community, becoming a revered exemplar of the Buddha's teachings.

Notes

1 Richman, Paula, ed. *Questioning Ramayanas: A South Asian Tradition.* Berkeley: University of California Press, 2001. p. 11.

2 I borrow this term from Werth, Paul. *Text Worlds: Representing Conceptual Space in Discourse.* Harlow, UK: Longman, 1999; but I do not use it in the strictly linguistic sense in which he developed it.

3 Thanissaro Bhikkhu. "Refuge: An Introduction to the Buddha, Dhamma, & Sangha." *Access to Insight (BCBS Edition)*, 30 November 2013. Accessed on 25 November 2025. www.accesstoinsight.org/lib/authors/thanissaro/refuge.html.

4 Monier-Williams, M. *Sanskrit-English Dictionary*, entry for "*saṃsāra.*" Oxford: Clarendon Press, 1899. Accessed on 10 May 2024. www.sanskrit-lexicon.uni-koeln.de/scans/MWScan/2020/web/webtc/indexcaller.php.

5 "Anusota Sutta: With the Flow" (AN 4.5), translated from the Pāli by Thanissaro Bhikkhu. *Access to Insight (BCBS Edition)*, 3 July 2010. Accessed on 10 May 2024. www.accesstoinsight.org/tipitaka/an/an04/an04.005.than.html.

6 Lopez, Donald, Jr. "Buddhism in the Real World," *Tricycle: The Buddhist Review* (Summer 2021). Accessed on 25 November 2025. https://tricycle.org/magazine/history-of-buddhism-and-activism/.

7 Heim, Maria. *Voice of the Buddha: Buddhaghosa on the Immeasurable Words.* New York: Oxford University Press, 2018. p. 50 ff.

8 Hills, David. "Metaphor." In Edward N. Zalta and Uri Nodelman, eds., *The Stanford Encyclopedia of Philosophy.* Stanford, CA: The Metaphysics Research Lab, 2022. Entry last revised 12 August 2022. Accessed on 25 November 2025. https://plato.stanford.edu/archives/fall2024/entries/metaphor/.

9 Substantial text in this section is drawn from Kilby, Christina, "'The World is Without Shelter, Without Protector': Buddhism, the Protection of Displaced People, and International Humanitarian Law." In Deniz Coşan Eke and Eric M. Trinka, eds. *Religion, Religious Groups and Migration*, pp. 9–28. London: Transnational Press, 2023.

10 International Rescue Committee. "Is it Legal to Cross the U.S. Border to Seek Asylum?" 1 July 2022. Accessed on 8 May 2024. www.rescue.org/article/it-legal-cross-us-border-seek-asylum.

11 Holy Bible, New Revised Standard Version, Anglicised. Accessed on 20 May 2026. https://www.biblegateway.com/versions/New-Revised-Standard-Version-Anglicised-NRSVA-Bible/. Genesis 12:1.

12 Holy Bible, New Revised Standard Version, Anglicised. Accessed on 20 May 2026. https://www.biblegateway.com/versions/New-Revised-Standard-Version-Anglicised-NRSVA-Bible/. Exodus 14:11–12. New Revised Standard Version, Anglicised.

They said to Moses, "Was it because there were no graves in Egypt that you have taken us away to die in the wilderness? What have you done to us, bringing us out of Egypt? Is this not the very thing we told you in Egypt, 'Let us alone and let us serve the Egyptians'? For it would have been better for us to serve the Egyptians than to die in the wilderness."

13 Zornberg, Avivah Gottlieb. *The Particulars of Rapture: Reflections on Exodus.* New York: Doubleday, 2011. p. 3.

14 *Quran.* Translation by M.A.S. Abdel Haleem. Accessed on 6 May 2026. https://quran.com/an-nisa/97?translations=85. An-Nisa 4:97.

15 Gould, Rebecca Ruth. "The Obligation to Migrate and the Impulse to Narrate: Soviet Narratives of Forced Migration in the Nineteenth Century Caucasus." In Ray Jureidini, Hamad Bin, and Said Fares Hassan, eds. *Migration and Islamic Ethics*, pp. 154–173. Leiden: Brill, 2019. p. 156.

16 "Kacchapa-Jātaka" (The Tortoise That Loved His Home Too Much). In *The Jataka; or, Stories of the Buddha's Former Births,* edited by E.B. Cowell, vol. 2. no. 178, pp. 55–56. Translated from the Pāli by W.H.D. Rouse. Cambridge: Cambridge University Press, 1895. Accessed on 10 May 2024. www.pitt.edu/~dash/jataka.html#tortoiserefused.

17 "Kacchapa-Jātaka" (The Tortoise That Loved His Home Too Much). In *The Jataka; or, Stories of the Buddha's Former Births,* edited by E.B. Cowell, vol. 2. no. 178, pp. 55–56. Translated from the Pāli by W.H.D. Rouse. Cambridge: Cambridge University Press, 1895. Accessed on 10 May 2024. www.pitt.edu/~dash/jataka.html#tortoiserefused. p. 55.

18 "Kacchapa-Jātaka" (The Tortoise That Loved His Home Too Much). In *The Jataka; or, Stories of the Buddha's Former Births,* edited by E.B. Cowell, vol. 2. no. 178, pp. 55–56. Translated from the Pāli by W.H.D. Rouse. Cambridge: Cambridge University Press, 1895. Accessed on 10 May 2024. www.pitt.edu/~dash/jataka.html#tortoiserefused. p. 56.

19 "Kacchapa-Jātaka" (The Tortoise That Loved His Home Too Much). In *The Jataka; or, Stories of the Buddha's Former Births,* edited by E.B. Cowell, vol. 2. no. 178, pp. 55–56. Translated from the Pāli by W.H.D. Rouse. Cambridge: Cambridge University Press, 1895. Accessed on 10 May 2024. www.pitt.edu/~dash/jataka.html#tortoiserefused. p. 56.

20 Hein, Jeremy and Tarique Niazi. "The Primordial Refugees: Religious Traditions, Global Forced Migration, and State-Society Relations." *International Sociology* 31, no. 6 (2016): 726–741. DOI: 10.1177/0268580916662388.

21 Collins, Steven, ed. *Readings of the Vessantara Jātaka.* New York: Columbia University Press, 2016.

22 "Vessantara-Jātaka." *The Jataka, Vol. VI*, translated by E.B. Cowell and W.H.D. Rouse, 1907. No. 547, pp. 246–306. Accessed on 3 January 2026. https://sacred-texts.com/bud/j6/j6013.htm.

23 "Vessantara-Jātaka." *The Jataka, Vol. VI*, translated by E.B. Cowell and W.H.D. Rouse, 1907. No. 547, pp. 246–306. Accessed on 3 January 2026. https://sacred-texts.com/bud/j6/j6013.htm. p. 250.

24 Makidono, Tomoko. "The Vessantara Jātaka in the Maṇi bka' 'bum and the Fifth Dalai Lama's 'Khrung rab," *The Indian International Journal of Buddhist Studies* 21 (2021), article 5. Accessed on 1 May 2024. https://digitalcommons.linfield.edu/iijbs/vol21/iss1/5. p 2.

25 Ladwig, Patrice. "Emotions and Narrative: Excessive Giving and Ethical Ambivalence in the Lao Vessantara Jātaka." In Steven Collins, ed., *Readings of the Vessantara Jātaka*, pp. 57–76. New York: Columbia University Press, 2016. p. 57.

26 "Vessantara-Jātaka." *The Jataka, Vol. VI*, translated by E.B. Cowell and W.H.D. Rouse, 1907. No. 547, pp. 246–306. Accessed on 3 January 2026. https://sacred-texts.com/bud/j6/j6013.htm. p. 255.

27 "Vessantara-Jātaka." *The Jataka, Vol. VI*, translated by E.B. Cowell and W.H.D. Rouse, 1907. No. 547, pp. 246–306. Accessed on 3 January 2026. https://sacred-texts.com/bud/j6/j6013.htm. p. 259.

28 "Vessantara-Jātaka." *The Jataka, Vol. VI*, translated by E.B. Cowell and W.H.D. Rouse, 1907. No. 547, pp. 246–306. Accessed on 3 January 2026. https://sacred-texts.com/bud/j6/j6013.htm. p. 260.

29 Hallisey, Charles, translator. *Poems of the First Buddhist Women: A Translation of the Therigatha*. Cambridge, MA: Harvard University Press, 2021.

30 "Alīnacitta-Jātaka." *The Jataka, Vol. II*, translated by W.H.D. Rouse [1895]. No. 156, pp. 13–17. Accessed on 3 January 2026. https://sacred-texts.com/bud/j2/j2009.htm.

31 Ladwig, Patrice. "Emotions and Narrative: Excessive Giving and Ethical Ambivalence in the Lao Vessantara Jātaka." In Steven Collins, ed., *Readings of the Vessantara Jātaka*, pp. 57–76. New York: Columbia University Press, 2016. pp. 57–76.

32 Collins, Steven, ed. *Readings of the Vessantara Jātaka*. New York: Columbia University Press, 2016.

33 Adapted from Kilby, Christina. "A Humanitarian Reading of the Vessantara Jataka." International Committee of the Red Cross, *Religion and Humanitarian Principles*. 7 October 2022. Accessed on 8 May 2024. https://blogs.icrc.org/religion-humanitarianprinciples/humanitarian-reading-vessantara-jataka/.

34 This discussion is based on the author's conference presentation on "The Limits of Karma: Humanitarian Crises and the Ethics of Governmental Responsibility," presented at the American Academy of Religion annual meeting in November 2021.

35 Hallisey, Charles and Anne Hansen. "Narrative, Sub-Ethics, and the Moral Life: Some Evidence from Theravāda Buddhism." *Journal of Religious Ethics* 24, no. 2 (1996): 305–327. p. 319. Their use of the term "opacity" hearkens to Clifford Geertz' characterization of the problem of suffering: "[…] the strange opacity of events, the dumb senselessness of intense or inexorable pain, and the enigmatic unaccountability of gross iniquity." Refer to Sharma, Ursula, "Theodicy and the Doctrine of Karma," *Man New Series* 8, no. 3 (Sep. 1973): 347–364. p. 347.

36 Hallisey, Charles and Anne Hansen. "Narrative, Sub-Ethics, and the Moral Life: Some Evidence from Theravāda Buddhism." *The Journal of Religious Ethics* 24, no. 2 (1996): 305–327.

37 Hallisey, Charles and Anne Hansen. "Narrative, Sub-Ethics, and the Moral Life: Some Evidence from Theravāda Buddhism." *Journal of Religious Ethics* 24, no. 2 (1996): 305–327. p. 319.

38 Hallisey, Charles and Anne Hansen. "Narrative, Sub-Ethics, and the Moral Life: Some Evidence from Theravāda Buddhism." *Journal of Religious Ethics* 24, no. 2 (1996): 305–327. p. 321.

39 King, Sallie. "The Problems and Promise of Karma from an Engaged Buddhist Perspective." In Jake Davis, ed., *A Mirror is for Reflection: Understanding Buddhist Ethics*, pp. 166–183. Oxford: Oxford University Press, 2017. p. 167.

40 King, Sallie. "The Problems and Promise of Karma from an Engaged Buddhist Perspective." In Jake Davis, ed., *A Mirror is for Reflection: Understanding Buddhist Ethics*, pp. 166–183. Oxford: Oxford University Press, 2017. Refer to p. 173 for a discussion of Ambedkar's society-level interpretation of karma.

41 King, Sallie. "The Problems and Promise of Karma from an Engaged Buddhist Perspective." In Jake Davis, ed., *A Mirror is for Reflection: Understanding Buddhist Ethics*, pp. 166–183. Oxford: Oxford University Press, 2017. p. 178.

42 Harvey, Peter. "'Freedom of the Will' in the Light of Theravada Buddhist Teachings." *Journal of Buddhist Ethics* 14, no. 1 (2007): 35–98. p. 56.

43 King, Sallie. "The Problems and Promise of Karma from an Engaged Buddhist Perspective." In Jake Davis, ed., *A Mirror is for Reflection: Understanding Buddhist Ethics*, pp. 166–183. Oxford: Oxford University Press, 2017. p. 176.

44 Hallisey, Charles and Anne Hansen. "Narrative, Sub-Ethics, and the Moral Life: Some Evidence from Theravāda Buddhism." *Journal of Religious Ethics* 24, no. 2 (1996): 305–327. p. 321.

45 King, Sallie. "The Problems and Promise of Karma from an Engaged Buddhist Perspective." In Jake Davis, ed., *A Mirror is for Reflection: Understanding Buddhist Ethics*, pp. 166–183. Oxford: Oxford University Press, 2017. p. 176.

46 Nāgārjuna. "bShes pa'i spring yig (Letter to a Friend)." *bsTan 'gyur* (sde dge), edited by zhu chen tshul khrims rin chen, translated from the Sanskrit by sKa ba dpal brtsegs, vol. 173, Delhi Karmapae Choedhey, Gyalwae Sungrab Partun Khang, 1982–1985, pp. 82–94. Buddhist Digital Resource Center (BDRC), purl.bdrc.io/resource/MW23703_4182. Stanza 46 (English translation mine).

47 sum pa mkhan po ye shes dpal 'byor (Sumpa Khenpo Yeshé Penjor). *Expressing the Conduct of the Supreme Pandita Sumpa Yeshé Penjor: Alchemy for the Ear (paN+Di ta sum pa ye shes dpal 'byor mchog gi spyod tshul brjod pa sgra 'dzin bcud len)*. In *Collected Works* 8 (nya), 373–960. Beijing: Tibetan Civilization Publishing House of China, 2001. Buddhist Digital Resource Center work ID W25006. Accessed on 6 May 2026. Buddhist Digital Resource Center (BDRC), purl.bdrc.io/resource/MW25006. p. 471 (English translation mine).

3 Place and Displacement in Buddhist Life Worlds

Introduction

Scholarship on religion and displacement has traced a variety of ways that people engage with their religious traditions when experiencing the cosmological rupture of displacement. They may pray or seek blessings, carry sacred objects with them for protection, search scriptural narratives for meaning or direction, request rituals from religious specialists, adapt rituals to new settings, follow pilgrimage routes on their paths to safety, erect religious structures, tap international religious networks for tangible support, or attribute success on their journey to miracles. People's relationships to religion often shift when they experience life-changing events like displacement: they may become more deeply religious, convert to another religion,[1] become internally pluralistic in terms of the religious resources they access,[2] or reject a religious orientation altogether.

Several English-language anthologies have gathered case studies that span this variety of religious responses to the experience of displacement.[3] They have highlighted the constructive roles that religion can play in making sense of suffering, providing hope, healing trauma, connecting communities, adapting to new homes, and motivating assistance and hospitality. Buddhism has been largely absent from these multireligious anthologies, despite the existence of a healthy field of ethnographic and social scientific studies of the experiences of Buddhist refugees in the modern world. Buddhism has also been largely absent from global academic conferences, humanitarian convenings, and policy discussions that seek to compare and synthesize findings across religions in order to facilitate more effective and culturally sensitive responses to displacement.[4]

In this chapter, I offer some arguments and several case studies to examine how people in contexts of displacement have drawn upon Buddhist teachings and practices as they have attempted to cope with loss and to bring their traditions with them into new places. These case studies address different schools of Buddhism, different historical moments, different cultural contexts, and different challenges. The shared Buddhist identity of the people featured in these case studies does not determine any single type of response to their

DOI: 10.4324/9781003318149-3

displacement; the ways in which people respond to their circumstances are emergent, contingent, variable. My hope in offering this study of particularities is that some overarching reorientations toward the intersection of religion and displacement might present themselves, particularly to those who want to improve humanitarian assistance and psychological care for displaced people in Buddhist contexts.

Case Study: Japanese-American Internees

During World War II, the U.S. government forced more than 110,000 Japanese Americans into internment camps. About sixty percent of the internees were U.S. citizens; half of the internees were children. In *American Sutra,* his expertly documented study of the experiences of Japanese Buddhist internees, Duncan Ryūken Williams observes a variety of roles that Buddhism played for the internees as they endured abduction, confiscation of their property, separation from their families, forced labor, inhumane living conditions, repression of religious practice, lack of appropriate medical care, and extrajudicial executions.[5]

Buddhism served as a source of great comfort and hope to many of the internees, but Buddhists in the camps were provided with scant resources to facilitate their religious practice in comparison to Japanese Christians in the camps. Meditation could only happen before wake-up and after lights-out. Buddhist priests had to work menial jobs in the camps to make necessary income, and in some cases, their traditional religious implements and texts were banned from the camps.[6] Still, they found ways to adapt their Buddhist practice to the constraints they faced.

Celebrating the Buddha's birthday was one ritual occasion that required creative adaptation. Williams records the observations of one of the detainees at Camp McCoy in Wisconsin that:

> We did not, of course, have a single religious implement to use for Buddhist services. We did not have a *tanjobutsu* [Baby Buddha statue], *butsu-gu* [Buddhist ritual tools], flowers, incense, or any of the implements used in Hanamatsuri [Buddha's birthday] celebration. Fortunately, we were with many people who were clever with their hands. Arthur Yamabe "borrowed" a carrot from the kitchen and carved a splendid image of the Buddha.[7]

The internees used coffee rather than the traditional tea to bathe the carrot Buddha.[8]

> Priests surrounded the carrot Buddha with "a cherry blossom flower arrangement" crafted by a Nishi Hongwanji priest using beet-dyed toilet paper, while a Jōdo sect priest officiated the intersectarian birthday

> ceremony at an altar created by transforming bread wrapping paper and labels from canned goods.[9]

Carrots, coffee, and can labels served as the mud in which the lotus of practice could take root in the camps. As Williams observes,

> Making do was, of course, part of the Buddhist tradition. Throughout Buddhist teachings, there are examples of people using whatever ingredients they could assemble. Consider this, for instance, from a thirteenth-century cooking manual written by Zen Master Dōgen, the founder of Sōtō Zen Buddhism in Japan:
>
> "If you only have wild grasses with which to make a broth, do not disdain them. If you have ingredients for a creamy soup do not be delighted. Where there is no attachment, there can be no aversion. Do not be careless with poor ingredients and do not depend on fine ingredients to do your work for you but work with everything with the same sincerity."[10]

Making do became a manifestation of *upāya* (skillful means) for priests and other practitioners in the camps. One priest wrote of how the internment experience helped him appreciate the hardships of those who had traveled in difficult conditions to bring Buddhism from India to China and from China to Japan.[11] Others expressed that their internment enabled a newfound intimacy with other teachers or saints in their lineages who endured hardship. One priest noted how his sense of vocational identity shifted in the camps; the indignities that the priests endured in the camps (for example, filthy clothes, no privacy in the shower or toilet, and invasive medical exams) could also be perceived as credentials for them to minister to people who suffer. From his diary entry:

> March 23—Because of our robes, we Buddhist priests are usually isolated from larger society, but being put in a place like this, we are just regular human beings who experience suffering just like everyone else. Indeed, without this kind of experience we priests should not talk to others about the purpose of life.[12]

Another priest saw his internment as an opportunity to enable the "eastward expansion of the dharma" (from Japan to the Americas), which he saw as a fulfillment of Buddhist prophecy.[13]

Thus, not only did Japanese Buddhists in the camps adapt their religious practices to conditions of deprivation, but those adaptations served in many cases to deepen their understanding of key Buddhist concepts, including detachment, skillful means, identity, prophecy, and the karmic links between suffering and liberation.[14] The internees' experience in the camps changed Buddhism for them.

Due to the unhygienic, crowded, and mosquito-ridden living conditions, 1,862 people died from disease while in the camps. Therefore, funerals were a regular feature of the intern experience and proved an extremely important ritual for internees. In one case, when a group of internees were forced to walk two miles through the desert to a camp in New Mexico, two men who were elderly and in poor health were shot and killed by a U.S. Army officer because they were not able to keep up with the group.

> The Army refused to allow Japanese doctors in the group to perform autopsies. The authorities also refused to allow a Buddhist funeral for the two men. In protest, the Buddhists in the camp refused orders to assemble at 4 pm the day after the shooting, stating that they would "pay their respects in their own barracks." After the Japanese complained to the Spanish consul, who was an international monitor charged with overseeing the treatment of Japanese internees, the Army permitted a small funeral, limited to forty people, three weeks later.[15]

The internees' willingness to defy U.S. Army orders and register a formal complaint with the Spanish consul to insist on a proper funeral for their elders speaks to the centrality of the funeral ritual for the human dignity of those interned. As in other Buddhist contexts, the role of monastics or priests in guiding the deceased toward a favorable rebirth made funerary rituals central to coping with the grief of loss.

While familiar practices like meditation, sutra recitation, funerals, and Buddhist holiday celebrations provided comfort to many, due to the scrutiny and intimidation that Buddhists in the camps faced, some internees "maintained their Buddhist affiliation only quietly, or even converted to Christianity."[16] For one devoted Buddhist, "fear of government reprisal had forced her to burn her Buddha and the tablets of the family dead," which she later "deeply regretted."[17]

Case Study: Tibetan Refugees

Since the People's Liberation Army invaded Tibet in 1950 and the Dalai Lama took refuge in India in 1959, more than one hundred thousand Tibetans have fled their communities on the Tibetan Plateau for a life in exile. The majority of Tibetan refugees have settled in India, where the Dalai Lama still resides, with a fair number in Nepal and smaller numbers in Bhutan and western countries. One atypical aspect of the Tibetan exile experience (compared to the experiences of other Buddhist refugees) has been that the majority of Tibetan refugees now live in the ancestral homeland of Buddhism and find themselves near their tradition's major pilgrimage sites and temples. When free to choose, Tibetans have often chosen to settle near sites such as the Great Stupa at Boudhanath in Kathmandu, linking themselves to the ancient sacred history of their host countries and viewing their exile as a homecoming.

Tibetans have also added to these sacred landscapes by constructing new shrines, stupas, temples, monasteries, and hospitals wherever they settle in large enough numbers. Hundreds of Tibetan Buddhist temples have been built around the world under the leadership of exiled lamas (more than fifty have been built near the Great Stupa at Boudhanath alone).

These extensive building projects serve as emplacement strategies, whereby Tibetans weave themselves into a sacred geography that extends beyond the Plateau and make new countries into "central lands"[18] or Buddhist homelands. These building projects create the tangible supports for Tibetans to engage in familiar merit-making practices, rituals, and festivals. Institutions (such as monasteries, schools, and hospitals) that Tibetans have built in exile have also enabled the continuity of traditional Tibetan Buddhist forms of education and medical practice for the younger generations to maintain their cultural and religious identities in exile.[19] The emplacement that many Tibetan refugee communities have achieved through their building projects—and the ritual and educational life they enable—has relied on several factors, including international attention and donor support, a strong sense of national identity anchored in the person of the Dalai Lama, and the assumption that their exile will be long-term and therefore worth investing in.

One surprising consequence of Tibetan building projects across the globe has been the occasional conflict with local religious or indigenous communities. For example, Sally McAra documented an Aboriginal woman's protest against the construction of a nearly fifty-meter-high stupa near Bendigo, Australia, at the intersection of two ancestral songlines.[20] While most Aboriginal people in the area appear to have supported the stupa's construction, after the woman's complaint, the stupa developers proposed a compromise that the stupa contain a hole on one side to allow the songlines to pass through, or that a garden be planted at its base to honor the Aboriginal ancestors of the locale.[21] This case highlights the compromises that Buddhist refugees must sometimes consider as they pursue emplacement strategies, particularly fascinating in Australia because of the collision of indigenous-colonized identities that both Aboriginal and Tibetan communities carry.

In another example of conflict with local religious communities, Laura Harrington has analyzed neo-Pentecostal responses to the Kālacakra for World Peace mass empowerment that the Dalai Lama offered in Ontario, Canada, in 2004.[22] The Dalai Lama, following on a 100-year-old tradition, has led tantric initiations into the Kālacakra system of practice for hundreds of thousands of people across his decades in exile. These mass empowerments serve to consecrate new places where Tibetan refugees live, to bring blessings and protection to those places, to provide proximity to the central figure of the Dalai Lama (to whom many Tibetans are deeply devoted), to draw together Tibetan nationals into a powerful identity-building experience, and to situate Tibetans within a larger cosmology of history and nationhood that extends beyond their exile experience.

The *Kālacakra Tantra*, or *Wheel of Time*, is a scriptural text detailing, among other things, an eschatological vision of a battle between a Buddhist kingdom and an enemy army; the auto-commentary interprets this violence metaphorically.[23] The eleven-day initiation program in Ontario involved teachings, rituals, dances, and the construction of an intricate nine-foot-wide sand mandala that was ritually disposed into Lake Ontario to bless the natural environment.[24] The mandala's construction and ritual disposal into Lake Ontario spurred a neo-Pentecostal Christian apostle to action to spiritually combat its effects. Part of the Spiritual Mapping movement within Christianity, this apostle (identified by the pseudonym Jim Gosa) saw the Kālacakra empowerment as part of the Dalai Lama's plan to colonize the earth with demonic, anti-Christ spirit beings—establishing a Buddhocracy called "Shambala" in preparation for the end times. Gosa was "leading a team in a chain of prayer sessions around the perimeter of the Lake to prevent the Tibetan spirits that would be poured into the waters from being dispersed into the adjacent lands. 'With the authority and dominion by God' and 'in the name of the Holy Spirit,' Apostle Gosa later explained, 'I commanded the spirits of the lake to shut their mouths … .' "[25]

While the Bendigo and Ontario cases differ significantly, they are both conflicts that relate to the indwelling of spiritual forces in the physical landscape and competition between them (through the ritual action of their supplicants) for territorial primacy. These cases demonstrate that the conflicts that can emerge between displaced Buddhists and their host societies are not limited to those over material resources or political policies; they include concerns about how spirit beings migrate and potentially displace or compete with other spirit beings. These concerns and their ritual ramifications might easily be missed by outsiders, yet they matter to displaced people and their hosts in many cultural contexts—in Asian and western contexts alike.

The Tibetan exile experience has not only been an optimistic story of building, continuity of tradition, and cultural resilience, but of course, also a story of pain. During the invasion of the 1950s and the Great Leap Forward years of famine and persecution, many Tibetans lost their lives or endured torture or forced disappearances. One of the most keenly felt losses of those years among Tibetan refugees was identified by one clinical study as "witnessing the destruction of religious signs," such as temples, sacred images, scriptures, and monastic robes.[26] Buddhism's role in the Tibetan exile has therefore also been one of healing trauma, especially for monastics who were heavily targeted in the anti-religion campaigns of the Maoist years. Violence, persecution, and disappearances continue to deeply affect Tibetan communities in the People's Republic of China today.

While many Buddhists and non-Buddhists alike may assume that meditation would be a useful tool for Tibetans coping with trauma and managing post-traumatic stress disorder (PTSD), one study of Tibetan refugee monks in Boston suggests otherwise. The 2009 study showed that for the eight refugee monks presenting with PTSD symptoms, meditation proved a great struggle. When sitting for meditation, the monks were overwhelmed by intrusive thoughts, painful memories, anxiety about nightmares, and worry about family members abroad. Their inability to meditate—a skill in which they were highly expert and which they associated with mental well-being—caused them further distress as well as feelings of shame and helplessness, exacerbating their intrusive symptoms.

These monks had been diagnosed by traditional Tibetan doctors as having a disorder of the central life-wind (*srog rlung*), caused in part by intellectual overexertion and resulting in symptoms like depression, anxiety, heart palpitations, and dysphoria.[27] Clinicians in the Boston study chose to approach a dual diagnosis of *srog rlung* disorder and PTSD in an attempt to find a model of well-being that bridged biomedical and religiocultural frameworks. As they consulted with traditional Tibetan medical experts, the Boston clinicians learned that

> traditional healing recommends against the use of meditation as a therapy for mental illness, warning against the greater anxiety that might be induced, and recommending that if one does attempt to meditate, that it would best be practiced in exceptionally brief sessions (which have a greater chance of being successful) as opposed to the usual longer sessions.[28]

In fact, Tibetan doctors advised that meditation could make *srog rlung* conditions much worse:

> If strain develops in the mind's attempt to concentrate itself on the object of meditation, if rather than being gently guided into one-pointedness the mind is forced into submission, if the mind squeezes and tightens in its attempt at concentration, then the mind is said to "rise up" in its attempt to find the object. As the mind rises up, the *pranic* current on which it is mounted rises with it, producing the symptoms and signs of sok-rlung [srog-rLung]. This same rise in sok-rlung will also occur when obsessive inner thoughts about progress in meditation arise in a mind already concentrated to the degree that external sensory inputs no longer occur.
>
> Remarkably, this symptom-as-stressor convolution resembles the very same "pathogenic spiral that deepened the patients' chronicity and despair, and exacerbated their dysfunctional behavior" as a result of undiagnosed and misdiagnosed PTSD, which was at the core of the argument for the creation of a new diagnostic category in the DSM-III.[29]

Research suggests that culturally sensitive care is vitally important for achieving mental health outcomes for refugees and traumatized immigrants.[30] Yet for Buddhist refugees, meditation may not constitute a low-risk, culturally sensitive therapy for PTSD. This study suggests that the religious worldview of the patient, the type of meditation practiced (since meditation takes manifold forms),[31] and the emic disease etiology (in this case, overexertion of the mind) should all be considered by clinicians working with Buddhist refugees seeking to provide culturally competent care. A clinically significant religious impairment—such as the inability to meditate—should be identified not only as a *symptom* of mental unwellness, but as a potential *cause* for unwellness.

Buddhism offers many resources other than meditation that may be helpful for healing trauma and cultivating resilience in the face of loss. In the case of the Tibetan diaspora community, Diane Denis has shown how the concept of spaciousness or limitlessness, a frequent metaphor in Tibetan-Himalayan Buddhist texts and prayers, has served to enhance Tibetans' resilience in the face of displacement and its losses.[32] She links her claims both to western clinical understandings of resilience and to Tibetan-Himalayan traditions of mind training (Tibetan *blo sbyong*) and the bodhisattva ideal, emphasizing in particular how metaphors of spaciousness (the sky, space, the vast ocean, and so forth) enable perspective-taking and help people resist victimization. Denis finds that

> within the Tibetan settlements according to [Sarah] Lewis, people do not necessarily see themselves as victims, even as victims of forced displacement. They also do not necessarily see themselves as damaged persons needing restoration. Kaye et al., in their research on justice, invite us to rethink the notion of trauma with its implicit tripartite structure featuring a division between three characters, that of victim, villain, and hero. Yet within the context of the Bodhisattva path, one could be said to embody these three within oneself, in other words, one is the present "victim" of one's past ignorance, the "villain" caught with past disturbed emotions responsible (at least in part) for the actual situation, and, depending on one's present state of mind, the hero oriented toward liberation from suffering.[33]

This powerful form of perspective-taking can be accessed without engaging directly in meditation; rather, it arises as a result of repeated encounters with familiar verses and teachings. Denis' study suggests that clinicians might seek more wide-ranging discussion with the communities they serve about which resources in their traditions may serve the cultivation of resilience.

Case Study: Cambodian Genocide Survivors

Displacement was integral to many layers of Cambodia's painful history during the civil war (1967–1975) and the reign of the Khmer Rouge (1975–1979). Not only were an estimated one million rural Cambodians displaced by U.S. bombing during the civil war, but when the war ended and the Khmer Rouge seized power, the regime systematically expelled more than two million people from Phnom Penh. About one million people fled Cambodia as refugees in the following years. For Cambodians, this displacement is intertwined with the trauma of mass violence, and their responses to both are likewise intertwined.

A number of clinical studies over the last several decades have sought to understand how Cambodians have coped with their trauma and the role Buddhism has played for many of them in their continued quest for healing. Devon E. Hinton and colleagues[34] have conducted numerous studies of the mental health of Cambodian and Vietnamese refugees who continue to suffer distress from their experiences of violence during the 1960s and 1970s. Hinton's group worked to bridge emic descriptions of psychological symptoms with the categories in the *Diagnostic and Statistical Manual* (*DSM*). In the Cambodian cultural context, describing oneself as "thinking too much" (*kut caraeun*) was one of the chief indicators for what the *DSM* identifies as "post-traumatic stress disorder."[35] Thinking too much was characterized by recalling upsetting topics, ruminating on past traumatic events, and thinking constantly about loved ones who had died, and included symptoms such as headaches, dizzy spells, "wind attacks," lethargy, and "overheating of the brain."[36] One key factor that led to thinking too much was nightmares, especially those featuring ghosts of loved ones who were violently killed.[37] Nightmares were not seen merely as symptoms of thinking too much, but also as causes for thinking too much because they were believed to actively decrease the soul's strength or rupture some of the soul's protective layers:

> For a Cambodian refugee, a nightmare raises concerns that a protective layer of the self is defective, that forces that should protect one are not intact—or at least are not the equal to the assaulting forces. It indicates low "good luck" (*riesey*), weakness and a dislodged soul; the nightmare itself, by bringing about fright, a dangerous emotion, may also weaken the body and dislodge the soul. After a bad dream, the patient will expect to be ill for several days.[38]

Hinton's team identified fifteen layers of protection that form a Cambodian model of concentric ontological security: the stable soul (at the center), and then in concentric circles, energy, body coolness, normal blood flow, good mental state, merit, high *riesey* (good luck), tattoos, holy water, talismans, *baasey/slaathoa* deities, house spirit, Buddha, ancestors, and local deities.[39] If too many of these layers are weakened or ruptured, the soul can wander away from the body and will need to be called back or resecured.

Each of these layers of protection can be enhanced through ritual techniques, such as applying holy water to one's body, offering it to one's ancestors, or imbibing it; generating positive thoughts; making offerings to monks; reciting Pāli verses; wearing amulets, talismans, or tattoos; or praying to the Buddha, ancestors, or other deities. In the diagrams that Hinton et al. provide in their study, they locate these ritual techniques in different physical places: inside one's body, on the surface of one's body, on the house post of one's home, at one's home altar, or at shrines or temples outside the home.[40] Most of the fifteen layers are activated within the confines of the home, where the person is located in the diagram. This model implies that a safe home and practices of emplacement are integral to Cambodian notions of ontological security. Home is where a person can nourish, wash, and ornament their body; where they enjoy the protection of household gods as well as ancestors; and where they can cultivate feelings of safety and other positive thoughts. These protective techniques are additional to the physical security, shelter, and family functions that the home provides.

For the several layers that are activated by ritual activity at temples or shrines outside the home, this model also indicates that home is not enough; Cambodians also rely on community spaces beyond their homes, spaces that might be difficult to recreate in a resettlement context, where shrines to the land and spirit deities will not likely exist or where community centers in strip malls might serve as poor substitutes for peaceful pagodas.

Inger Agger, an activist and clinical psychologist, has conducted extensive research with victims of torture, including Cambodians who survived the Khmer Rouge. One of her studies involved seven months of fieldwork where she interviewed thirty-six survivors, five NGO psychotherapy providers, six staff members of the Extraordinary Chambers in the Courts of Cambodia (the Khmer Rouge tribunal), ten Buddhist monks, four Buddhist nuns (*donchee),* and six traditional healers.[41] Agger's analysis found that, despite the widescale destruction of Buddhist institutions under the Khmer Rouge, as Buddhism has gradually taken root again, "many Cambodians pin their hopes of coping with the past and restoring 'moral order' in the future on Buddhism."[42]

Agger found that many of her informants turned to the practice of calming meditation (*samatha*) in order to "calm my feelings," "cool my body," relieve "thinking too much," and steady their breathing.[43] Some chose a meditation object to hold in mind, such as a deity (*tevada*), also chanting the word *tevada* to help them recall "the goodness of the Buddha."[44] Her research found that the Pāli language itself was held to have a protective power (*monakum*), so that even if the monks could not translate the Pāli healing rituals they were chanting, the rituals were nonetheless believed to offer protection. Pāli-language tattoos were believed to serve as additional forms of protection.[45]

Monks figured importantly among Agger's informants for their role in offering not only rituals or meditative instruction, but also personal advice about how to respond to experiences of mental distress.[46] Monks tended to emphasize the ubiquity of suffering, the benefits of restraining anger and cultivating a calm mind, and the discipline of morality offered in the eightfold path.[47]

> When an individual pursues the Noble Eightfold Path of Buddhism, they reduce not only their own suffering but also the chances of causing suffering for others by performing wrong actions. Ultimately, then, this helps heal relationships and build trust within the community.[48]

(According to one study, broken trust, or "broken courage" (*baksbat*), is one of the top struggles that Cambodians have identified in their experience of post-traumatic stress.[49])

Thus far, Agger's findings sound not too dissimilar from grief coping mechanisms in western clinical contexts: they appear to be focused on individual symptoms and their relief, with some assistance and comfort from respected experts (in this case, monks). Agger's study began with a simple question about the role of Buddhist meditation in helping Cambodian survivors cope with their past, but her study became more complex when she began to identify the connections between meditation, merit, and the dead:

> In Cambodia, it is recognized that healthy grieving involves maintaining a good relationship with the dead and perhaps assisting the dead towards rebirth. The spirits of those who died a violent death or whose bodies were not ritually handled by monks may continue to experience distress and unfulfilled needs even after death and they may continue to disturb their surviving relatives. Therefore, efforts to "calm the mind" may need to be directed not simply to the living individual but also to their relationship with the dead. This means that the dead are treated as an extension of the moral community of the living and attending to their wellbeing and tranquility is integral to the wellbeing of the living as well. The "currency" by which this is achieved is that of *bon* [merit]. After performing meditation, it is common practice for Cambodians to pour a cup of water onto the earth while thinking of their dead. This symbolically enacts the transfer of the merit accumulated through meditation to the spirits of the dead, thus enhancing their karmic status and aiding their passage along the chain of being.[50]

Visiting the pagoda to make offerings, hear a sermon, or meditate is not simply about cultivating peace of mind for the living, but also about pacifying the grievances of the dead in order to achieve mutual peace. For the Cambodian survivors that Agger worked with, the dead are a constant presence and essential actors in their matrix of social relationships as they seek collective healing. One informant reported,

> The purpose of the monks' praying and chanting is to make all the dead people and the victims calm down their feelings. It helps us to feel relief to offer to the dead, relief from grief, because our relatives were killed during the Khmer Rouge regime, because the dead people died without the monks chanting for them. They were just abducted and killed.[51]

Rituals led by bhikkhus allow the living to transfer merit to the dead, aiding them in their journey to find rebirth, especially if deceased loved ones are feared to have become hungry ghosts. This service that monastics offer is critical to community life and well-being and in Cambodia finds its most dramatic expression in the Festival of the Dead (*p'chum ben*), which is celebrated at pagodas across the country for two weeks in the fall. At the conclusion of the festival, people throw ritually prepared rice balls across the *sima* boundary of the temple to the area beyond, where hungry ghosts are thought to gather. Further offerings are made at home, where people ask their ancestors for protection. The festival concludes by sending representations of the hungry ghosts down the river on banana tree stems. Agger observes that "the rapid revival of *p'chum ben* since the end of the war may be understood partly as an attempt to ritually reinstate the distinction between the realms of the dead and of the living,"[52] even as it creates positive relationships between those realms.

These studies led by Agger and by Hinton shed new light for humanitarian practitioners on the role of merit-making, which might be overlooked by outsiders as less important for psychological healing than, for example, calming meditation or receiving counseling. Merit-making activities create a psychological sense of security and connect the living with the dead, who are a constant presence and often a source of anxiety and stress. Merit-making rituals that involve monastics may engender more confidence in the living that their merit will be successfully transferred to the dead and will be effective in bringing peace.

The Cambodian case also brings to light an important point about the boundaries between canonical Buddhism and other cultural or spiritual traditions. Lived Buddhism often includes practices that are centered on spiritual entities not described in the Buddhist canons, whether stove gods, personal souls, or ancestors who do not seem to adhere to the cosmology of rebirth, but instead linger to trouble the living. Buddhism in Asia has always been integrated with traditions such as veneration of local spirits, ancestor worship, and notions of sacred landscape; Buddhists have used soul-calling rituals, house consecrations, mountain god offerings, ancestor veneration, and more to establish their relationships to particular buildings, particular pieces of land, and local lineages and histories. A culturally responsive understanding of Buddhism and displacement in any community should account for the wide spectrum of practices and logic systems encompassing the "Buddhism" that people engage when seeking to create or maintain their notions of home, security, and belonging.

Case Study: Sri Lankan Monastics and Disaster Relief

When a tsunami struck the coast of Sri Lanka on December 26, 2004, the destruction was immense: "an estimated 30,000 were killed, 800,000 were made homeless, and 70 percent of the island's coastline was devastated."[53] This calamity, the deadliest tsunami in recorded history, occurred at a time when Sri Lanka remained embroiled in ethnic tensions as part of the civil war that would not be formally ended until 2009; it also occurred at a time of heightened mistrust between Buddhist actors and Christian NGOs, over the practice of converting Buddhists to Christianity by promising material support.[54]

Despite these tensions, when the tsunami wreaked its havoc on the island nation, the Sri Lankan people showed indiscriminate compassion and generosity. Elizabeth Harris notes that people walked for miles carrying food to distribute to affected communities on the coastlines, without regard for their ethnic or religious identities. Several civil society organizations made important contributions to the humanitarian response to the tsunami by drawing on Buddhist insights. Among many others, the Damrivi Foundation, which had just established a diploma in Counselling with Buddhist Insights, deployed a team of medical doctors, psychologists, art therapists, and monastics to several of the camps for internally displaced people (IDPs) to offer psychological support.[55] Harris believes that these trauma counseling services would not have been as effective coming from other NGOs because of the stigma around mental health care in Sri Lankan culture; the involvement of monastics and the Buddhist orientation of the counseling made such care more appealing and accessible to the affected population.[56]

Damrivi also offered a more expedient version of Sri Lanka's Buddhist funerary rituals, which typically consist of a series of visits to the deceased's family home for sermons, prayers, and ritual offerings of white cloth and water to the monastic sangha, activities whose scope is impractical when tens of thousands of people are impacted by loss. By bringing white cloth to the IDP camps and organizing monks' sermons for the community, along with the dedication of merit to the deceased, larger groups of bereaved people could participate in the ritual together and gain a greater sense of closure after the tragic loss of their family members.[57]

NGOs were not the only civil society actors leading humanitarian assistance after the tsunami; Buddhist monastics also organized relief efforts individually or through their monasteries. Ven. Pinnawala Sangasumana observed that after the tsunami, Buddhist monastics engaged in the following activities: emergency relief (providing food, clothing, medicine, and sanitation); establishing welfare centers in their temples; mental health support; sheltering; schooling; livelihood assistance; and representation for policy making (on a limited basis).[58] As Harris describes,

> Most significantly, in the south, Buddhist temples became a focus for providing immediate palliative aid. Tents were erected in *vihāras* (Buddhist monasteries) to house refugees. Members of the monastic sangha used bicycles to ride around the affected areas, inviting everyone in need to come to the *vihāras*, whether Buddhist, Christian, Hindu, or Muslim. Traditionally, food and material requisites are brought by laypeople into the *vihāras*. In the immediate aftermath of the tsunami, this action was reversed. Laypeople came to the monks to be fed and sheltered.[59]

Buddhist monastics also took on significant rebuilding projects for displaced lay people. Not content with accepting support for his own temple's reconstruction, Ven. Uluwitike Bodhisiha at the Kacchiwatte Purana Vihāra also organized funding for sixteen houses to be built for the local villagers. Harris writes,

> I asked Ven. Bodhisiha what had motivated this activity. He immediately referred to the Buddha's insistence that people needed food, dwelling, medicine, and clothes in order to progress along the spiritual path. A central message of the Pāli texts is that the fourfold community of monks, nuns, laymen, and laywomen will function effectively and holistically only when laypeople can access the basic amenities for a secure life. The traditional role of the monk as teacher of the *dhamma*, has always been dependent on this, nurturing a sense of responsibility for laypeople among members of the monastic sangha.[60]

In this quotation, Ven. Bodhisiha reframes the monastic code's provisions of the four requisites—food, dwelling, medicine, and clothes—as basic needs for all humans, including laypeople. A monk that Ven. Sangasumana interviewed described how his temple repurposed their alms rounds to collect food and supplies for the IDPs they were housing.[61] The sense of nurture and caretaking that the lay community typically expresses toward the monastic sangha, enshrined in the ritual of alms-giving, was reflected back to the lay community in an articulation of reciprocity. Although monastics' activities in response to the tsunami involved leaving their monasteries and performing work outside the expectations of the monastic code, the monastics that Harris and Ven. Sangasumana interviewed did not describe their actions as innovative: in their eyes, compassion to the lay community has always been part of the sangha's role in society.

Merit-Making, Time Bindedness, and Emplacement

Virtually all forms of Buddhist practice, from making offerings to meditation to chanting, can be associated with the accumulation of merit. When Alexandra Kent studied how Cambodians work to create security for themselves in a post-genocide context that continues to be shaped by poverty, corruption, and mistrust, she discovered that merit-making plays a pivotal role:

> At the very beginning of my fieldwork, I spent time in Phnom Penh. There, I met a Western woman who had been running a nongovernmental organization in Cambodia for many years. She mentioned to me that, after all the efforts of her organization to alleviate rural poverty, she remained nonplussed by the villagers' continued interest in donating so much of their scarce resources to monks and the pagoda. Sometimes, she told me,

villagers would even borrow money through one of her organization's micro-credit facilities to make a donation, and would then be unable to repay. Why, she wondered, could they not see that it made far more sense for them to invest in a cow or seed grain?[62]

The foundational form of merit-making in Buddhist communities is offering food, money, or other tangible gifts to the monastic community. There are many reasons why displaced people experiencing trauma might choose to give from their meager resources to make donations to temples. One reason is that monastic institutions perform many security-enhancing functions in the community: they offer spiritual teachings that help people make sense of their suffering; they offer personal counseling and sometimes healing services; they offer serene physical spaces for people to feel safe; and they represent the teachings of the Buddha, which transcend individual circumstances of suffering and appeal to what is ultimately secure. As gathering places for the community, temples can offer the comforts of social cohesion and identity-making, even nation-making. Monastics help create security in the relationship between the living and the dead through the funerary rituals that they offer; they are also often the most trusted experts for dealing with ghosts and other supernatural sources of affliction. Considering all these roles that monastics and temple spaces can play in community well-being, it may be quite pragmatic for rural Cambodians, on occasion, to give to the pagoda before they invest in seed grain.

A second reason that merit-making is a security-enhancing measure for many Buddhists who have experienced displacement or trauma is that acts of merit empower people to invest in a positive future and to play an active role in bringing that future about. As discussed in Chapter 2, framing one's experiences of injustice through the lens of karma can lead to inaction if one focuses too much on the past, which can't be changed, but can generate a strong sense of agency if directed toward the future, which can be changed. Even if there is very little one can do to change one's immediate situation, and even if the fruits of one's merit may not mature until a future lifetime, planting positive seeds of merit is seen as an effective way to change the trajectory of one's existence, investing in the long-term future when one's immediate future may remain uncertain.

The role of karma in reconfiguring one's relationship to the future echoes psychological research on the phenomenon of "time bindedness": the ability to integrate the past, present, and future in a coherent way into one's psychology.[63] Strengthening time bindedness can involve narratives, material objects, personal relationships, and ritual practices. For example, the Vietnamese tradition of placing ancestor tablets in one's home is one way of binding the past to the present; planting a fruit tree binds the present with the future.

Yet with a deeply traumatic past, achieving time bindedness can be complicated and fraught with risk. Several studies of Southeast Asian refugees' mental health conducted by Morton Beiser found that refugees in camps were more successful if they split the past from the present and future (displaying an "atomistic" orientation toward time) in order to focus on short-term survival, since "the reemergence of the past and its reconnection with the present and future are mental processes that create a risk for depression."[64] Still, memory is a critical part of mourning the compounded losses that accompany displacement; Beiser argued later that

> whenever a severe disjuncture occurs between past and present, the retrieval of memory is necessary to enable mourning and recognition of loss, and if refugees do not move toward a healthy pattern of integrating the past (time-bindedness), their risk for PTSD is radically increased.[65]

An atomistic orientation toward time can only be sustained for so long before having deleterious effects. Thomas Feeny's study of Rohingya children experiencing decades-long stays in refugee camps in Bangladesh emphasizes the harms of the "monotonous now" that children endure without secondary schooling, work opportunities, or ritual events to mark time in their progress toward adulthood.[66] At some point, time bindedness becomes necessary for psychological well-being.

The psychological research on time bindedness links well with Leaning and Arie's articulation of three psychosocial domains of human security for the United States Agency for International Development (USAID):

> (1) Relationships with location (a sustainable sense of home and safety) ... (2) Relationships with community (a network of constructive social or family support) ... (3) Relationships with time (an acceptance of the past and a positive grasp of the future).[67]

From an economic perspective, an insecure relationship with time manifests in "a foreshortened planning horizon and a tendency to dismiss the value of the future," also known as a high discount rate.[68] When the future feels highly uncertain, people are more likely to make detrimental tradeoffs between current and future well-being.

> For example, the more parents fear that their children will not survive into adulthood, and the more they doubt that their community or social group will support them into their own old age, the stronger will be their incentives to raise large families. [...] High birth rates can be seen as attempts of one generation to pass on the costs of insecurity to their children.[69]

Similarly, child marriage, the overextraction of environmental resources, and choosing lower-return enterprises (selling one's land) over those that mature in the future (such as planting an orchard) are all manifestations of a high discount rate; lack of trust in the future leads to behaviors that ultimately undermine security.

Merit-making activities are typically more future- than past-oriented and may prove a constructive way for displaced Buddhists to rebuild their time bindedness. When there might be little to visualize for one's future, merit-making constitutes a kind of planning that doesn't require a specific vision or hope in a particular outcome. In cases where merit-making draws upon connections to a traumatic past, such as transferring merit to loved ones who died violently, the predictable role of familiar rituals, the protective oversight of monastic experts, and community support may help mitigate the risks of engagement with that past. As Agger observes, collective memorial ceremonies at sacred sites in Cambodia involve a simultaneous forgetting and remembering of the atrocities of the genocide, rendered safer by the community context in which this selective commemoration occurs.[70] The karmic narrative that many Tibetans in exile have adopted about their plight—recognizing that they may have displaced others in the past, and that their current diaspora community has a precious opportunity to spread Buddhism and increase merit in the world—may be effective precisely because it is a communal narrative rather than one of individual suffering.

By performing actions that are recognized by their community as inherently meritorious, people may feel an increased sense of personal agency even in the midst of circumstances that are constraining. Performing deeds of charity can also help to reframe a person's experience of suffering as part of the broader human condition, not uniquely theirs as victims of a particular injustice. The three marks of existence, according to the foundational Buddhist teachings, are *anicca* (impermanence), *dukkha* (suffering), and *anattā* (essenceless); all beings experience these realities. There is a story from the Pāli canon in which the Buddha, trying to help a woman named Kisā Gotamī who was inconsolable with grief after losing her child, asks her to gather a mustard seed from any household she can find that has not lost someone to death.[71] She cannot collect a single seed; her gradual acclimation to the universality of grief is the first step in her healing.

The financing and construction of religious monuments or institutions such as stupas, statues, temples, or monasteries is a highly resource-intensive form of merit-making. Building projects can serve as emplacement strategies that mark new places as Buddhist and root displaced people in the protective power of their religious spaces and symbols. Just as Tibetans have engaged in extensive building projects across India, Nepal, and elsewhere, Buddhist Karen refugees on the Thai–Burmese border have built Buddhist structures as a form of homemaking in their displacement context. Prasert Rangkla studied the emplacement strategies of self-settled Buddhist Karen refugees, including their impressive construction of new monasteries. In particular, Rangkla found that the construction of stupas, or *cedi,* formed a powerful placemaking strategy for many Karen:

> To live in proximity to the *cedi* creates a sense of living under the radiance of the Buddha's power. For people who have been displaced, they feel they are living in a secure place, in the Buddha's presence. Several new Karen settlements across the borderland have attempted to construct a *cedi* when building a place of worship.[72]

The emplacement symbolism of a *cedi* is hard to ignore. The spire reaches high as if to draw those near and far toward itself. In the Mon-Burmese style of Buddhism, the *cedi* is topped with an ornate gold spire that represents the abode of the god Indra on Mt. Meru, the center of the universe according to Buddhist cosmology: the ultimate "place."[73] With Buddhist relics or precious objects inside the *cedi,* the structure is consecrated and the Buddha's presence is spiritually activated there. A "nowhere" becomes a "here" when anchored by the spiritual power of this monument.

The Buddha is not the only sacred presence whose protection people seek at the *cedi.* In the Mon-Burmese tradition, *cedi* are surrounded by eight chambers that house eight planetary deities that protect the *cedi* in the eight directions. Lay people make offerings to the *cedi* at the chamber representing the day of the week they were born (Wednesday has two deities, one for day and one for night); they then expect to receive special protection from that deity. For Karen refugees, the *cedi* integrates Buddhist cosmology with the planetary deity traditions and plays a strong role in orienting followers in time as well as in space, which is simultaneously local and cosmic.

Rangkla also found that the robes-offering ceremony (*kathay pwe)* forms an important emplacement practice for Karen Buddhist refugees. The ceremony involves several days of preparations (building a wishing tree) as well as processions, dancing, offerings, and chanting, serving as an opportunity for building social cohesion among dispersed Karen refugees.[74]

> For these Buddhist Karen, locality is recreated through strategies of material symbols of cosmological security, sociality and festive structures of affect that are reconstituted across the geographical boundary. These Karen have strong attachments and commitments to a religiously constituted locality rather than to ethno-nationalist and millenarian yearnings for a "lost" homeland or ethnic identity.[75]

New Rituals to Address the Losses of Displacement and Violence

Although displacement has always been part of human experience, contemporary experiences of displacement have sparked the development of new religious rituals to help communities cope. Ritual innovation is sometimes controversial, because the currency of ritual tends to be its rootedness in tradition and its perceived stability across the vicissitudes of time and history. Still, when circumstances change, sometimes new rituals emerge to meet new needs (or to create new ways of meeting old needs). Here, I discuss two studies of Buddhist ritual innovation that address the grief accompanying displacement, violence, and loss.

Alex Wakefield conducted a study of how new Buddhist rituals could facilitate coping with the complicated grief experienced by the families of missing persons.[76] Focusing on contexts of internal displacement due to armed conflict, Wakefield highlights the prevalence of disappearances (whether killings, abductions, or forced or accidental separation of families) in conflict zones and the role of the International Committee of the Red Cross in tracing missing persons and reunifying families.[77] Drawing on Pauline Boss's work on ambiguous loss, Wakefield observes,

> when an individual goes missing, no certainty of death can be conclusively established, leaving relatives in a state of ongoing limbo and unable to effectively process or resolve their grief. It will often be impossible for a body or remains to be recovered.[78]

In contexts where those who die without proper ritual treatment are feared to become ghosts, the lack of a funeral can be deeply distressing. Unresolved grief, without the comfort of customary funerals, burials, or other death rituals, takes a heavy toll on families of the missing not only because they receive no psychological closure or resolution, but also because they are denied the community validation of their loss that funerals and death certificates may confer. Without the typical social ties of support, families of the missing may withdraw further from the very relationships that could have tended them through their loss.[79] Damrivi's creative efforts to organize public funerary rituals in Sri Lanka after the tsunami may have been particularly effective because they provided the public validation of and witness to the families' grief that Wakefield describes as essential.

Wakefield cites reports from the International Committee of the Red Cross explaining that humanitarian organizations do not usually identify families of the missing as vulnerable populations in need of assistance, and that their needs are often overlooked.[80] Wakefield also notes that in certain cultural contexts, asking for blessings or making merit on behalf of the missing may be perceived as bad luck, or as having a negative effect on the person if they are in fact still alive.[81] In some cases, mere association with a missing person may be perceived as a sign of bad karma and lead to stigmatization, especially for women whose husbands are missing.[82] Each of these factors poses hindrances to assistance for grieving families of missing persons, underscoring the value that ritual innovation could offer people in these sorrowful circumstances.

While Wakefield does not propose a specific ritual formula for grieving the missing, he seeks to inspire Buddhist groups to consider creating such rituals themselves with consideration for individual, family, and community dimensions of healing, as well as with attention to the political statement that such ceremonies could make in highlighting the plight of missing persons and resisting dehumanization.[83] He cites examples of Sicilian Catholic women mourning at the graves of unidentified migrants who die at sea[84] as well as "counterfeit" funerals in Thailand after the 2004 tsunami, when photos of the missing were featured in place of coffins or the names of the missing were laid in coffins.[85] Buddhist communities already have the ritual resources and trusted leadership necessary to create new rituals for grieving missing persons and providing public recognition for their families.

In a second example of ritual innovation, Inger Agger organized a series of workshops for community leaders to create testimony ceremonies, in which torture survivors participated in thoughtfully crafted legal rituals of presenting their documented accounts of torture and receiving affirmation from their communities.[86] Survivors received assistance from community workers to document their testimonies of human rights violations, and then heard their narratives read aloud and received official copies of their testimony documents in an honor ceremony. Agger recounts the key elements of the ceremonies that she and her collaborators constructed (original emphasis):

1 The ceremony is performed at a symbolic *location*, such as a sacred space, a place of remembrance, or a place representing oppressive forces.
2 A few key *actors* perform the ritual elements of the ceremony. This may include representatives of religious or local communities, or other respected persons who can give the ritual a higher significance.
3 An *audience* of significance to the survivor is present. It can include members of the community, family, friends, colleagues, and the media.
4 There is a visually impressive *document* containing the narrative to reflect that the "bad" story has been symbolically reframed by inscribing it on fine, nicely bound paper.
5 A community worker reads out the document in the first person, so that the survivor gets an *auditory* impression of his or her story, thus facilitating mindfulness and acceptance by hearing the anxiety-provoking story in another person's "safe" voice.
6 The document is presented to the survivor by someone of importance, together with other *symbols of honour* such as flowers, shawls, protective bands, etc. The story is "given back" to the survivor to keep in its new and positive version, which the survivor can use as he or she wishes for advocacy, remembrance, or family history.
7 The document is symbolically *purified* by one of the key actors in the ceremony: The priest, imam, or monk says a prayer over the document, or the human rights leader gives a speech honouring the struggle of the survivor.
8 Interventions *embodied with spiritual significance* are performed, such as singing, dancing, chanting, hugging, touching, and *sharing of a meal*. Emotional release is facilitated through expressions of love, kindness, and compassion.[87]

The Cambodian ceremony that Agger and her team co-organized honored sixteen survivors who were applicants in the first case of the Khmer Rouge Tribunal.[88] The ceremony included a pilgrimage from Phnom Penh to the nearby Killing Fields at Choeung Ek, where three Buddhist monks made offerings at a stupa that contained 5,000 skulls of executed victims.

> This was a symbolic offering to the ancestors made through the monks, addressing people who had been killed and praying for them to "be in a peaceful place." The survivors also prayed for divine forces to help them obtain justice at the tribunal. Survivors and staff knelt down in front of the monks and offered three burning incense sticks symbolizing three generations: parents, children, and themselves. They also offered flowers and prayed. The Achar led the audience in chanting with some participants using the sacred language Pali, and others in their own Khmer language, while some people remained silent, keeping their hands in a *sampheas*, that is, held together in front of their heart. The monks joined the chanting in the sacred languages of Pali and Sanskrit, and sang about life and death. They sprinkled holy water on the audience in a ritual of purification and a blessing. The audience offered money to the monks on a dish, and two survivors stood up and spoke.[89]

After the ceremony at the Killing Fields, which evoked strong emotions, the ceremony participants continued to a nearby pagoda where incense was lit, the atmosphere calmed, and summaries of each testimony were read aloud in the presence of the Buddha statue.[90] Each survivor had a counselor standing beside them, touching their arm or shoulder while their testimony was being read. Then each survivor handed their testimony document to a monk to receive it back with a blessing, made tangible in an orange thread of protection tied around their right wrist. Finally, the whole audience was blessed, and the monks sprinkled holy water and white jasmine flowers, symbolizing purity, over the audience.

In this testimony ceremony, familiar symbols and merit-making activities—like making offerings to the Buddha and to monks—are more deeply meaningful because of their power to transfer merit from the living to the dead as well as to confer powerful protection upon those sharing this sacred space. Some of the rituals were performed by monks, while the offerings at the Killing Fields were performed by the survivors themselves, which enabled survivors to actively participate in building their own positive karma with faith that a better future may unfold out of tragedy.

Conclusions

These case studies and my interpretive arguments accompanying them have illuminated some of the challenges that Buddhists have faced in displacement situations and the variety of ways they might seek to address those challenges.

These cases bring to light several themes that can be useful guideposts for humanitarian workers and clinicians providing care for displaced Buddhists. These recommendations will not be relevant or effective in every situation, but rather are considerations that I recommend taking into account, subject to the input of those affected and to the particulars of each displacement situation.

First: displaced people in Buddhist contexts should have access to funerals and other death-marking rituals. These rituals play an important role not only in grieving and dignifying the deceased, but also in addressing the anxiety people may have about the afterlife fate of their loved ones, especially those who die violent deaths. Access to monastics or other clergy (in Japan, for example, some Buddhist priests marry) is critical for death rituals; these specialists often provide a sense of safety and assurance because in certain contexts, they are believed to have the power to transfer merit to the dead or to pacify adverse supernatural forces, such as ghosts. They symbolize the Buddha's presence and protection in the community. They also serve the important functions of counseling, meditation instruction, and receiving alms so that lay people can perform merit-making activities.

One area of concern in my promoting the importance of monastics and other (predominantly male) Buddhist clergy is that female religious specialists are likely to be further marginalized, even if unintentionally, by outsider organizations. In the Theravāda and Tibetan–Himalayan lineages, full monastic ordination for women in the contemporary world is rare, and when it occurs, it is usually considered controversial because the lineages are deemed to have died out. Nuns do not enjoy the same status as monks in much of the Buddhist world. Female religious specialists in Theravāda and Tibetan–Himalayan contexts—such as novice nuns, ascetics who take eight or ten precepts (*maechi* in Thailand), or householder tantric practitioners—are less likely to be recognized by humanitarian organizations, as well as by most Buddhists, as legitimate authorities for performing rituals on behalf of a community. Given this reality, humanitarian and clinical practitioners should strive to balance responsiveness to the preferences of the people they serve with gender-equity principles. Where feasible, they should seek out the perspectives of female as well as male specialists (both ordained and lay) as they carry out their work among Buddhist communities, even when women's status is not officially recognized by those they are serving. Beyond the ethical question of gender equality, paying attention to women leaders makes for more effective humanitarian action. As Sid Brown has shown, for example, *maechi* communities in Thailand lead very active organizations in social work, elder care, and job training for troubled youth; their expertise and their established infrastructure for serving their communities are important assets that outsider organizations should engage for more efficient and effective humanitarian response.[91]

Second: merit-making practices are centrally important resources for many displaced Buddhists facing trauma. Practices of charity and commemoration facilitate a sense of personal agency and social recognition in the midst of hardship. They connect communities and provide collective expressions of grief, aspiration, or celebration. They provide safe links between the living and the dead, helping to ease nightmares and fears that may accompany the belief that the deceased have not yet found a favorable rebirth. They provide gentle ways to begin achieving time bindedness by offering a vision of the future that is both distal and proximate. They cultivate non-violence and build community trust. They also lead to tangible benefits, such as religious structures or monuments that help Buddhists emplace in new settings and enjoy spaces to perform their rituals and festivals. When displaced Buddhists have even the most minimal resources to pursue merit-making activities, they often choose to pursue them. Humanitarian and clinical practitioners should not discount the value of these practices and should, where feasible, create access to sacred spaces and objects that can facilitate merit-making activities that are meaningful to the community in question. In cases where new rituals might provide special benefit to displaced communities, aid workers should consult with relevant local specialists to explore the possibility of ritual innovation, including by presenting successful examples that others have crafted.

Third: meditation can sometimes benefit Buddhists in healing their trauma, but can sometimes cause harm. The benefits of meditation for displaced communities are highly contingent on the religious training and worldview of the client, the type of meditation practiced, and the etiology of trauma that is operative in the cultural context. Not all Buddhists meditate, and not all Buddhists agree on what qualifies as meditation (for example, listening to chants or praying with prayer beads could be considered forms of meditation because they cultivate mental calm and focus). Humanitarian and clinical practitioners should try to bracket their own assumptions about the therapeutic benefits of meditation or mindfulness practices and remain responsive to their clients' perspectives on the potential benefits or harms of meditation. Consulting with culturally relevant experts, care providers should consider what forms of meditation, if any, might be beneficial to recommend to their clients; care providers must be receptive to the possibility that some forms of meditation may do more harm than good in a particular case.

Fourth: non-canonical deities are integral actors in Buddhist cosmologies and may play an important role for Buddhists in displacement situations. From the concept that many cultures share of one or more souls that can wander away from the body, to the eight planetary deities in Mon-Burmese cosmology, to the various deities contributing to Cambodians' sense of ontological security, to ancestors that seem to elude the wheel of rebirth, a variety of non-canonical spirit beings are part of many Buddhists' sense of community, safety, and selfhood. An approach that defines what is "Buddhist" based solely on scriptural precedent will not adequately recognize the relevance of these many deities to the spiritual lives of Buddhists and to their constructions of well-being. Humanitarian and medical practitioners who are seeking to respond to the cultural and spiritual contexts of their clients should leave space for unexpected spirit beings in their clients' constructions of Buddhism.

Notes

1 McLellan, Janet. "Religious Responses to Bereavement, Grief, and Loss Among Refugees." *Journal of Loss and Trauma* 20, no. 2 (2014): 131–138. DOI: 10.1080/15325024.2013.833807. p. 136.

2 Trinka, Eric M. "Migration and Internal Religious Pluralism: A Review of Present Findings." *The Journal of Interreligious Studies* 28 (2019): 20–37.

3 Meyer, Birgit, and Peter van der Veer, eds. *Refugees and Religion: Ethnographic Studies of Global Trajectories*. London: Bloomsbury Academic, 2021; Mavelli, Luca, and Erin K. Wilson, eds. *The Refugee Crisis and Religion: Secularism, Security and Hospitality in Question*. New York: Rowman and Littlefield, 2017; Beckford, James A., ed. *Migration and Religion*. London: Edward Elgar Publishing, 2016; Horstmann, Alexander, and Jin-Heon Jung, eds. *Building Noah's Ark for Migrants, Refugees, and Religious Communities*. New York: Palgrave Macmillan, 2015.

4 This reality is slowly changing. For example, the UNHCR–Religions for Peace Multi-Religious Council of Leaders, formed in 2021, includes two Buddhist clergy among its nineteen members. Religions for Peace. "UNHCR-Religions for Peace Multi-Religious Council of Leaders." 13 April 2021. Accessed on 12 July 2024. www.rfp.org/unhcr-religions-for-peace-multi-religious-council-of-leaders/.

5 Williams, Duncan Ryūken. *American Sutra: A Story of Faith and Freedom in the Second World War*. Cambridge, MA: Harvard University Press, 2019.

6 Williams, Duncan Ryūken. *American Sutra: A Story of Faith and Freedom in the Second World War*. Cambridge, MA: Harvard University Press, 2019. p. 103.

7 Williams, Duncan Ryūken. *American Sutra: A Story of Faith and Freedom in the Second World War*. Cambridge, MA: Harvard University Press, 2019. p. 86.

8 Williams, Duncan Ryūken. *American Sutra: A Story of Faith and Freedom in the Second World War*. Cambridge, MA: Harvard University Press, 2019. p. 87.

9 Williams, Duncan Ryūken. *American Sutra: A Story of Faith and Freedom in the Second World War*. Cambridge, MA: Harvard University Press, 2019. p. 87.

10 Williams, Duncan Ryūken. *American Sutra: A Story of Faith and Freedom in the Second World War*. Cambridge, MA: Harvard University Press, 2019. p. 87.

11 Williams, Duncan Ryūken. *American Sutra: A Story of Faith and Freedom in the Second World War*. Cambridge, MA: Harvard University Press, 2019. p. 95.

12 Williams, Duncan Ryūken. *American Sutra: A Story of Faith and Freedom in the Second World War*. Cambridge, MA: Harvard University Press, 2019. p. 91.

13 Williams, Duncan Ryūken. *American Sutra: A Story of Faith and Freedom in the Second World War*. Cambridge, MA: Harvard University Press, 2019. p. 90.

14 Williams, Duncan Ryūken. *American Sutra: A Story of Faith and Freedom in the Second World War*. Cambridge, MA: Harvard University Press, 2019. pp. 85–86.

15 Williams, Duncan Ryūken. *American Sutra: A Story of Faith and Freedom in the Second World War*. Cambridge, MA: Harvard University Press, 2019. p. 94.

16 Williams, Duncan Ryūken. *American Sutra: A Story of Faith and Freedom in the Second World War*. Cambridge, MA: Harvard University Press, 2019. p. 112.

17 Williams, Duncan Ryūken. *American Sutra: A Story of Faith and Freedom in the Second World War.* Cambridge, MA: Harvard University Press, 2019. p. 113.

18 In Tibetan Buddhism, one of the ten advantages that characterize a precious human birth is to be born in a land where Buddhism is taught, making it a "central land." Refer to Patrul Rinpoche. *Words of My Perfect Teacher: A Complete Translation of a Classic Introduction to Tibetan Buddhism.* Translated by the Padmakara Translation Group. New Haven: Yale University Press, 2011. p. 22.

19 Tibetan institutions have not only continued, but have changed significantly in the exile context. For example, nuns have gained access to more educational opportunities and the Tibetan Government in Exile has transitioned to a fully democratic system.

20 McAra, S.A. "Indigenizing or Adapting? Importing Buddhism into a Settler-Colonial Society." *Journal of Global Buddhism* 8 (2007): 132–156. It is not clear at this time of writing whether either of the two proposed solutions has been implemented.

21 McAra, S.A. "Indigenizing or Adapting? Importing Buddhism into a Settler-Colonial Society." *Journal of Global Buddhism* 8 (2007): 132–156. p. 148.

22 Harrington, Laura. "Exorcising the Mandala: Kālacakra and the Neo-Pentecostal Response." *Journal of Global Buddhism* 13 (2012): 147–171.

23 Harrington, Laura. "Exorcising the Mandala: Kālacakra and the Neo-Pentecostal Response." *Journal of Global Buddhism* 13 (2012): 147–171. p. 152.

24 Harrington, Laura. "Exorcising the Mandala: Kālacakra and the Neo-Pentecostal Response." *Journal of Global Buddhism* 13 (2012): 147–171. p. 147.

25 Harrington, Laura. "Exorcising the Mandala: Kālacakra and the Neo-Pentecostal Response." *Journal of Global Buddhism* 13 (2012): 147–171. p. 148.

26 Benedict, Adriana Lee, Linda Mancini, and Michael A. Grodin. "Struggling to Meditate: Contextualising Integrated Treatment of Traumatised Tibetan Refugee Monks." *Mental Health, Religion and Culture* 12, no. 5 (2009): 485–499. DOI: 10.1080/13674670902788908. p. 491.

27 Benedict, Adriana Lee, Linda Mancini, and Michael A. Grodin. "Struggling to Meditate: Contextualising Integrated Treatment of Traumatised Tibetan Refugee Monks." *Mental Health, Religion and Culture* 12, no. 5 (2009): 485–499. DOI: 10.1080/13674670902788908. p. 489.

28 Benedict, Adriana Lee, Linda Mancini, and Michael A. Grodin. "Struggling to Meditate: Contextualising Integrated Treatment of Traumatised Tibetan Refugee Monks." *Mental Health, Religion and Culture* 12, no. 5 (2009): 485–499. DOI: 10.1080/13674670902788908. pp. 489–490.

29 Benedict, Adriana Lee, Linda Mancini, and Michael A. Grodin. "Struggling to Meditate: Contextualising Integrated Treatment of Traumatised Tibetan Refugee Monks." *Mental Health, Religion and Culture* 12, no. 5 (2009): 485–499. DOI: 10.1080/13674670902788908. p. 490.

30 Among others, Benedict et al 2009 ("Struggling to Meditate") cite Shah, S.A. "Ethnomedical Best Practices for International Psychosocial Efforts in Disaster and Trauma." In J.P. Wilson and C.S. Tang, eds., *Cross-Cultural Assessment of Psychological Trauma and PTSD*, pp. 51–64. New York: Springer, 2007.

31 Hinton, Devon E.,Rebecca A. Ojserkis, Baland Jalal, Sonith Peou, and Stefan G. Hofmann. "Loving-Kindness in the Treatment of Traumatized Refugees and Minority Groups: A Typology of Mindfulness and the Nodal Network Model of Affect and Affect Regulation." *Journal of Clinical Psychology* (2013) 69: 817–828.

The researchers had successful results from integrating loving-kindness (*mettā*) meditation into their care of several Cambodian refugees presenting with PTSD.

32 Denis, Diane. "From Metaphors to Life in Tibetan Settlements and Back Again: Space, an Important Factor for Resilient Response to the Suffering Caused by Armed Conflict." *Journal of Buddhist Ethics* 31 (2024): 51–80.

33 Denis, Diane. "From Metaphors to Life in Tibetan Settlements and Back Again: Space, an Important Factor for Resilient Response to the Suffering Caused by Armed Conflict." *Journal of Buddhist Ethics* 31 (2024): 51–80. Refer to pp. 65–66.

34 Hinton, D.E.; Hinton, A.; Eng, K.-T.; and Choung, S. "PTSD Severity and Key Idioms of Distress Among Rural Cambodians: The Results of a Needs Assessment Survey." Pp. 47–68 in *Cambodia's Hidden Scars: Trauma Psychology in the Wake of the Khmer Rouge*. Ed. B. van Schaack, D. Reicherter, and Y. Chhang. Phnom Penh, Cambodia: Documentation Center of Cambodia (DC-Cam), 2011. Also, refer to Hinton, D.E.; Hinton, A.L.; Eng, K.-T.; and Choung, S. (2012). "PTSD and Key Somatic Complaints and Cultural Syndromes Among Rural Cambodians: The Results of a Needs Assessment Survey." *Medical Anthropology Quarterly* 26 (3): 383–407.

35 Hinton, D.E.; Hinton, A.L.; Eng, K.-T.; and Choung, S. "PTSD and Key Somatic Complaints and Cultural Syndromes among Rural Cambodians: The Results of a Needs Assessment Survey." *Medical Anthropology Quarterly*, 26 (2012): 383–407. p. 395.

36 Agger, Inger. "Calming the Mind: Healing after Mass Atrocity in Cambodia." *Transcultural Psychiatry* 52, no. 4 (2015): 543–560. p. 545, referring to Hinton et al 2011 ("PTSD Severity") and to Hinton, D.E., M.A. Kredlow, V. Pich, E. Bui, and S.G. Hofmann. "The Relationship of PTSD to Key Somatic Complaints and Cultural Syndromes Among Cambodian Refugees Attending a Psychiatric Clinic: The Cambodian Somatic Symptom and Syndrome Inventory (CSSI)." *Transcultural Psychiatry* 50, no. 3 (2013): 347–370.

37 Hinton, D.E.; Hinton, A.L; Pich, V.; Loeum, J.R.; and Pollack, M.H. "Nightmares Among Cambodian Refugees: The Breaching of Concentric Ontological Security." *Culture, Medicine, and Psychiatry* 33 (2009): 219–265.

38 Hinton, D.E.; Hinton, A.L; Pich, V.; Loeum, J.R.; and Pollack, M.H. "Nightmares Among Cambodian Refugees: The Breaching of Concentric Ontological Security." *Culture, Medicine, and Psychiatry* 33 (2009): 219–265. p. 222.

39 Hinton, D.E.; Hinton, A.L; Pich, V.; Loeum, J.R.; and Pollack, M.H. "Nightmares Among Cambodian Refugees: The Breaching of Concentric Ontological Security." *Culture, Medicine, and Psychiatry* 33 (2009): 219–265. p. 223.

40 Hinton, D.E.; Hinton, A.L; Pich, V.; Loeum, J.R.; and Pollack, M.H. "Nightmares Among Cambodian Refugees: The Breaching of Concentric Ontological Security." *Culture, Medicine, and Psychiatry* 33 (2009): 219–265. p. 224.

41 Agger, Inger. "Calming the Mind: Healing after Mass Atrocity in Cambodia." *Transcultural Psychiatry* 52, no. 4 (2015): 543–560. p. 547.

42 Agger, Inger. "Calming the Mind: Healing after Mass Atrocity in Cambodia." *Transcultural Psychiatry* 52, no. 4 (2015): 543–560. p. 544.

43 Agger, Inger. "Calming the Mind: Healing after Mass Atrocity in Cambodia." *Transcultural Psychiatry* 52, no. 4 (2015): 543–560. p. 548.

44 Agger, Inger. "Calming the Mind: Healing after Mass Atrocity in Cambodia." *Transcultural Psychiatry* 52, no. 4 (2015): 543–560. p. 548.

45 Agger, Inger. "Calming the Mind: Healing after Mass Atrocity in Cambodia." *Transcultural Psychiatry* 52, no. 4 (2015): 543–560. p. 548.
46 Agger, Inger. "Calming the Mind: Healing after Mass Atrocity in Cambodia." *Transcultural Psychiatry* 52, no. 4 (2015): 543–560. p. 548.
47 Agger, Inger. "Calming the Mind: Healing after Mass Atrocity in Cambodia." *Transcultural Psychiatry* 52, no. 4 (2015): 543–560. pp. 546–548.
48 Agger, Inger. "Calming the Mind: Healing after Mass Atrocity in Cambodia." *Transcultural Psychiatry* 52, no. 4 (2015): 543–560. p. 549.
49 Agger, Inger. "Calming the Mind: Healing after Mass Atrocity in Cambodia." *Transcultural Psychiatry* 52, no. 4 (2015): 543–560. p. 545. Agger cites Chhim, S. "Baksbat (Broken Courage): A Trauma-Based Cultural Syndrome in Cambodia." *Medical Anthropology* 32, no. 2 (2013): 160–173.
50 Agger, Inger. "Calming the Mind: Healing after Mass Atrocity in Cambodia." *Transcultural Psychiatry* 52, no. 4 (2015): 543–560. p. 550.
51 Agger, Inger. "Calming the Mind: Healing after Mass Atrocity in Cambodia." *Transcultural Psychiatry* 52, no. 4 (2015): 543–560. p. 551.
52 Agger, Inger. "Calming the Mind: Healing after Mass Atrocity in Cambodia." *Transcultural Psychiatry* 52, no. 4 (2015): 543–560. p. 552.
53 Harris, Elizabeth J. "Buddhism and International Aid: A Case Study from Post-Tsunami Sri Lanka." In Hiroko Kawanami and Geoffrey Samuel, eds., *Buddhism, International Relief Work, and Civil Society*, pp. 1–26. New York: Palgrave Macmillan, 2013. p. 1. Overall, the tsunami killed more than 200,000 people in fourteen countries. It is widely considered one of the deadliest natural disasters of all time.
54 Harris, Elizabeth J. "Buddhism and International Aid: A Case Study from Post-Tsunami Sri Lanka." In Hiroko Kawanami and Geoffrey Samuel, eds., *Buddhism, International Relief Work, and Civil Society*, pp. 1–26. New York: Palgrave Macmillan, 2013. pp. 3–4.
55 Harris, Elizabeth J. "Buddhism and International Aid: A Case Study from Post-Tsunami Sri Lanka." In Hiroko Kawanami and Geoffrey Samuel, eds., *Buddhism, International Relief Work, and Civil Society*, pp. 1–26. New York: Palgrave Macmillan, 2013. p. 8.
56 Harris, Elizabeth J. "Buddhism and International Aid: A Case Study from Post-Tsunami Sri Lanka." In Hiroko Kawanami and Geoffrey Samuel, eds., *Buddhism, International Relief Work, and Civil Society*, pp. 1–26. New York: Palgrave Macmillan, 2013. p. 9.
57 Harris, Elizabeth J. "Buddhism and International Aid: A Case Study from Post-Tsunami Sri Lanka." In Hiroko Kawanami and Geoffrey Samuel, eds., *Buddhism, International Relief Work, and Civil Society*, pp. 1–26. New York: Palgrave Macmillan, 2013. p. 8. For a description and analysis of Buddhist funerary rituals in Sri Lanka, including the transfer of merit to the dead, refer to Langer, Rita. *Buddhist Rituals of Death and Rebirth: Contemporary Sri Lankan Practice and Its Origins*. London: Routledge, 2007.
58 Sangasumana, Ven. Pinnawala. "The Role of Buddhist Monks in Disaster Management: A Case Study from Sri Lanka." United Nations Day of Vesak Conference. *Social Science Research Network*, 6 May 2011. https://papers.ssrn.com/sol3/papers.cfm?abstract_id=3455602. p. 7, table 02.
59 Harris, Elizabeth J. "Buddhism and International Aid: A Case Study from Post-Tsunami Sri Lanka." In Hiroko Kawanami and Geoffrey Samuel, eds., *Buddhism,*

International Relief Work, and Civil Society, pp. 1–26. New York: Palgrave Macmillan, 2013. p. 4.

60 Harris, Elizabeth J. "Buddhism and International Aid: A Case Study from Post-Tsunami Sri Lanka." In Hiroko Kawanami and Geoffrey Samuel, eds., *Buddhism, International Relief Work, and Civil Society*, pp. 1–26. New York: Palgrave Macmillan, 2013. p. 16.

61 Sangasumana, Ven. Pinnawala. "The Role of Buddhist Monks in Disaster Management: A Case Study from Sri Lanka." United Nations Day of Vesak Conference. *Social Science Research Network*, 6 May 2011. https://papers.ssrn.com/sol3/papers.cfm?abstract_id=3455602. p 7.

62 Kent, Alexandra. "Reconfiguring Security: Buddhism and Moral Legitimacy in Cambodia." *Security Dialogue* 37, no. 3 (2006): 343–361. p. 344.

63 Al-Issa, Ihsan and Michel Tousignant, eds. *Ethnicity, Immigration, and Psychopathology*. Dordrecht, Netherlands: Springer, 1997. p. 49.

64 Beiser, Morton, and Ilene Hyman. "Southeast Asian Refugees in Canada." In Ihsan Al-Issa and Michel Tousignant, eds., *Ethnicity, Immigration, and Psychopathology*, pp. 35–41. Dordrecht: Springer, 1997. Refer to pp. 48–49. Also refer to Beiser, Morton. "Changing Time Perspective and Mental Health Among Southeast Asian Refugees." *Culture, Medicine and Psychiatry* 11 (1987): 437–464; and Beiser, Morton, and K.A.S. Wickrama. "Trauma, Time and Mental Health: A Study of Temporal Reintegration and Depressive Disorder Among Southeast Asian Refugees." *Psychological Medicine* 34, no. 5 (2004): 899–910.

65 McLellan, Janet. "Religious Responses to Bereavement, Grief, and Loss Among Refugees." *Journal of Loss and Trauma* 20, no. 2 (2014): 131–38. p. 134.

66 Feeny, Thomas. "Caught Between a Crocodile and a Snake: Childhood in a Rohingya Refugee Camp, Bangladesh." In *Childhood in South Asia: A Critical Look at Issues, Policies, and Programs*, ed. Jyotsna Pattnaik, pp. 1–18. Greenwich, CT: Information Age Publishing, 2005. p. 1.

67 Leaning, Jennifer, and Sam Arie. *Human Security: A Framework for Assessment in Conflict and Transition*. USAID Complex Emergency Response and Transition Initiative, December 2000. p. 18.

68 Leaning, Jennifer, and Sam Arie. *Human Security: A Framework for Assessment in Conflict and Transition*. USAID Complex Emergency Response and Transition Initiative, December 2000. pp. 32–33.

69 Leaning, Jennifer, and Sam Arie. *Human Security: A Framework for Assessment in Conflict and Transition*. USAID Complex Emergency Response and Transition Initiative, December 2000. p. 34.

70 Agger, Inger. "Calming the Mind: Healing after Mass Atrocity in Cambodia." *Transcultural Psychiatry* 52, no. 4 (2015): 543–560. DOI: 10.1177/1363461514568336. p. 553.

71 "Skinny Gotami & the Mustard Seed" (Commentary to the *Therīgāthā* 10.1). Translated by Andrew Olendzki. *Access to Insight (BCBS Edition)*, 30 November 2013. Accessed on 25 November 2025. www.accesstoinsight.org/noncanon/comy/thiga-10-01-ao0.html.

72 Rangkla, Prasert. "Refuge and Emplacement through Buddhism: Karen Refugees and Religious Practices in a Northwestern Border Town of Thailand." *The Asia Pacific Journal of Anthropology* 14, no. 1 (2013): 8–22. p. 17.

73 Rangkla, Prasert. "Refuge and Emplacement through Buddhism: Karen Refugees and Religious Practices in a Northwestern Border Town of Thailand." *The Asia Pacific Journal of Anthropology* 14, no. 1 (2013): 8–22. p. 17.

74 Rangkla, Prasert. "Refuge and Emplacement through Buddhism: Karen Refugees and Religious Practices in a Northwestern Border Town of Thailand." *The Asia Pacific Journal of Anthropology* 14, no. 1 (2013): 8–22. p. 19.
75 Rangkla, Prasert. "Refuge and Emplacement through Buddhism: Karen Refugees and Religious Practices in a Northwestern Border Town of Thailand." *The Asia Pacific Journal of Anthropology* 14, no. 1 (2013): 8–22. p. 22.
76 Wakefield, Alex. "The Missing and Their Families: Buddhism and the Role of Ritual in Processing Grief and Ambiguous Loss." *Journal of Buddhist Ethics* 30 (2023): 255–283.
77 The International Committee of the Red Cross reports that the Family Links Network's register of missing persons rose to about 284,400 in the year 2024, an increase of almost seventy percent across five years. International Committee of the Red Cross. "Number of Missing People Registered with the Red Cross and Red Crescent Movement up Nearly 70% in Five Years." 29 August 2025. Accessed on 25 November 2025. www.icrc.org/en/statement/tragedy-of-missing-persons-urgently-requires-more-determined-international-response.
78 Wakefield, Alex. "The Missing and Their Families: Buddhism and the Role of Ritual in Processing Grief and Ambiguous Loss." *Journal of Buddhist Ethics* 30 (2023): 255–283. p. 260.
79 Wakefield, Alex. "The Missing and Their Families: Buddhism and the Role of Ritual in Processing Grief and Ambiguous Loss." *Journal of Buddhist Ethics* 30 (2023): 255–283. p. 262.
80 Wakefield, Alex. "The Missing and Their Families: Buddhism and the Role of Ritual in Processing Grief and Ambiguous Loss." *Journal of Buddhist Ethics* 30 (2023): 255–283. p. 262.
81 Wakefield, Alex. "The Missing and Their Families: Buddhism and the Role of Ritual in Processing Grief and Ambiguous Loss." *Journal of Buddhist Ethics* 30 (2023): 255–283. pp. 267–268.
82 Wakefield, Alex. "The Missing and Their Families: Buddhism and the Role of Ritual in Processing Grief and Ambiguous Loss." *Journal of Buddhist Ethics* 30 (2023): 255–283. p. 268.
83 Wakefield, Alex. "The Missing and Their Families: Buddhism and the Role of Ritual in Processing Grief and Ambiguous Loss." *Journal of Buddhist Ethics* 30 (2023): 255–283. p. 274.
84 Wakefield, Alex. "The Missing and Their Families: Buddhism and the Role of Ritual in Processing Grief and Ambiguous Loss." *Journal of Buddhist Ethics* 30 (2023): 255–283. p. 276.
85 Wakefield, Alex. "The Missing and Their Families: Buddhism and the Role of Ritual in Processing Grief and Ambiguous Loss." *Journal of Buddhist Ethics* 30 (2023): 255–283. p. 277.
86 Agger, Inger. "Testimony Ceremonies in Asia: Integrating Spirituality in Testimonial Therapy for Torture Survivors in India, Sri Lanka, Cambodia, and the Philippines." *Transcultural Psychiatry* 49, no. 3–4 (2012): 568–589.
87 Agger, Inger. "Testimony Ceremonies in Asia: Integrating Spirituality in Testimonial Therapy for Torture Survivors in India, Sri Lanka, Cambodia, and the Philippines." *Transcultural Psychiatry* 49, no. 3–4 (2012): 568–589. , p. 575.
88 Agger, Inger. "Testimony Ceremonies in Asia: Integrating Spirituality in Testimonial Therapy for Torture Survivors in India, Sri Lanka, Cambodia, and the Philippines." *Transcultural Psychiatry* 49, no. 3–4 (2012): 568–589. p. 579.

89 Agger, Inger. "Testimony Ceremonies in Asia: Integrating Spirituality in Testimonial Therapy for Torture Survivors in India, Sri Lanka, Cambodia, and the Philippines." *Transcultural Psychiatry* 49, no. 3–4 (2012): 568–589. p. 580.
90 Agger, Inger. "Testimony Ceremonies in Asia: Integrating Spirituality in Testimonial Therapy for Torture Survivors in India, Sri Lanka, Cambodia, and the Philippines." *Transcultural Psychiatry* 49, no. 3–4 (2012): 568–589. p. 580.
91 Brown, Sid. *The Journey of One Buddhist Nun: Even Against the Wind*. Albany, NY: State University of New York Press, 2001. Refer to chapters 10 and 11 (p. 106 ff.).

4 Buddhism, Displacement, and Law[1]

Introduction

In the previous chapters, we have focused on the inherited scriptural traditions and historical experiences of displaced people across diverse Buddhist communities. Our lens has been a phenomenological one, focused closely on creativity, meaning making, and moral agency within the constraints that shape the particularities of human lives and possibilities. At this juncture in the book, we widen our focus by turning to the larger structures of law, governance, ethics, and internationalism that impact displaced people and host communities. We will trace Buddhist ways of imagining law so that displacement and its sufferings may be reduced. Our goal remains twofold: to uncover new insights about Buddhism by looking through the lens of displacement, and to explore how Buddhist legal perspectives can contribute to contemporary solutions to displacement.

What exactly is "Buddhist law?" As Miguel Alvarez Ortega points out, the common English translation of "dharma" (Pāli *dhamma*) as "law" has not helped clarify this question, nor does the intriguing ambivalence of the eight-spoked wheel of dharma, which can be turned by either a world-conquering king or a world-renouncing sage.[2] Scholars have used the phrase "Buddhist law" to refer to various bodies of literature and practice, both broad and narrow, including: the entirety of the Buddha's teaching, Buddhist philosophy and epistemology, the monastic discipline, traditional notions of Buddhist kingship, domestic law in Buddhist-majority states, Buddhist constitutionalism, Buddhist-interest litigation, Buddhist approaches to international law, Buddhist ethics, and Buddhist normative approaches to "the problem of power and its legitimation."[3]

Among such a wide-ranging scope of concerns, this chapter first explores concerns about place, displacement, and security that are embedded in the Buddhist monastic codes of discipline. Unlike Islam's *sharia* and Judaism's *halakha*, the Buddhist canons do not offer a body of law intended to govern the whole of society. Instead, while Buddhist traditions have greatly influenced the development of state law in many societies, the only body of law fully articulated in the Buddhist canons is monastic law. The principles

DOI: 10.4324/9781003318149-4

and habits that are enshrined in Buddhist monastic law are considered conducive to the spiritual life, but are not necessarily pragmatic for or ethically incumbent upon the broader lay society. Thus, Buddhist monastic law should not be viewed as an ideal moral standard for all people. Some of its provisions have influenced the formation of secular law in Buddhist societies, but many have not.

As we move into a discussion that ranges from the ancient legal codes of the Buddhist monastic discipline to the modern Geneva Conventions, it is worth pausing to introduce the state of the current scholarship on Buddhism, law, and law's close relative, politics. Far from a "settled line of research," Buddhism and law "make up quite a controversial couple," at least among western scholars, because of the seeming incongruity between the transcendent aims of Buddhism on the one hand and the mundane aims of law and politics on the other.[4] In his comparative study *Buddhism and Political Theory,* Matthew Moore summarizes the controversy by observing,

> Some scholars argue that any politics in the early [Buddhist] texts is relatively peripheral to the main concerns of Buddhism, which are primarily about individual transformation, while other scholars argue that politics and salvation cannot be separated in the Buddhist theory, and thus that politics should be understood as central to Buddhism.[5]

Moore sides with the former group of scholars, going so far as to argue that Buddhism is "radically deflationary about the importance of politics to human life."[6]

The question of whether law and politics are either central or peripheral to Buddhism rests largely on what we understand "Buddhism" to mean. Moore defines Buddhism as the "religious/philosophical system taught by Siddhattha Gotama"[7] and identifies the central goal of Buddhism as "individual salvation."[8] I take a civilizational view of Buddhism,[9] which accounts not only for the Buddha's system of teachings, but also for the artistic, cultural, social, political, legal, scientific, and economic ways in which societies have been shaped by those teachings. Also differing from Moore, I understand the central goal of Buddhism to be the reduction of suffering,[10] with "individual salvation" or enlightenment as a worthy pursuit because it means the end of suffering—both for oneself and for the others whom one causes to suffer when acting out of ignorance. I also take a different stance on social change than does Moore, who posits that "real social and political change and improvement will come from the transformation of individuals, which is only modestly affected by politics and is largely the responsibility of each person."[11] I find strong evidence, particularly in the Mahāyāna traditions, that the authors of Buddhist scriptures were concerned by how profoundly kings shape the social order and how much responsibility they bear for their people's suffering. I argue in Chapter 5, "The Gift of Fearlessness," that monarchs and governments can even impede their people's spiritual development if they oppress their subjects to such a degree that their basic needs are not met and they lose the precious opportunity for spiritual advancement afforded by a human birth. This debate links to the core premise of this book, which is that displacement and its sufferings are relevant to the central concerns of the Buddhist tradition and that for many Buddhists, these worldly realities have spiritual ramifications.

Displacement in Buddhist Monastic Law

We will begin by analyzing the system of law and governance that the Buddha himself is said to have authored: his monastic community's rules of discipline. What might this body of law reveal about how the Buddha and his renunciant community understood the value of home and the sufferings of displacement?

There are three living bodies of *vinaya* ("discipline") literature in use today by Buddhist monastic lineages: the Theravāda (prominent in Sri Lanka and Southeast Asia), the Mūlasarvāstivāda (prominent in Tibetan, Mongolian, and Himalayan communities), and the Dharmaguptaka (prominent in East Asia and the Pacific).[12] The scale of this body of literature is significant; for example, the Tibetan text of the *Mūlasarvāstivāda Vinaya* alone numbers almost 8,000 pages.[13] Furthermore, even though the Buddhist *vinayas* are the most visible legal texts in Buddhist monastic life, such that some scholars have made the term "Buddhist law" equivalent with the *vinaya* literature,[14] in practice, Buddhist monastics apply a range of legal sources beyond the *vinaya* to their lives. These extra-*vinaya* legal sources include commentarial literature, monastic handbooks, monastic constitutions (Tibetan *bca' yig*), local monastic ordinances (Sanskrit *kriyākāras*), rules of purity (Chinese 禪苑清規 *chányuàn qīngguī*), and more. To add further complexity to the study of Buddhist monastic law, the *vinaya* texts themselves are not merely legal codes. They encompass narratives, case studies, rebirth genealogies, and proverbs: a range of genres that inform legal practice in diverse ways and must be interpreted with diverse methodologies. Finally, we should remember that monastic discipline is located not only in written documents, but also in what is "unwritten, local, and contextual: the normative control and expectations emanating directly and indirectly from laity."[15] *Vinaya* is a living discipline shaped by its surrounding social and political contexts.

In this chapter, I do not have the capacity to address the enormous body of legal texts and social contexts of Buddhism's many monastic communities. Instead, to make a beginning of an exploration, here I rely primarily on the Theravāda tradition's rules of monastic discipline, the *Pāṭimokkha,* with some references to studies of Mūlasarvāstivāda and Chan *vinaya* literature. There remain many promising areas for future study regarding the relationship between the Buddhist monastic discipline and other legal traditions; I hope that others with scholarly as well as lived expertise in these traditions will undertake more in-depth studies in the future and that the current work inspires them in that direction.

The Buddhist Monastic Codes on the Requisite of Shelter

To reframe our initial questions about displacement by focusing specifically on the monastic codes of discipline, we may ask: given that Buddhist monastics voluntarily embrace a life of quasi-homelessness, how much value do the Buddhist *vinayas* ascribe to place and home? How much harm do they ascribe to displacement? How might the *vinayas* spark a productive dialogue with other bodies of law regarding displacement?

The three Buddhist monastic traditions whose lineages are alive today differ somewhat from one another, but they each provide Buddhist monastics with four requisites of food, shelter, clothing, and medicine. These basic provisions support the safety and comfort of members of the order. Notably, they set Buddhist monastics in contrast to stricter ascetic orders that required their members to wander naked or to sleep out of doors.[16] A story in the *Mūlasarvāstivāda Vinaya* relates,

> When the Blessed One had trained the first five monks they lived in the forest, but while living there they were vulnerable to lions, tigers, leopards, and hyenas. The Blessed One then thought to himself: "Where have the disciples of past Fully and Completely Awakened Buddhas made their home?" He saw that it was in a *vihāra* [a dwelling, later coming to mean "monastery"]. The gods also told the Blessed One that it was so.[17]

In the judgment of the Buddha, who sought a middle way between the extremes of indulgence and deprivation, shelter is a basic security provision, appropriate not only for lay people but also for those who embrace the so-called "homeless" life. His decision to provide homes for his monastic disciples set the Buddha and his community apart.

Home and Habitat

What considerations do the *vinayas* make regarding "home?" Specific regulations in the *vinaya* literature govern the construction of monastic dwellings in terms of the proper choice of building sites, the materials to be used, and the size and simplicity of structures. According to the Theravāda *Pāṭimokkha*, sites for monastic dwellings should be "free of disturbances" and have "adequate space."[18] Thānissaro Bhikkhu, drawing from the Theravāda *vinaya* commentarial literature, explains that:

> A site free of disturbances is (1) not the abode of such creatures as termites, ants, or rats who might do harm to the building. (2) It is not the abode of those—such as snakes, scorpions, tigers, lions, elephants, or bears—who

might do harm to its inhabitant. The Commentary states that the [Sutta] Vibhanga's purpose in forbidding a bhikkhu from building on a site where termites and other small animals have their home is to show compassion to these and other small creatures like them by not destroying their nests. As for the stipulation against building where snakes and other dangerous animals live, this also extends, it says, to the areas where they regularly forage for food. [...]

Adequate space means that there is enough room on the site for a yoked wagon or a man carrying a ladder to go around the proposed hut. [...] The Sub-commentary states that the stipulation for adequate space is so that the hut will not be built on the edge of a precipice or next to a cliff wall, and the Vinaya-mukha notes that the Vibhanga here is following the *Laws of Manu* (an ancient Indian legal text) in ensuring that the dwelling not be built right against someone else's property.[19]

The considerations undergirding these rules about shelter for monastics involve not only safety and comfort (not building a hut in a place where there are dangerous poisonous animals or many annoying insects),[20] sustainability (assessing environmental factors that will allow the building to last), and compassion for the site's animal inhabitants (refraining from destroying animals' habitats and food sources), but also respect for the private property of other people, because infringing on others' property would not only be morally questionable but may invite legal action against the sangha.

Respect for private property also informs the rule that entails expulsion from the sangha "should any bhikkhu, in what is reckoned a theft, take what is not given from an inhabited area or from the wilderness," established when the monk Dhaniya built himself a meditation hut out of wood that had not been properly permitted by the king.[21] Stories like this one that place the sangha in a legally precarious position may explain why in the *Pāṭimokkha*, before building a hut or dwelling, a bhikkhu must "assemble the bhikkhus to designate the site."[22] The monastic community ensures that the building site is legitimately acquired without encroaching on the property of others. The *Pāṭimokkha* also attends to crops: not building where there are crops[23] and not polluting nearby crops with saliva, urine, or feces.[24] The Chinese Chan tradition's rules of purity, the *Chanyuan Qinggui,* are particularly attentive to the protection of others' cropland and the delineation of boundaries between monastic fields and other property because monastics in the Chan tradition have often engaged in agriculture.[25]

Just as the *vinayas* make provisions for home and shelter for Buddhist monastics, they are also keenly aware that "home" is contingent on legal, economic, and social relationships that require respect and compromise with others. The principles of site assessment and compromise with the local community and governing authorities exemplified in the *vinaya* literature are resonant with contemporary United Nations High Commissioner for Refugees guidelines for siting and planning camps for displaced people, promoting the aims of safety, sustainability, and respecting the needs and rights of host communities.[26] One major difference between the two models is that camps for displaced people are often designed to promote productive integration with the local host community, whereas the *vinayas* seek to maintain clear divisions between monastic and lay communities. Still, monastic dwellings should usually be close enough to lay communities to enable the giving of alms.

Danger and Security

The Buddhist monastic codes account for the dangers of being away from home and on the road. There are rules in each of the three *vinaya* traditions that make special exceptions for monastics who are traveling and subjected to heightened risks. In the *Bhikkhu Pāṭimokkha*, for example, monastics are instructed to travel in groups where possible and are permitted to engage in behaviors while traveling that otherwise would not be permitted, such as a bhikkhu (male monastic) traveling with a bhikkhuṇī (female monastic) when "the road is to be traveled by caravan and is considered dubious and risky."[27] The *Bhikkhuṇī Pāṭimokkha* even prohibits bhikkhuṇīs from undertaking a journey *without* joining a merchant caravan in a territory "considered dubious and risky."[28] Here, the *vinaya* is pragmatic in its assessment of the need not only for shelter, but also for security—two connected needs that remain at the center of the displacement crisis today. The *Pāṭimokkha* is attuned to the increased vulnerability to gender-based violence that female monastics face, compared to their male counterparts.[29] Unfortunately, this injustice persists among displaced people today.[30]

Not only does traveling away from home entail heightened risk, but staying in place can also be risky if environmental factors render home unsafe. As further evidence of the security concerns central to the formation of the *vinaya*, the Buddha allows for exceptions to the rules when encountering dangerous obstacles during the monsoon season retreat. In the *Pāṭimokkha*, breaking the rains retreat is not an offense if practitioners encounter danger to their well-being, such as being "harassed by beasts who seize and attack them, harassed by creeping things who bite and attack them, harassed by criminals who rob and beat them, or harassed by demons who possess them and zap their vitality."[31] Thānissaro Bhikkhu clarifies that "With regard to the beasts, the Commentary notes that 'seize and attack' also includes cases where the beasts, having surrounded one, chase one away, frighten one, or kill someone else in the vicinity."[32] Reasonable evidence of danger is enough to justify breaking the retreat; one needn't reach the point of shedding blood. There are also provisions for bhikkhus on retreat whose dwellings are burned or flooded, with permission for them to leave what is otherwise a strictly residential retreat to pursue their four requisites of food, shelter, clothing, and medicine elsewhere. Sometimes even a dangerous road is safer than home, a truth that displaced people know all too well.

Eviction and Displacement

More closely related to the act of forced displacement, the monastic codes prohibit monastics from intruding upon other monastics' dwellings and from evicting one another.[33] There are rules instructing monastics how to mark certain dwelling places or cells as their own, as well as rules requiring them to forfeit their spaces in community-owned dwellings when vacating them[34] and erasing their marks to enable other monastics to use the spaces.[35] Interestingly, in the *Dharmaguptaka Vinaya*, these instructions are paired with a story about a rebellion at the border that displaced many monastics, causing overcrowding in a nearby monastery—a reminder that for much of Buddhist history, monasteries have served as sites of refuge in times of conflict or disaster, as they do today in Myanmar, for example.

In the monastic codes, we also find a sense of responsibility and duty to make restitution for accidental displacement of local animals and spirits. According to the *Suttavibhanga*, the monastic precept against injury to living plants came about because monks in one region were cutting down trees to build their huts.[36] One of those trees was home to a tree spirit and her child. When a monk struck the tree, he unknowingly struck the arm of her child. Distraught, the mother tree spirit decided to approach the Buddha, who promptly found a vacant tree for her and her son to inhabit. The stories usually portray her new home as a better tree than the first: the Buddha's restitution for her losses was generous.

Including Local Inhabitants

The *Mūlasarvāstivāda Vinaya* acknowledges and accounts for the local protector deities (Tibetan *srung ma*) who inhabit the land where a monastery is built. According to that *vinaya* tradition, a special verse is to be recited daily for the local deity protecting the monastery, and when monastics travel, they should recite a verse for the deity of any well or spring they use for drawing water.[37] The text instructs that when monastics gather to stay in a particular place for the rains retreat, each member agrees to be "counted in" and bound by the local monastic ordinances by taking a counting stick. The sticks are then to be placed in a box and counted at each fortnightly confessional meeting in order to take attendance. In the *Mūlasarvāstivāda Vinaya*, the local deity of that place also receives a counting stick, indicating that the deity's presence is acknowledged and accounted for—and perhaps also encouraging the deity's cooperation with the retreat ordinances. This ritual procedure indicates respect for the prior inhabitants of a locale and enacts an inclusive rather than dispossessive posture toward these spiritual "others."

There is also a story in the *Mūlasarvāstivāda Vinaya* about the founding of Jetavana Monastery, which a donor built as an offering to the Buddha on land that the donor had deceptively acquired from a local prince.[38] When the Buddha's chief disciple Śāriputra and his attendant group of bhikkhus were invited to move in, a rival religious order who went for alms rounds in that locale were worried about being displaced. They explained to the donor that they had already divided up the towns for alms rounds: Rājagṛha was Gautama Buddha's and Śrāvastī was theirs. The donor replied, "you may have divided up the towns [for alms rounds], but not my private property. I will have a religious foundation built for whomever I want."[39] The rival group cried out to the donor,

> You, householder, have completely cut off all the foundations of our livelihood. Have some pity on us! We will work for wages on your *vihāra*. We have been here a long time. Surely you will not make us abandon our country![40]

While the donor wasn't particularly moved, Śāriputra considered their plight kindly by contemplating the question, "do they have some roots of merit, or do they not?" Seeing that the rival religious group had roots of merit, he then asked, "On whom are they dependent?—me myself."[41] Reasoning thus, he secured them paid employment on the property.

This story acknowledges the property rights of the donor (a necessary feature of the monastic community's economic sustainability, which depends on private gifts), yet nevertheless takes a clear position on the importance of compromise and of accommodating prior inhabitants of the place to enable their livelihood. Śāriputra's two questions spur his community both to recognize merit in the others against whom they are competing for territory, and to acknowledge their rivals' position of economic dependency. Śāriputra's answer to the question of dependency— "me myself" —is unexpected; surely what he should have said is that the rival group is dependent on the local landlord, or on the almsgivers in the local community. Yet in this moment of reflection, Śāriputra takes responsibility for them and claims agency in creating a sustainable solution for them.

Displacement as Equal in Penalty to Killing

The ethic of constant care modeled in the Buddhist *vinaya*s shows us not only that shelter and security are necessary for well-being, but also that preventing the foreseeable causes of displacement is weighed just as importantly as refraining from direct or forcible displacement. The *vinayas* are highly attuned to the fact that home and habitat are critical to survival. Monastics are enjoined not only to exhibit non-violence toward animals but also to protect animals' habitats, the necessary conditions for their life.

The *vinayas* treat several instances of destroying animal homes or displacing them from their habitats as equal in penalty to killing animals directly. To quote from the *Bhikkhuṇī Pāṭimokkha* (with equivalent rules from the *Bhikkhu Pāṭimokkha* in brackets):

106 [10]. Should any bhikkhuṇi dig soil or have it dug, it is to be confessed.

116 [20]. Should any bhikkhuṇi knowingly pour water containing living beings—or have it poured—on grass or on clay, it is to be confessed.

142 [61]. Should any bhikkhuṇi intentionally deprive an animal of life, it is to be confessed.

143 [62]. Should any bhikkhuṇi knowingly make use of water containing living beings, it is to be confessed.[42]

Here, the implication is that digging soil will expose underground-dwelling insects, removing them from their primary habitat and subjecting them to danger; pouring out water containing living beings likewise removes them from the conditions on which they immediately depend for survival. To honor the prohibition against using water containing living beings, Buddhist monastics in some traditions carry water filters to remove small organisms before consuming water.

What is significant regarding the *vinayas'* legal reasoning here is that displacement is weighed as a form of violence. The lifestyle of "constant care" exemplified in the *vinayas* enables monastics to evaluate their surroundings and to consider how their actions can cause harm to others living in the same place. This legal tradition enjoins monastics to acknowledge the close relationship between habitat and life, as well as to carefully reflect on how one's actions upon the environment impact other beings' security.

To summarize, the Buddhist codes of discipline for male and female monastics have much to say about place and displacement. They take both implicit and explicit positions on issues such as the essential importance of shelter and security; the dangers of being on the road or away from home; the need to migrate when local dangers emerge; respect for private property, especially that of lay people; acknowledgement of and cooperation with local inhabitants of a territory; the duty to avoid displacing others from their dwellings or rendering them insecure, whether they are religious rivals, deities, animals, or insects; and the duty to take responsibility for one's role in causing displacement and to make generous restitution when displacement occurs. Each of these themes, while there is room for debate within them, contributes to a Buddhist legal perspective on the importance of place and the collective duty to prevent or reduce the sufferings of displacement.

The *Vinaya* and State Law

Buddhist monastics are subject not only to the authority of the *vinayas* but also to state law and international law. The codes of monastic discipline constitute but one layer of law in a multivalent reality of legal pluralism that characterizes Buddhist life (and life for most everyone).[43] The Buddhist *vinayas* should be understood not only as coexisting with other bodies of law, but also as interdependent with them. The Buddhist *vinayas* do not constitute fully self-sufficient systems of law; they were developed to govern communities operating within broader polities structured by their own laws and governance systems.[44] The *vinayas* depend on state law for such essential roles as setting the calendar (for the rains retreats), protecting property rights (of monasteries, temples, and stupas), enabling transnational migration (for monastics who travel to study, teach, and fundraise), and enforcing penalties against lay people who violate the rights of monastics or their institutions (the *vinayas* do not prescribe penalties for crimes committed by anyone outside the monastic community). The monastic community also depends on states for military protection in times of war.

In turn, states exert legal control over Buddhist monastic life in various ways, from China's 2007 State Religious Affairs Bureau Order No. 5 prohibiting Tibetan lamas from reincarnating without pre-approval from the central government,[45] to the governments of Southeast Asia managing ordination quotas. In Myanmar in recent years, under the guise of violations of state law, the military government has arrested many monastics for protesting junta rule.[46] It is worth stating that in contexts of authoritarianism, Buddhist monastics' ability to exercise their rights under state law can be heavily curtailed and legal engagement can be dangerous. Within this tapestry, the ways that Buddhist monastic communities have engaged various bodies of law regarding displacement are complex. An example from Myanmar showcases some of this complexity.

Case Study: Myanmar's Protestors Facing Displacement

After the military coup of February 1, 2021, Theravāda monk Sayadaw U Yaw Gyi began leading pro-democracy protests.[47] The military government—the State Administrative Council (SAC)—charged him with violating Section 505A of Myanmar's Penal Code, a provision that the junta added to the code soon after they seized power, which prohibits "causing fear, spreading false news and agitating crimes against a government employee, all punishable by up to three years' imprisonment." 505A is among several revisions to Myanmar's legal code that the Centre for Law and Democracy has judged as violating international human rights standards.[48] The SAC pursued Ven. U Yaw by raiding his monastery; he evaded capture by hiding in a toilet, fearing for his life.

In April 2021, Ven. U Yaw moved to Mandalay to continue his pro-democracy activism. Several times, he and his fellow protestors were attacked by the military. They fled gunshots, taking cover in swamps and rivers and sometimes being sheltered by brave lay people who opened their doors to them. Ven. U Yaw explains, "I still have to wear a Buddhist monk robe even when I protest. Because of its bright colour, it is so easy to spot me in the crowd," he said. "Because of kind people like that, I could escape from life-threatening danger."[49] One time he and fellow monks took refuge in a mosque. "They gave us their clothes, including *kufi* hats, so that we could escape from the crackdown," he said. "I will always remember that."[50]

The military has destroyed many religious buildings across the country, including Buddhist monasteries, "accusing them of sheltering those associated with the anti-coup movement or who have been displaced by military attacks."[51] When the military raided the monastery where Ven. U Yaw was staying in September 2021, he once again evaded capture by fleeing. The military government responded by sealing the monastery (evacuating and closing it).

This case study illuminates how several bodies of law can intersect regarding displacement in a Buddhist context. A monk exercises his right to free expression as defined by international human rights law, but is charged with violating state law. He is displaced many times by the military; those who shelter him are liable to being charged with criminal activity against the state. Despite the extreme insecurity of his situation, the monk maintains his adherence to the *vinaya* requirement to wear his brightly colored monastic robes, even when they easily identify him in a crowd and endanger his life. On at least one occasion, however, he is willing to violate the *vinaya* robe requirements by donning Muslim garb and a *kufi* hat offered to him by courageous allies. Finally, the monastery where Ven. U Yaw takes shelter is forcibly closed by the state, which renders his fellow monks displaced—a violation of international human rights law.

Ven. U Yaw's story reveals how military attacks after an unlawful regime change caused wide-scale displacement and how different bodies of law articulated the legality of that displacement differently. His story also showcases the different roles that Buddhist monasteries are serving in the displacement crisis in Myanmar (almost five million people have been displaced since the 2021 coup as of this writing, including internally displaced people and refugees who have fled abroad).[52] Monasteries in Myanmar serve as refuges for displaced monks, as shelters for displaced lay people (including non-Buddhists), and as sites of displacement when they are attacked, destroyed, or forcibly closed. The *vinaya* continues to guide monastics' actions in these extreme situations, but does not provide sufficient guidance to cover all the decisions monastics must make and is sometimes violated for the sake of safety. While Buddhist monastics in this context can appeal to both the *vinaya* and to international law to justify their actions, they are severely impacted by state law and its (right or wrongful) implementation and adjudication.

Case Study: Myanmar's Monks Influencing Rohingya Displacement

Our case study of Buddhism and displacement in Myanmar would be grossly incomplete without highlighting some Buddhist monastics' role in the mass displacement of primarily Muslim Rohingya people. Over one million Rohingya have been displaced in and from Myanmar across the past several decades due to increasingly marginalizing policies. A series of violent attacks and the destruction of entire villages in August 2017 were responsible for more than 742,000 Rohingya people fleeing to neighboring Bangladesh, where around one million continue to reside as refugees in the world's largest refugee camp.[53] Buddhism and law both played leading roles in instigating this violence, which the UN Human Rights Chief has called a "textbook case of ethnic cleansing."[54] As of 2024, an estimated 636,000 Rohingya people remained in Myanmar, many of them internally displaced.[55] The SAC keeps tight control over their movement and has arrested many hundreds of Rohingya, including children, who try to flee the military-controlled refugee camps (which are effectively detention centers) for safer options elsewhere.[56]

There are several rules in the *vinaya* that virtually prohibit Buddhist monks and nuns from entanglement in politics. For example, in the Theravāda *Pāṭimokkha*, monastics are prohibited from spending prolonged time with armies, from criticizing government officials, from handling money, and from engaging in divisive talk. To cement their apolitical status in society, monastics are prohibited from voting in Myanmar as well as in Thailand. (By contrast, in Tibet, a monk—the Dalai Lama—served as head of state from 1642 to 2011.)

Despite the rules and customs designed to keep monastics removed from political involvement, particularly in Theravāda contexts, such involvement nevertheless occurs. In Myanmar, a group of nationalist Buddhist monks convened in 2014 to form Ma Ba Tha, the Association for the Protection of Race and Religion. Some prominent members of the group have stoked fear of Muslims' taking over the country by "outbreeding" the majority-Buddhist citizenry (Muslims continue to comprise around four percent of Myanmar's population at this time of writing).[57] In 2015, Ma Ba Tha drafted and lobbied for the passage of four national Race and Religion Protection Laws that limit religious conversion, limit interreligious marriage, prohibit polygamy, and limit procreation. These laws disproportionately impact Muslim communities in Myanmar and have been decried by human rights organizations like Amnesty International as discriminatory.[58]

Although the Rohingya's precarious position in Myanmar had been mounting for decades, rendering them stateless by the time those laws were passed,[59] the laws played a critical role in swelling the tide of anti-Rohingya sentiment in Myanmar that culminated in an explosion of hate speech on Facebook and the August 2017 attacks. Amnesty International warned that the proposed laws could fuel "discrimination and violence," and they did.[60] Prominent Ma Ba Tha spokesman, Buddhist monk Ashin Wirathu—who had served a seven-year jail sentence for inciting violence against Muslims in 2003—denied any responsibility for 2017's violent attacks.[61]

In 2016, the government-appointed State Saṃgha Mahā Nāyaka Committee, which oversees monastic affairs in Myanmar, issued a public statement that "Ma Ba Tha is not a Buddhist organisation that was formed in accordance with the basic Sangha rules, regulations and directives of the State Sangha authority."[62] This rebuke of Ma Ba Tha from the state sangha council had a detrimental effect on the group's influence, although their statement did not prevent the escalation of violence in 2017. The displacement and insecurity of Rohingya people both abroad and within Myanmar continue to remain acute.

This case study illuminates how Buddhist monastics may involve themselves in state law and politics, even in cases where *vinaya* rules and social customs discourage them from doing so. In Myanmar's case, monastic political involvement has had major implications for the Rohingya displacement crisis: both for the violence of August 2017 leading to the largest exodus of Rohingya from Myanmar, and for the deflation of Ma Ba Tha's influence in the public sphere. Given the ongoing conflict and displacement promulgated by the SAC, solutions for the Rohingya and other displaced people in Myanmar do not appear to be forthcoming at the time of this writing.

The *Vinaya* and International Law

Displacement and refuge-seeking in our modern world are regulated by several bodies of law. State or domestic law governs many aspects of human movement, including state immigration policies and refugee admission quotas. International refugee law (IRL), international humanitarian law (IHL), and international human rights law (IHRL) are three global bodies of law that apply to situations of displacement both within and across state borders.[63] These three bodies of international law overlap and complement one another. IRL applies to people who have crossed international borders due to fear of persecution for specifically delineated reasons; IHL applies to all situations of armed conflict; and IHRL applies universally, at least in theory. These interlocking bodies of law establish the rights of people to flee unsafe conditions, to receive protection and assistance when displaced, to seek asylum, to retain their personal property when displaced, and not to be forcibly returned to a home that remains unsafe (the principle of *non-refoulement*).

It is not difficult to find echoes in the Buddhist *vinaya* traditions of these basic security provisions for displaced people. What is more difficult is adjudicating between the needs and rights of displaced people and the needs and rights of others—whether host communities, host governments, or arms bearers. In the remainder of this chapter, I explore resonances between the Buddhist *vinayas* and IHL. IHL guides the lawful conduct of hostilities by seeking a proportionate balance between minimizing the civilian harms of war and respecting the prerogative of arms bearers to engage in hostilities. In the search for justice within the balance, I find the dialogue between the monastic disciplines and IHL regarding displacement to be particularly fruitful.

The *Vinaya* and IHL

IHL, also known as the law of war, is the body of law that, during times of armed conflict, protects those who are not or no longer in the fight and restricts the means and methods of warfare. Its purpose is to establish minimum standards of humane conduct in order to lessen the sufferings of war, particularly on civilian populations and regarding civilian infrastructure. Displacement is a common occurrence during times of armed conflict. IHL contains critical provisions to help prevent unnecessary displacement from occurring and to provide for the safe passage, protection, and assistance of displaced people in cases when displacement occurs.

The majority of displaced people today are forced to flee due to armed conflict where they live, and contexts of armed conflict often involve the breakdown of basic government services and a curtailment of rights. For people who are displaced due to conflict, the protection afforded to them by state law and national agencies may be severely limited. In many cases, IHL may provide the only meaningful legal protection on which displaced people can draw. This reality lends a sense of urgency and significance to the role of IHL and its steward, the International Committee of the Red Cross (ICRC), in protecting displaced people and in preventing and reducing displacement in times of armed conflict. IHL should be understood as a critical lever that can help change the trajectory of our current displacement crisis, both because of the outsized role that conflict plays in displacement and because of the frequent failure of other legal protections for displaced people in conflict zones.

My research, in collaboration with the ICRC's Global Affairs division, addresses the roles that Buddhist teachings and IHL can play in mitigating the sufferings of displaced people in times of armed conflict.[64] Approaching the topic of displacement from a Buddhist perspective confronts us with several interesting questions about how to balance the needs and rights of various parties in contexts of displacement. These questions are not merely speculative, but are practically relevant for several sets of actors: for Buddhist religious leaders and civil society leaders who are on the ground assisting displaced people and encouraging local communities to be generous to those in need; for Buddhist government leaders and policy makers who decide which groups of displaced people will be provided state assistance and for how long; and for Buddhists in the military or non-state armed groups whose professional duties obligate them to assess the severity of incidental civilian harm in attacks that are likely to cause displacement. A Buddhist legal exploration of displacement, even though it may not yield univocal answers to these questions, can help Buddhists operating at many levels of society strengthen their capacity to reduce the suffering of displacement in times of conflict.

The Buddhist monastic codes may at first glance seem unsuited to a dialogue with IHL because they are aimed at such high ethical conduct, far higher than is expected for lay people in peacetime, much less in times of war with its attendant moral compromises. However, despite the important differences between monastic and military life, there are also generative resonances between the two. Both monastics and military professionals play special roles in society—roles that are even marked by the uniforms and haircuts that visually distinguish these professionals from ordinary citizens—and both are bound by cultures of strict discipline and by rules that supersede the obligations of lay citizens. Additionally, both monastics and military professionals practice in environments of legal pluralism, where their unique rules of conduct are layered with other bodies of law issued by national and international bodies. Immersed in these legal pluralist environments, both monastic and military communities cultivate complex habits of legal reasoning. Just as Buddhist monastics carefully balance the harms (toward insects, animals, plants, and deities) inherent to daily life with the requirements of their spiritual duties, so must parties to armed conflict balance the harms inherent to war with their professional obligations as arms bearers. At their best, monastics and military personnel both entrust themselves to livelihoods of constant care and vigilance as they perform their respective roles in society, taking responsibility for harm, the causes of harm, and the reverberating consequences of harm as they serve causes greater than their own individual well-being. Further dialogue between the Buddhist monastic discipline and IHL may better illuminate the ethical values and reasoning habits these two traditions hold in common and may motivate Buddhist actors—in both military and civil society—to analyze more thoroughly the causes and consequences of displacement in order to reduce and prevent conflict-induced displacement.

Here, I hope to make the case that Buddhist monastic codes of discipline are relevant to the discourse on displacement from a global legal perspective, and for two main reasons. First, the monastic codes—even though they are designed to support what is called the "homeless" life—nevertheless provide for the shelter and security of monastics, facilitating their basic dignity and humanity, which are also centrally important concepts in IHL.[65] Second, the Buddhist monastic codes exhibit a high level of conscientiousness, or what in IHL is called "constant care."[66] The codes attend exhaustively to the causes and conditions that give rise to unwholesome behavior, not merely to unwholesome behavior itself. The codes of discipline cultivate in the monastic community habits of legal reasoning that take responsibility for the behaviors that cause harm, as well as for the cascading consequences of those behaviors, requiring a practice of mindful analysis that can be useful for the application of IHL in preventing and reducing displacement.

In IHL, we find concerns similar to those in the Buddhist *vinayas* about the importance of home and shelter for human dignity, legal limits on displacement, the humane treatment of displaced persons, the protection of people's right to return home in safety, and the protection of the property rights of the displaced:

> IHL expressly prohibits parties to an armed conflict from forcibly displacing civilians in both international and non-international armed conflicts, unless the security of the civilians involved or imperative military reasons so demand (*Geneva Convention IV* Articles 49 and 147; *AP I* Article 85(4)(a); *AP II* Article 17; *Customary IHL* Rule 129. See also *AP*

> *I* Articles 51(7) and 78(1) and *AP II* Article 4(3)(e)). Like other rules of IHL that can prevent displacement from occurring in the first place, this prohibition also protects civilians against the risk of secondary displacement. Furthermore, internally displaced persons have a right to voluntary return in safety to their homes or places of habitual residence as soon as the reasons for their displacement cease to exist (*Geneva Convention IV* Article 49 and *Customary IHL* Rule 132).[67]

We also find in IHL habits of legal reasoning about actions that are likely to cause human displacement, habits that resonate with the way the *vinaya*s consider building activities that are likely to displace animals. In IHL, parties to a conflict are prohibited not only from "ordering" a population's removal or "forcibly transferring" people,[68] but also from taking actions that serve as direct causes for displacement.[69] Some of these causes of displacement, such as cutting off water supply or food transport, destroying civilian homes, damaging critical infrastructure, or terrorizing the local population, are already illegal in their own right (at least, as primary objectives). Other actions that lead to civilian displacement may not be explicitly prohibited, but may nonetheless be foreseeable causes of displacement for which military decision-makers must take account as they weigh the legality of their actions.

Although military attacks that target civilians or whose primary objective is to displace civilians are illegal under IHL, many attacks that result in civilian displacement fall in a gray area where the attack's legality is not objectively clear. The principle of proportionality is the mechanism in IHL that helps to guide decision makers through this gray area of legality, as described in rule 14 of the ICRC's study of customary IHL:

> Launching an attack which may be expected to cause incidental loss of civilian life, injury to civilians, damage to civilian objects, or a combination thereof, which would be excessive in relation to the concrete and direct military advantage anticipated, is prohibited.[70]

Assessing the proportional relationship between the "concrete and direct military advantage anticipated" and incidental civilian harm is a notoriously ambiguous area of IHL, one that cannot rely on a simple mathematical formula. Instead, this assessment requires a "value judgment," which renders decision-making in conflict zones more complex, but which also leaves space for Buddhist values to help guide decision makers whose actions on the battlefield have the potential to cause or prevent enormous suffering.[71]

The ICRC's report on the *Gendered Impacts of Armed Conflict* confirms that "proportionality assessments must consider incidental civilian harm that is foreseeable—for example, the spread of disease due to incidental damage to municipal sewage systems in an attack."[72] Just as Buddhist monastics take legal responsibility for damaging habitats or displacing animals because such actions lead to foreseeable consequences of harm, military personnel must take legal responsibility for the foreseeable consequences of their actions, such as fighting in close proximity to villages or cities, that are likely to cause human displacement.

The ICRC *Gendered Impacts* report also emphasizes the importance of "the military practitioner's understanding of the kind of harm that might result from an attack [...] including the indirect or 'reverberating' effects, that may be expected."[73] Regarding displacement, this means that decision makers in times of conflict should consider not only how their actions might lead to displacement, but also how any displacement they cause may lead to a variety of other forms of harm. We know a lot about the foreseeable, indirect harms of displacement:

1. Displacement subjects people to a higher risk of violence, including sexual and gender-based violence; at least one in five refugee women have experienced sexual violence, for example.[74]
2. Rates of child marriage and forced marriage increase significantly in certain contexts of displacement because marriage is viewed in many communities as a mechanism for enhancing short-term security, even though it presents serious obstacles to children's education and health outcomes.[75]
3. Loss of civilian property and the loss of herds or harvest are well-documented implications of displacement whose effects can be felt for a lifetime, or even for generations.
4. Family separation is a great risk among displaced populations. IHL customary rule 131 requires that civilians affected by conflict are provided "satisfactory conditions of shelter, hygiene, health, safety and nutrition and that members of the same family are not separated,"[76] and the fourth Geneva Convention also makes strong commitments toward respecting family life and protecting the unity of families.[77] In reality, parties to armed conflict often do not fulfill these requirements. The ICRC works to restore missing family links for thousands of people every year. Family separation is a foreseeable reality of displacement that must be factored into assessments of civilian harm.
5. When civilians are compelled to flee their homes, some cannot flee as easily as others. The disabled, ill, elderly, and very young, as well as their (usually female) caregivers, all face additional risks and difficulties in situations where flight becomes necessary.[78] These groups are even more vulnerable when on the road, and if they are unable to flee, they may be forced to remain home in a conflict zone where their community structures of support have disappeared.

Decision makers in contexts of armed conflict must weigh the harms of displacement, its causes, and its consequences very heavily. The principles of "constant care" and "foreseeable precaution" in IHL enjoin decision makers to minimize attacks that cause displacement because of the severe immediate and reverberating harms that displacement causes. Both the Buddhist *vinayas* and IHL are legal reasoning traditions that take into account responsibility for the prior causes of harm, for direct harm, and for the reverberating consequences of harm.

The Buddhist tradition is a psychologically rich tradition that offers an array of contemplative methods for analyzing internal as well as external phenomena. Several scholars have explored the possible applications for Buddhist mindfulness techniques for military professionals in order to enhance compliance with IHL.[79] By integrating IHL with the rigorous analytical tools as well as the ethical legitimacy that Buddhism offers its followers, Buddhist decision makers during times of war could be better prepared to foresee and reduce displacement.

Moore has articulated well the reasons why the stewards of international law should pay more attention to Buddhism:

> The ideal of the system of international law is that it would be similar to successful national systems of law, which are seen by those bound by them as not merely the commands of the powerful backed by threats for noncompliance, but rather as legitimate and binding rules that represent reasons for acting in certain ways. [...] Such a system's legitimacy and efficacy ultimately rest on the consent of the states and/or individuals that are bound by it, for the same reasons that national legal systems rest on the consent or acquiescence of subnational political units and the general population [...]. Because of this need for consent, the international law regime has a strong interest in demonstrating how its various principles and institutions are consistent with, and perhaps even required by, the major religious and philosophical systems of the world. For that reason, international law has a profound interest in engaging in comparative philosophical analysis, both to demonstrate to Buddhists (for example) that international law is consistent with Buddhism and to identify and hopefully resolve any inconsistencies, in the interests of both universality and getting the laws right.[80]

The ICRC project on *Religion and Humanitarian Principles* seeks to encourage Buddhists to identify more closely with and therefore to self-implement IHL, while also seeking to improve the law through dialogue and critique from Buddhist actors. This brief comparison of the *vinayas* and IHL regarding displacement indicates that IHL could benefit from increased attention to the dynamics of habitats and ecosystems; to the long-term, multi-generational consequences of attacks; and to the role of religious actors in spreading awareness, understanding, and support for the law.

In Chapter 5, we explore how a Buddhist ethical framework called the "gift of fearlessness" can shed new light on IRL and state refugee admissions policies.

Notes

1 Portions of this chapter are adapted or reproduced from Kilby, Christina. "Legal Reasoning about Displacement and Responsibility: A Dialogue Between the Buddhist Monastic Discipline and IHL." *Journal of Buddhist Ethics* 30 (2023): 231–254. Accessed on 20 May 2026. https://blogs.dickinson.edu/buddhistethics/category/volume-26-2019/
2 Alvarez Ortega, Miguel. "Buddhism and Law." In Courtney Bruntz, ed. *Oxford Bibliographies in Buddhism.* Oxford University Press, 2016. "Introduction." Accessed on 11 June 2024.
3 Alvarez Ortega, Miguel. "Buddhism and Law." *In Courtney Bruntz, ed.Oxford Bibliographies in Buddhism.* Oxford University Press, 2016. "Introduction." Accessed on 11 June 2024.
4 Alvarez Ortega, Miguel. "Buddhism and Law." *In Courtney Bruntz, ed.Oxford Bibliographies in Buddhism.* Oxford University Press, 2016. "Introduction." Accessed on 11 June 2024.
5 Moore, Matthew J. *Buddhism and Political Theory.* New York: Oxford University Press, 2016. p. 16.
6 Moore, Matthew J. *Buddhism and Political Theory.* New York: Oxford University Press, 2016. p. 2.
7 Moore, Matthew J. *Buddhism and Political Theory.* New York: Oxford University Press, 2016. p. 6.
8 Moore, Matthew J. *Buddhism and Political Theory.* New York: Oxford University Press, 2016. p. 29.
9 My approach is influenced by Ninian Smart's seven dimensions of religions. Refer to Smart, Ninian. *The World's Religions.* Cambridge University Press, 1998.
10 In the *Anuradha Sutta*, the Buddha claims that he teaches only two things: suffering and the end of suffering. Refer to "Anuradha Sutta: To Anuradha" (SN 22.86), translated from the Pāli by Thānissaro Bhikkhu. *Access to Insight (BCBS Edition)*, 30 November 2013. Accessed on 11 June 2024. www.accesstoinsight.org/tipitaka/sn/sn22/sn22.086.than.html.
11 Moore, Matthew J. *Buddhism and Political Theory.* New York: Oxford University Press, 2016. p. 30.
12 In this chapter, I do not address the *vinaya* texts from traditions that are no longer practiced.
13 Csoma Körösi, Alexander. "An Analysis of the Dulva, A Portion of the Tibetan Work Entitled the Kah-gyur." *Asiatic Researches* 20 (1836): 41–93.
14 French, Rebecca R. "What is Buddhist Law?" *Buffalo Law Review,* 63 (2015): 833–872. Refer to p. 835.
15 Schonthal, Benjamin. "Buddhist Legal Pluralism: Looking Again at Monastic Governance in Modern South and Southeast Asia." *Buddhism, Law & Society* 3 (2017–18): vii–xxxvii. Refer to p. xxiv.
16 Some Buddhist ascetics, such as masters in the Thai forest tradition or yogic masters in the Tibetan–Himalayan tradition, may opt to live in the wilderness without the comforts of shelter in order more rigorously to pursue their meditative goals. However, this level of asceticism is voluntary, not an expectation set by the Buddha for all his monastics.

17 Schopen, Gregory. "Hierarchy and Housing in a Buddhist Monastic Code: A Translation of the Sanskrit Text of the *Śayanāsanavastu* of the *Mūlasarvāstivāda-vinaya* – Part 1." *Buddhist Literature* 2 (2000): 92–196. Refer to p. 108.

18 *Bhikkhu Pāṭimokkha: The Bhikkhus' Code of Discipline*. Trans. Thānissaro Bhikkhu. *Access to Insight (BCBS Edition)*, 17 December 2013. Accessed on 20 June 2023 at www.accesstoinsight.org/tipitaka/vin/sv/bhikkhu-pati.html. Refer to Saṅghādisesa rules 6–7.

19 Thānissaro Bhikkhu. *The Buddhist Monastic Code I: The Pāṭimokkha Rules Translated and Explained*. Valley Center, CA: Metta Forest Monastery, 1994. p. 128.

20 For a fascinating discussion of how the *vinaya* addresses these creatures, refer to Hierman, Ann. "How to Deal with Dangerous and Annoying Animals: A *Vinaya* Perspective." *Religions* 10, no. 113 (2019): 1–17.

21 Heim, Maria. *The Forerunner of All Things: Buddhaghosa on Mind, Intention, and Agency*. New York: Oxford University Press, 2014. p. 159. This narrative relates to the Theravāda *Pāṭimokkha* Pārājika rule 2. A similar case occurred in 2024 when a Khmer temple was destroyed by government authorities in Vietnam due to a claim that the structure had been built illegally. Refer to "Buddhist Community Hall Destroyed and Four Khmer Krom Monks Arrested in Crackdown," *CSW*. Accessed on 20 June 2024. www.csw.org.uk/2024/04/03/press/6201/article.htm.

22 "Bhikkhu Pāṭimokkha: The Bhikkhus' Code of Discipline." Trans. Thānissaro Bhikkhu. Access to Insight (BCBS Edition), 17 December 2013. Accessed on 20 June 2023. www.accesstoinsight.org/tipitaka/vin/sv/bhikkhu-pati.html. Saṅghādisesa rules 6–7.

23 "Bhikkhu Pāṭimokkha: The Bhikkhus' Code of Discipline." Trans. Thānissaro Bhikkhu. Access to Insight (BCBS Edition), 17 December 2013. Accessed on 20 June 2023. www.accesstoinsight.org/tipitaka/vin/sv/bhikkhu-pati.html. Pācittiya rule 19.

24 "Bhikkhu Pāṭimokkha: The Bhikkhus' Code of Discipline." Trans. Thānissaro Bhikkhu. Access to Insight (BCBS Edition), 17 December 2013. Accessed on 20 June 2023. www.accesstoinsight.org/tipitaka/vin/sv/bhikkhu-pati.html. Sekhyia rule 74.

25 Yifa. *The Origins of Buddhist Monastic Codes in China: An Annotated Translation and Study of the Chanyuan Qinggui*. Honolulu: University of Hawai'i Press, 2002. "Chanyuan Qinggui in Translation," pp. 112–220. Refer especially to p. 166.

26 United Nations High Commissioner for Refugees. *Principles and Standards for Settlement Planning*. Updated 26 June 2025. Accessed on 26 November 2025. https://emergency.unhcr.org/emergency-assistance/settlement-and-shelter/guidance-settlements/principles-standards-settlement-planning.

27 "Bhikkhu Pāṭimokkha: The Bhikkhus' Code of Discipline." Trans. Thānissaro Bhikkhu. Access to Insight (BCBS Edition), 17 December 2013. Accessed on 20 June 2023. www.accesstoinsight.org/tipitaka/vin/sv/bhikkhu-pati.html. Pācittiya rule 27.

28 "Bhikkhunī Pāṭimokkha: The Bhikkhunīs' Code of Discipline." Trans. Thānissaro Bhikkhu. Access to Insight (BCBS Edition), 17 December 2013. Accessed on 20 June 2023. www.accesstoinsight.org/tipitaka/vin/sv/Bhikkhunī-pati.html. [Pācittiya rules 37–38.

29 The ICRC report on *Gendered Dimensions of Armed Conflict* also explores the gender-based vulnerabilities that males tend to face, such as forced conscription and boys being categorized as adults in detention situations at younger ages than girls are. Refer to the International Committee of the Red Cross. *Gendered Impacts of Armed Conflict and Implications for the Application of International Humanitarian Law.* Geneva, 2022.

30 Vu, A; Adam, A; Wirtz, A; Pham, K; Rubenstein, L; Glass, N; Beyrer, C; and Singh, S. "The Prevalence of Sexual Violence among Female Refugees in Complex Humanitarian Emergencies: A Systematic Review and Meta-analysis." *PLoS Currents* 6 (18 March 2014). PMID: 24818066.

31 Thānissaro Bhikkhu. *The Buddhist Monastic Code II: The Khandhaka Rules Translated and Explained.* Valley Center, CA: Metta Forest Monastery, 2001. Accessed on 26 November 2025 at www.accesstoinsight.org/lib/authors/thanissaro/bmc2.pdf. pp. 138–139.

32 Thānissaro Bhikkhu. *The Buddhist Monastic Code II: The Khandhaka Rules Translated and Explained.* Valley Center, CA: Metta Forest Monastery, 2001. Accessed on 26 November 2025 at www.accesstoinsight.org/lib/authors/thanissaro/bmc2.pdf, p. 139.

33 Rules relevant to monastic evictions include "Bhikkhu Pāṭimokkha: The Bhikkhus' Code of Discipline." Trans. Thānissaro Bhikkhu. Access to Insight (BCBS Edition), 17 December 2013. Accessed on 20 June 2023. www.accesstoinsight.org/tipitaka/vin/sv/bhikkhu-pati.html. Pācittiya rules 16 and 17; "Bhikkhunī Pāṭimokkha: The Bhikkhunīs' Code of Discipline." Trans. Thānissaro Bhikkhu. Access to Insight (BCBS Edition), 17 December 2013. Accessed on 20 June 2023. www.accesstoinsight.org/tipitaka/vin/sv/Bhikkhunī-pati.html. Pācittiya rules 35, 112, and 113; and "Varṣa Skandhaka." *Dharmaguptaka Vinaya,* fascicle 37. Trans. Christie Chang, ed. Thubten Chodron and Thubten Damcho. *Taishō Tripiṭaka* (CBETA edition), vol. 22. Taipei: Bodhi Foundation for Culture and Education, 2014. Accessed on 20 May 2026. https://dharmaguptakavinaya.wordpress.com/wp-content/uploads/2014/06/varsa-skandhaka-2014-06-22-bilingual.pdf. p. 831a.

34 "Bhikkhunī Pāṭimokkha: The Bhikkhunīs' Code of Discipline." Trans. Thānissaro Bhikkhu. Access to Insight (BCBS Edition), 17 December 2013. Accessed on 20 June 2023. www.accesstoinsight.org/tipitaka/vin/sv/Bhikkhunī-pati.html, rule 48.

35 *Dharmaguptaka Vinaya* Varṣa Skandhaka, *Taishō Tripiṭaka*, Vol. 22, No. 1428, p. 831c.

36 Thānissaro Bhikkhu, *Buddhist Monastic Code I: The Pāṭimokkha Rules Translated and Explained.* Valley Center, CA: Metta Forest Monastery, 1994. p. 272.

37 Schopen, Gregory. "Counting the Buddha and the Local Spirits In: A Monastic Ritual of Inclusion for the Rain Retreat." *Journal of Indian Philosophy* 30, no. 4 (2002): 359–88. Refer to p. 380.

38 Schopen, Gregory. "Hierarchy and Housing in a Buddhist Monastic Code: A Translation of the Sanskrit Text of the *Śayanāsanavastu* of the *Mūlasarvāstivāda-vinaya*—Part 1." *Buddhist Literature* 2 (2000): 92–196. p. 117.

39 Schopen, Gregory. "Hierarchy and Housing in a Buddhist Monastic Code: A Translation of the Sanskrit Text of the *Śayanāsanavastu* of the *Mūlasarvāstivāda-vinaya*—Part 1." *Buddhist Literature* 2 (2000): 92–196. p. 119.

40 Schopen, Gregory. "Hierarchy and Housing in a Buddhist Monastic Code: A Translation of the Sanskrit Text of the *Śayanāsanavastu* of the *Mūlasarvāstivāda -vinaya*—Part 1." *Buddhist Literature* 2 (2000): 92–196. p. 121.

41 Schopen, Gregory. "Hierarchy and Housing in a Buddhist Monastic Code: A Translation of the Sanskrit Text of the *Śayanāsanavastu* of the *Mūlasarvāstivāda -vinaya*—Part 1." *Buddhist Literature* 2 (2000): 92–196. p. 122.

42 *Bhikkhunī Pāṭimokkha: The Bhikkhunīs' Code of Discipline.* Trans. Thānissaro Bhikkhu. *Access to Insight (BCBS Edition)*, 17 December 2013. Accessed 20 June 2024. www.accesstoinsight.org/tipitaka/vin/sv/Bhikkhunī-pati.html.

43 Schonthal, Benjamin. "Buddhist Legal Pluralism: Looking Again at Monastic Governance in Modern South and Southeast Asia," *Buddhism, Law & Society* 3 (2017–2018): vii–xxxviii. Refer to p. viii.

44 On this point, I disagree with the assessment that Buddhist legal culture is "a form of social and collective government that is at odds with our notions of the sovereign state." French, Rebecca R. "What is Buddhist Law?" *Buffalo Law Review* 63 (2015): 833–872. Refer to p. 839.

45 "Measures on the Management of the Reincarnation of Living Buddhas in Tibetan Buddhism" (State Religious Affairs Bureau Order Number 5). Translated by the International Campaign for Tibet. Congressional-Executive Commission on China. 18 July 2007. Accessed on 26 November 2025. www.cecc.gov/resources/legal-provisions/measures-on-the-management-of-the-reincarnation-of-living-buddhas-in-0.

46 Nu Nu Lusan. "In Myanmar, A Monk Takes on the Junta." *The New Humanitarian,* 20 October 2022. Accessed on 26 November 2025. www.thenewhumanitarian.org/feature/2022/10/20/Myanmar-protests-monks-junta-Buddhist.

47 Nu Nu Lusan. "In Myanmar, A Monk Takes on the Junta." *The New Humanitarian,* 20 October 2022. Accessed on 26 November 2025. www.thenewhumanitarian.org/feature/2022/10/20/Myanmar-protests-monks-junta-Buddhist.

48 Centre for Law and Democracy. "Myanmar: Analysis of the Military's Changes to the Penal Code." 10 May 2021. Accessed on 26 November 2026. www.law-democracy.org/live/myanmar-analysis-of-the-militarys-changes-to-the-penal-code/. This clause was used to charge an estimated 3,995 protestors within the first year of the coup. Many of those charged fled government-controlled areas, while some were imprisoned. Refer to Free Expression Myanmar, "New Report: 505A Act of Revenge." 31 January 2022. Accessed on 26 November 2025. https://freeexpressionmyanmar.org/505a-act-of-revenge/.

49 Nu Nu Lusan. "In Myanmar, A Monk Takes on the Junta." *The New Humanitarian,* 20 October 2022. Accessed on 26 November 2025. www.thenewhumanitarian.org/feature/2022/10/20/Myanmar-protests-monks-junta-Buddhist.

50 Nu Nu Lusan. "In Myanmar, A Monk Takes on the Junta." *The New Humanitarian,* 20 October 2022. Accessed on 26 November 2025. www.thenewhumanitarian.org/feature/2022/10/20/Myanmar-protests-monks-junta-Buddhist.

51 Nu Nu Lusan. "In Myanmar, A Monk Takes on the Junta." *The New Humanitarian,* 20 October 2022. Accessed on 26 November 2025. www.thenewhumanitarian.org/feature/2022/10/20/Myanmar-protests-monks-junta-Buddhist.

52 Amnesty International. "Myanmar: Four Years after Coup, World Must Demand Accountability for Atrocity Crimes." 31 January 2025. Accessed on 26 November 2025. www.amnesty.org/en/latest/news/2025/01/myanmar-four-years-after-coup-world-must-demand-accountability-for-atrocity-crimes/.

53 United Nations High Commissioner for Refugees. "Rohingya Refugee Crisis Explained." 22 August 2024. Accessed on 26 November 2025. www.unrefugees.org/news/rohingya-refugee-crisis-explained/.

54 "UN Human Rights Chief Points to 'Textbook Example of Ethnic Cleansing' in Myanmar." *UN News*, 11 September 2017. Accessed on 28 November 2025. https://news.un.org/en/story/2017/09/564622-un-human-rights-chief-points-textbook-example-ethnic-cleansing-myanmar.

55 van den Assum, Laetitia. "Out of the Spotlight, Myanmar's Rohingya Face Worst Violence in 7 Years." United States Institute of Peace. Accessed on 28 November 2025. www.usip.org/publications/2024/09/out-spotlight-myanmars-rohingya-face-worst-violence-7-years.

56 "More than 100 Rohingya Refugees Jailed for Trying to Flee Myanmar Camps." *The Guardian*. 11 January 2023. Accessed on 28 November 2025. www.theguardian.com/world/2023/jan/11/more-than-100-rohingya-refugees-jailed-for-trying-to-flee-myanmar-camps.

57 "Myanmar Passes 'Anti-Polygamy' Law." *Deutsche Welle*. 31 August 2015. Accessed on 3 December 2025. www.dw.com/en/myanmar-passes-controversial-anti-polygamy-law/a-18684571.

58 Amnesty International and the International Commission of Jurists. "Myanmar: Parliament Must Reject Discriminatory 'Race and Religion' Laws." 3 March 2015. Accessed on 7 May 2026. www.amnesty.org/en/documents/asa16/1107/2015/en/.

59 Curiously, analysts seem to have not determined whether the four laws apply to non-citizens, which, given the Rohingyas' barriers to citizenship, would undermine the intention of the legislation. Refer to Amnesty International, "Myanmar: Scrap 'Race and Religion' Laws that Could Fuel Discrimination and Violence." 3 March 2015. Accessed on 6 December 2025. www.amnesty.org/en/latest/news/2015/03/myanmar-race-and-religion-laws/.

60 Amnesty International. "Myanmar: Scrap 'Race and Religion' Laws that Could Fuel Discrimination and Violence." 3 March 2015. Accessed on 6 December 2025. www.amnesty.org/en/latest/news/2015/03/myanmar-race-and-religion-laws/.

61 Khin Khin Ei (trans. Khet Mar, English version by Joshua Lipes). "Myanmar Monk Rejects Terrorist Label Following Communal Clashes." *Radio Free Asia*. 21 June 2013. Accessed on 6 December 2025. www.rfa.org/english/news/myanmar/monk-06212013182954.html.

62 Abrahamian, Andray. "Myanmar's Ma Ba Tha Fades with Barely a Whimper." *The Interpreter*, 2 August 2016. Accessed on 6 December 2025. www.lowyinstitute.org/the-interpreter/myanmar-s-ma-ba-tha-fades-barely-whimper.

63 At times, international criminal law (which holds individual perpetrators of war crimes accountable for their actions) and the emerging area of international disaster response law (seeking to fill legal gaps to reduce communities' vulnerability to natural disasters) are also relevant legal instruments for situations of displacement.

64 International Committee of the Red Cross. "Project on the Interface Between Buddhism and IHL." *Religion and Humanitarian Principles*. 2 March 2020. Accessed on 20 June 2023. https://blogs.icrc.org/religion-humanitarianprinciples/project-on-the-interface-between-buddhism-and-ihl/.

65 International Committee of the Red Cross. "What is IHL?" 18 September 2015. Accessed on 20 June 2023. www.icrc.org/en/document/what-ihl.
66 International Committee of the Red Cross. "Rules." International Humanitarian Law Database. Accessed on 20 June 2023. https://ihl-databases.icrc.org/en/customary-ihl/v1. Refer to rule 15.
67 International Committee of the Red Cross. "Internally Displaced Persons and International Humanitarian Law (Factsheet)." 6 April 2022. Accessed on 25 July 2023. www.icrc.org/en/document/internally-displaced-persons-and-international-humanitarian-law-factsheet. Refer to p. 3.
68 The exceptions to this prohibition are when "the security of the civilians involved or imperative military reasons so demand." Refer to ICRC, "Rules," International Humanitarian Law Database. Accessed 20 June 2023. https://ihl-databases.icrc.org/en/customary-ihl/v1. Rule 129.
69 IHL involves a balance between humanity and military necessity; the prohibitions against displacement are not absolute but must be weighed against military necessity, while always attending to the distinction between combatants and those who are not or no longer in the fight and while preserving the humanity of those affected.
70 International Committee of the Red Cross. "Rules." International Humanitarian Law Database. Accessed 20 June 2023. https://ihl-databases.icrc.org/en/customary-ihl/v1. Rule 14.
71 Cohen, Amichai and David Zlotogorski. *Proportionality in International Humanitarian Law: Consequences, Precautions, and Procedures.* United Kingdom, Oxford University Press, 2021. p. 7.
72 International Committee of the Red Cross (ICRC). *Gendered Impacts of Armed Conflict and Implications for the Application of International Humanitarian Law.* Geneva, 2022. p. 16.
73 International Committee of the Red Cross (ICRC). *Gendered Impacts of Armed Conflict and Implications for the Application of International Humanitarian Law.* Geneva, 2022. p. 17.
74 Vu, A; Adam, A; Wirtz, A; Pham, K; Rubenstein, L; Glass, N; Beyrer, C; and Singh, S. "The Prevalence of Sexual Violence among Female Refugees in Complex Humanitarian Emergencies: A Systematic Review and Meta-analysis." *PLoS Currents* 6 (18 March 2014). PMID: 24818066.
75 Goers, M., K. Hunersen, L.S. Karim, A. Jeffery, A. Zedan, C. Robinson, J. Metzler. "Child Marriage Among Displaced Populations – A 2019 Study in Kurdistan Region of Iraq." *BMC Public Health* 22 (2022): 796. DOI: 10.1186/s12889-022-13220-x.
76 ICRC. "Rules." International Humanitarian Law Database. Accessed 20 June 2023. https://ihl-databases.icrc.org/en/customary-ihl/v1. Refer to rule 131.
77 ICRC. "Internally Displaced Persons and International Humanitarian Law(Factsheet)." 6 April 2022. Accessed on 25 July 2023. www.icrc.org/en/document/internally-displaced-persons-and-international-humanitarian-law-factsheet. p. 5.
78 ICRC. *Gendered Impacts of Armed Conflict and Implications for the Application of International Humanitarian Law*. Geneva, 2022. p. 19.
79 Refer to the following chapters from Andrew Bartles-Smith, Kate Crosby, Peter Harvey, Asanga Tilakaratne, Daniel Ratheiser, Noel Maurer Trew, Stefania Travagnin, Elizabeth J. Harris, Venerable Mahinda Deegalle, and

Christina A. Kilby, editors. *Buddhism and International Humanitarian Law.* New York: Routledge, 2023: Elizabeth J. Harris, "Buddhist Empirical Realism and the Conduct of Armed Conflict," pp. 147–166; Diane Denis, "Fundamental Intelligence, A Buddhist Justification for the Universal Principles Underlying IHL,"pp. 167–192; Noel Maurer Trew, " 'Not Knowing is Most Intimate'; Koan Practice and the Fog of War," pp. 228–256; Bhagya Samarakoon, "Restraint in Warfare and Appamāda: the Concept of Collateral Damage in International Humanitarian Law in Light of the Buddha's Last Words," pp. 307–329.

80 Moore, Matthew J. *Buddhism and Political Theory*. New York: Oxford University Press, 2016. p. 52.

5 The Gift of Fearlessness[1]

At the writing of this book, the number of displaced people is at its highest in recorded history and projected to continue increasing. International humanitarian organizations are strained, and the funding and resettlement commitments of states are falling far short of the current need. In 2024, a small fraction of the refugees identified as needing resettlement[2] were resettled in a safe third country. The UNHCR reports that

> In 2024, fewer than 5% of refugees who were in need of resettlement managed to start their life in a third country through UNHCR-assisted resettlement. In 2025, resettlement quotas are expected to be the lowest since 2003, falling below the levels seen even during the COVID-19 pandemic. This dramatic decline risks reversing the significant progress made in recent years, while also exposing refugee lives to danger. Meanwhile, resettlement needs have surged by 32% over the past two decades.[3]

The proportion of refugees resettled out of all needing resettlement in 2024 was half of the proportion resettled in 2014.[4] States are failing refugees.

Beyond its enormous humanitarian and human geographical consequences, the global refugee crisis has also become a focus of heated political debate as nationalist movements across the world promote the reduction or elimination of refugee resettlement by questioning the legitimacy of ethnic and religious minorities within their state boundaries. The drive to decrease refugee admissions is often presented as a dictate of national security; a 2016 Pew Research poll, for example, showed that the majority of Europeans believed that "incoming refugees increase the likelihood of terrorism in their country."[5] Rhetoric linking "refugee" to "terrorist" has indelibly marked the administrations of U.S. President Donald Trump, under whose leadership refugee admission levels fell to their lowest since the inception of the U.S. Refugee Admissions Program in 1980, even as the number of forcibly displaced people has climbed to its highest on record.[6]

It is evident that the identity of "refugee" is now a highly contested one: Is a refugee a victim or a villain? A moral obligation or a security risk?

DOI: 10.4324/9781003318149-5

Embedded in the very process of defining "refugee" are ethical and political consequences of significant import, both for displaced people and for potential resettlement states.

In this chapter, I turn to Buddhist political ethics to grapple with the role of states in the global refugee crisis. States play an outsized role both in *creating refugees* and in *offering refuge* to the endangered. While Buddhist traditions are far from univocal on important questions in political ethics—ranging from which form of government is ethically preferable, to whether politics is even a worthwhile arena in which to spend one's precious human life[7]—Buddhists have engaged in much reflection over the centuries about the ethics of state power and just governance. In many cases, Buddhist reflection on the ethics of governance is framed as advice to kings. Yet as Buddhist-majority states have adopted democratic governments across the last half century, many Buddhists have translated the traditional teachings on righteous kingship into frameworks of political ethics aimed at states, including those that are not monarchies.

While karma is generally understood among Buddhists as individuated, Buddhist morality is not merely an individual matter, but reflecting the reality of interdependence, it is also a matter of collectives. This is why the codes of monastic discipline regulate not only individual behavior, but also group behavior, concerning themselves with the effects of the sangha as a collective unit upon the lay community. Additionally, the teachings on the noble eightfold path have direct implications for collective activities, from economics (right livelihood) to communication and media (right speech). For these reasons, I find it appropriate to apply the ethical instruction originally aimed at kings not only to individuals who wield political power, but to states as collective entities.

My analysis here is centered on *abhayadāna*: the gift of fearlessness. Investigating classical Indic literary sources on the gift of fearlessness—typically glossed as the offer of refuge or protection to those in mortal danger—I present today's refugee as situated at the nexus of two types of fear: the fear that drives vulnerable people to flee from harm and the fear that drives a potential refuge-offering state to close its borders or build walls. I argue that the gift of fearlessness, if extended beyond its classical scope to include the challenges of xenophobia and terrorism, is a capacious framework through which to probe the moral contours of contemporary refugee policy as well as the legitimate security concerns of states.

The international refugee regime—the body of laws and policies governing refugee protection—has, over the past six decades, adopted a series of legal definitions of "refugee." The 1951 Refugee Convention articulates what has remained the foundational framework for international refugee protection.[8] Article 1A(2) of the Convention defines a refugee as

> any person who, owing to well-founded fear of being persecuted for reasons of race, religion, nationality, membership of a particular social

> group or political opinion, is outside the country of his [or her] nationality and is unable, or owing to such fear, is unwilling to avail him [or her] self of the protection of that country; or who, not having a nationality and being outside the country of his [or her] former habitual residence as a result of such events, is unable or, owing to such fear, is unwilling to return to it.[9]

In the tangle of language through which a displaced person is legally defined as a refugee, what is striking is the pivotal role of a particular emotion in the construction of this definition: fear. It is not merely flight that makes a refugee; according to the Convention, it is fear. A "well-founded fear of being persecuted" both propels refugees to flee the borders of a state and prevents them from seeking the protection of that state, opting instead for an uncertain future in an unknown land. Fear is the force behind forced migration.

Within the international legal framework established in 1951, refugees (who must qualify as refugees to receive certain forms of aid and life-saving asylum) are compelled to represent their fear in a concrete way for the international legal community. Media portrayals of refugees, especially those portrayals soliciting support for refugee relief and resettlement, often convey images of fearful faces and embodied desperation rather than images reflecting the resiliency and strength that are equally authentic characterizations of refugees. While there has emerged a growing awareness of the harms of "trauma-porn" (the graphic portrayal of others' suffering), the fact remains that refugees must narrate and renarrate their often-traumatic experiences of displacement and name their fears of persecution in order to participate effectively in the international refugee regime. International law constitutes the refugee as a living embodiment of fear.

In potential resettlement states that are dominated by nativist ideologies, fear amplifies as the refugee's fear of persecution meets xenophobia: fear of the stranger. The irony is that the refugee, a person legally defined as a victim of fear, can be simultaneously assumed to be an agent of fear ("terrorist").[10] Sara Ahmed discusses the position of the contemporary refugee by offering a phenomenology of fear's embodiment. In *The Cultural Politics of Emotion*, Ahmed writes, "fear works through and on the bodies of those who are transformed into its subjects, as well as its objects," so that "signs of affect seem to pass between bodies."[11] Fear is contagious, Ahmed argues, and one body's fearful affect stimulates a neighboring body to shrink, close, withdraw, or tighten its range of motion. The same phenomenology of fear is visible in nativist responses to the refugee crisis. When recognizing the refugee primarily in terms of "fear," a state exhibits the same responses that a fearful body does when it shrinks, closes, withdraws, or tightens its range of motion. The state slows refugee admissions, tightens its borders, and withdraws from the world stage.

The intertwining mechanisms of fear centering around the identity of "refugee" are fueled by political rhetoric and media imagery rather than by statistical realities. Xenophobia is sometimes strongest when actual arrival numbers are low. For example, during the campaign for the 2016 U.S. presidential election, popular outcries against illegal immigration from Mexico rose dramatically, despite the fact that undocumented crossings to the United States from Mexico actually declined by almost one-third between 2007 and 2017.[12] Regardless of the statistics, in this phenomenology of contagious fear, the international refugee regime fails to function. The dramatic reduction of refugee admissions in the United States during the Donald Trump administrations, for example, illustrates the twin movements of fear that leave refugees in increasingly vulnerable positions (and states that have signed the 1951 Refugee Convention in increasingly untenable ones).

The international refugee regime is not the only context in which an ontological link between flight and fear is embedded in the identity of the refugee. The role of fear as a primary determinant for refugee status intersects in a dynamic way with a classical Indic ethic for refugee protection: *abhayadāna*, the gift of fearlessness. *Abhayadāna* offers an alternative phenomenology of fear to that which is crippling refugee resettlement efforts today. In *abhayadāna*, we meet a dynamic shift in how states and societies can both perceive and respond to the fear of the displaced, transforming the image of "refugee" from an agent of fear to a domestic subject whose protection enhances state sovereignty.

The Gift of Fearlessness

The gift of fearlessness is described in Hindu, Jain, and Buddhist treatises on gift-giving that classify, sometimes in exhaustive detail, the various types of gifts with which one may practice the virtue of *dāna*, generosity. In Hindu digests, *dāna* typically pertains to tangible gifts: food, requisites for religious practitioners or, on a larger scale, community institutions. The gift of fearlessness is usually the only intangible gift listed in these texts, making for surprising juxtapositions; Hibbets notes that the digest writers often list the "nine types of superior gifts" as "food, curds, honey, protection [=fearlessness], cows, land, gold, horses, and elephants."[13] The gift of fearlessness is understood in these texts as the gift of "protection or security to those who fear threatened or inflicted violence," applicable both to individuals and to groups.[14] According to Hindu *dharmaśastra* tradition, "The king should offer amnesty to prisoners, grant his subjects protection from fear of mutilation, imprisonment, banishment, beatings, thievery, and dishonor, and should save anyone who comes to him for refuge."[15] In these texts, the gift of fearlessness is often assigned to the moral capacity of a king. Generosity is the first of the ten classically outlined duties of a king, whose position of authority imbues him with the power either to offer or to withhold protection, to make judgments about life and death. Hindu sources also extend the practice of *abhayadāna* to yogins, who undertake the discipline of refraining from harm of living creatures, as well as to ordinary lay people who, though perhaps powerless to save refugees, can at the very least protect the lives of certain insects and animals.[16] The extension of *abhayadāna* beyond the role of kingship contextualizes the gift of fearlessness within relationships of power. Fearlessness is a gift given by the powerful to the powerless, whether by rulers who hold power over the life and death of their subjects or by ordinary humans who hold power over the fates of the smallest animals.

Importantly, unlike gifts that are ritually exchanged in the context of a well-defined reciprocal relationship between two parties, fearlessness is a gift meant for strangers, and a gift that expects no reciprocity. As a form of public benefaction, fearlessness belongs to a class of gifts in which the recipient is not restricted, and the scrutiny to which the recipients are submitted in a relationship of esteem does not obtain.[17] When one establishes water reservoirs, endows temples, dams rivers, plants trees, provides healthcare, and vows to protect the protectorless, the recipients of those public benefits are for all purposes anonymous. Such gifts are given outside the religious boundaries of the sacrificial altar, without the usual procedure of reciting mantras, and to recipients who are not considered on the basis of their eligibility or worth.[18] In Indic treatises on gift-giving, the merit of the recipient is one of the defining criteria of the ethical value of a gift; a gift to a corrupt politician is karmically weighted with much less value than a gift to a renunciant, for example. For this reason, the Buddhist community continues to highly value gift-giving to monastic institutions. The wider social context in which Buddhist monks and nuns are valued as the ultimate field of merit brings the gift of fearlessness, meant for strangers and not based on any measure of their worthiness, into sharp relief: this gift is fundamentally different from the forms of giving most commonly associated with Buddhist community life.

In Buddhist commentarial texts on the perfection of generosity, gifts are typically classified as one of two or three types.[19] Most commonly discussed are gifts of material goods (the ultimate of which is a gift of one's own body sacrificed for others) and gifts of dharma (knowledge, truth, or spiritual edification);[20] the gift of fearlessness sometimes appears as a third type, the gift of life itself that makes material and spiritual well-being possible. The responsibility to give material gifts is either implicitly or explicitly assigned to the lay community, who are economically productive, and the responsibility to give dharmic gifts is assigned to the monastic community, who are spiritually productive. These gift-giving capacities reflect the reciprocal roles that lay society and sangha ideally play for one another: the lay community provides material support for religious practitioners, and the sangha propagates the dharma for the benefit of the wider society.[21]

The gift of fearlessness is treated far less often in Buddhist commentarial literature than are the first two gifts. Institutional priorities may explain this paucity because the economy of merit that sustains the relationship between the Buddhist sangha and lay society depends primarily on the reciprocal exchange of material supports and dharmic intangibles. In this context, the king acts more as leading lay patron rather than as the state, with all the moral compromises that a state must make to function. Indeed, despite rich Hindu elaborations on the gift of fearlessness as a duty of righteous kingship, many Buddhist textual references to *abhayadāna* ignore kingship as a distinct moral role, instead considering the gift of fearlessness within relationships of unequal power, up and down the social hierarchy. (Institutional priorities may explain this tendency as well; it is less risky for a Buddhist monastic to encourage all people to give the gift of protection to those in danger than to single out the king for a moral exhortation.) Although the relative silence on *abhayadāna* in Buddhist canonical and commentarial literature is puzzling, the concept promises such relevance for the ethical challenges of our contemporary moment as to invite closer examination.

In a nineteenth-century Tibetan commentarial discussion of the perfection of generosity, Patrul Rinpoché glosses the gift of fearlessness (*mi 'jigs pa skyabs kyi sbyin pa*) as

> actually doing whatever you can to help others in difficulty. It includes, for instance, providing a refuge for those without any place of safety, giving protection to those without any protector, and being with those who have no other companion. It refers particularly to such actions as forbidding hunting and fishing wherever you have the power to do so, buying back sheep on the way to the slaughter, and saving the lives of dying fish, worms, flies and other creatures.[22]

Patrul's mention of "forbidding hunting and fishing wherever you have the power to do so" refers to the practice, familiar in Tibet, of a political ruler's proclaiming a seal (*rgya*) on a mountain or forest, which serves to protect the designated territory and its non-human inhabitants (including animals, plants, minerals, nagas, and landscape deities) from destructive human activities. Although governance plays an integral role in Patrul's understanding of *abhayadāna*, Patrul follows the yogic tradition by extending the gift of fearlessness beyond the duties of rulership to the layperson's practice of showing mercy to animals and insects. This move reflects Patrul's larger agenda of lay ethical reform and the promotion of vegetarianism.[23]

A contemporary lama following in Patrul's tradition, Khenpo Tsultrim Lodrö (*tshul khrims blo gros*) of Larung Gar, took up Patrul's advocacy for vegetarianism and promoting life-release (*tshe thar*) rituals in order to save animals' lives and draw attention to their exploitation by humans. Tsultrim Lodrö situates the gift of fearlessness within the practice of the six perfections. He writes,

> Great Vehicle bodhisattvas have three [types of] gifts: the gift of fearlessness, the gift of dharma, and material gifts. Life release is fundamentally the gift of fearlessness. However, in order for the gift of fearlessness to become thoroughly pure, several conditions are necessary: a) an analysis of whether the site and environment of release and the being to be released

> are compatible or not. For example, in Tibetan areas, if there are mud-dwelling amphibians to be released, but the animals were imported from Chinese areas, the people will think they are fish, and will throw them in the water. In that area, the beds of the streams have rocks but no mud, and because the source of the water is snow, the water is extremely icy; after throwing the amphibians in the water, by force of the unsuitability of the environment, the animals cannot survive in the long term, and they all will die. [...] If they become killed by people for food, that gathers a great [store of] non-virtue. For that reason, however we can, we need to prevent this. We need to release them in a place that is safe and where people can't inflict harm on them.[24]

In response to the recognition that some life-release rituals in Tibetan and Han Chinese communities were being conducted without consideration as to environmental suitability, leading to the suffering not only of the released animals but also sometimes of the native fauna at the release site, Tsultrim Lodrö has

> continuously sought to make improvements and adjustments to his method to releasing lives in line with a "rigorous, careful attitude" and "scientific technique." In the past twenty years, billions of living beings have been saved from slaughter, earning him the respected moniker "Life release Khenpo."[25]

Humanitarian challenges are always rooted in political ecologies that include non-human beings as well as living natural environments. In these Indic textual traditions, refugee protection should not ultimately be separated from environmental protection or from policies of economic restraint. As Tsultrim Lodrö models, a thorough analysis of the wider conditions that make protection sustainable is essential for achieving its desired outcomes.

The gift of fearlessness is a form of restraint exercised on behalf of a particular class of vulnerable beings and over a particular terrain or landscape. While all people can apply the gift of fearlessness within the compass of their agency, it is political rulers who ultimately render a given landscape either secure or insecure for beings' welfare. As another Tibetan commentator of Patrul's day, Sumpa Khenpo, describes the role of the ruler,

> In any and every world system, the good and evil that befall people, both collectively and individually, is indeed the fruition of their karma that is shared or unshared; but, conventionally speaking, in any place, the waxing and waning of the Buddha's teachings, and the respective happiness or misery of beings, all follow as a consequence of the words and actions of the kings and ministers of that land. [... .] Therefore, [...] merit and non-merit and happiness and misery, whatever befalls [the inhabitants],

follows as a consequence of the powerful rulers of that place — and there is no place where that isn't the case.[26]

Moral Valences of Fear in Buddhism

While there are clear moral exhortations in the discourse on *abhayadāna* to offer fearlessness and protection to others where one can, Buddhist tradition offers varying perspectives on the moral valences of being afraid. Buddhadasa Bhikkhu argued that because fear is not a form of aversion or a form of attachment, it should be understood as a form of ignorance or delusion. He calls fear the fourth defilement:

> Fear comes from the instinct of egoism, fear is an instinctual necessity. If there is insufficient knowledge and wisdom, this instinct is impossible to control. Through the study and practice of Dhamma, necessary and sufficient wisdom is developed so that this instinct can be controlled and fear does not arise. Understanding and insight into anatta (not-self) allows us to be free of fear, helps us to uproot fear, and protects us from its future arising.[27]

Even though the Buddha is said to have achieved a state of fearlessness, the Buddha discusses his own experience of fear in the *Bhayabherava Sutta*. He recounts of his time dwelling in the forest,

> I stayed in the sort of places that are awe-inspiring and make your hair stand on end, such as park-shrines, forest-shrines, & tree-shrines. And while I was staying there a wild animal would come, or a peacock would make a twig fall, or wind would rustle the fallen leaves. The thought would occur to me: 'Is this that fear & terror coming?' Then the thought occurred to me: 'Why do I just keep waiting for fear?
>
> What if I, in whatever state I'm in when fear & terror come to me, were to subdue that fear & terror in that very state?' So when fear & terror came to me while I was walking back & forth, I would not stand or sit or lie down. I would keep walking back & forth until I had subdued that fear & terror. When fear & terror came to me while I was standing, I would not walk or sit or lie down. I would keep standing until I had subdued that fear & terror. When fear & terror came to me while I was sitting, I would not lie down or stand up or walk. I would keep sitting until I had subdued that fear & terror. When fear & terror came to me while I was lying down, I would not sit up or stand or walk. I would keep lying down until I had subdued that fear & terror. [28]

In these sources, fear is less of a fault to be righted than an instinct to be rehabituated. Drawing on modern neuroscience, Martha Nussbaum points out that,

> Unlike compassion, which requires perspectival thinking and is thus available only to a few species of animal, and even unlike anger, which requires causal thinking about who is to blame for causing harm, fear really does not require very elaborate mental apparatus. All it requires is some rudimentary orientation toward survival and wellbeing, and an ability to become aroused by what threatens them. Not surprisingly, then, recent research has associated fear with the amygdala, a part of the brain that is shared among all vertebrates and is not associated with higher cognition.[29]

Perhaps fear's rootedness in the most primal part of our brains explains the relative gentleness with which the Buddha taught about fear. While fear might cause attachment, aversion, or ignorance (or arise as a consequence of them), fear itself is not an appropriate site of moral transformation. For ordinary beings, fear may indeed be beneath the conscious mind's ability to change itself. In the Buddha's trope about a rope being mistaken for a snake, he does not chide the person who recoils in fear of the perceived snake, nor does he praise the fearlessness of the person who recognizes that what looks like a snake is actually a rope. Fear and fearlessness arise out of perceptions; the Buddha's teachings are aimed at cultivating right perceptions.

Thānissaro Bhikkhu elaborates on both skillful and unskillful dimensions of fear. In his essay "Freedom from Fear," he proposes that

> These five elements—confusion, aversion, a sense of danger, a sense of weakness, and a desire to escape—are present, to a greater or lesser extent, in every fear. The confusion and aversion are the unskillful elements. Even if the deer has many openings to escape from the hunter, its confusion and aversion might cause it to miss them. The same holds true for human beings. The mistakes and evils we commit when finding ourselves weak in the face of danger come from confusion and aversion.
>
> Maddeningly, however, there are also evils that we commit out of complacency, when oblivious to actual dangers: the callous things we do when we feel we can get away with them. Thus the last three elements of fear—the perception of weakness, the perception of danger, and the desire to escape it—are needed to avoid the evils coming from complacency. If stripped of confusion and aversion, these three elements become a positive quality, heedfulness—something so essential to the practice that the Buddha devoted his last words to it.[30]

Abhayadāna is directed toward beings experiencing mortal fear, but their fear is not a moral failing; it is a logical response of the ordinary mind to perceptions of insecurity and danger. Some dimensions of fear are skillful and lead to heedfulness, while others are unskillful and lead to ineffective action. In all its dimensions, both skillful and unskillful, fear entails suffering. This discussion on the moral valences of fear is an important contribution to the contemporary discourse on displacement, where those who migrate are often villainized. Despite the links in Buddhist tradition between fearlessness and enlightenment and between fear and ignorance, the teachings on *abhayadāna* make no judgment about the moral standing of the recipients of protection but, in light of their suffering, urge compassion.

Fearlessness and Security

Thus far, our investigation of *abhayadāna* has brought Buddhist ethics to bear on the humanitarian concern for refugee protection, but what of the security concerns that are raised in contemporary refugee policy debates? *Abhayadāna* does offer a logic that links the question of refugee protection to domestic security concerns, but it is not the logic of xenophobia and exclusion; instead, it is a more capacious understanding of what security truly entails.

The gift of fearlessness is not only classically explained as the offer of protection to outsiders who otherwise have no protection: fearlessness is also explained as "the gift that kings give when they ensure that their subjects live in security."[31] *Abhayadāna* deconstructs the false dichotomy between providing asylum to foreigners on the one hand and providing domestic security on the other hand, which is one of the key logics of nativist movements. In *abhayadāna* discourse, asylum and security are expressions of a single type of political power: the capacity to offer fearlessness and protection.

If each state offered its population real security, it could be argued that there would be no refugees in the first place. In particular, "a king should protect his subjects from fear of imprisonment, exile, beatings, robbery, and dishonor" at the hands of the state, the arbitrary use of which may cause fear-based flight.[32] This dimension of *abhayadāna* validates the moral prerogative of a king or state to ensure security: to protect his subjects, to defend the nation, to uphold the rule of law, and even to wield violence in moderation and when appropriate to his duties—but the gift of fearlessness also compels the righteous king to refrain from the capricious or abusive use of force that instills fear in those under his care. Indeed, when the *Upāsakaśīlasūtra* enumerates the many dangers that sentient beings may fear, from tigers and wolves to floods and fires, kings are first on the list.[33]

This reading of *abhayadāna* affirms the value of domestic security while challenging any security agenda that relies on fear. Fear tactics undermine the very nature of security as this discourse defines it. Such protection, in the context of the contemporary refugee crisis, extends to minority groups as well as to the majority group, to immigrants and asylees as well as to the native population. Here we should question whether xenophobic rhetoric and inaccurate portrayals of the dangers posed by refugees serve to alleviate domestic fears or, rather, to magnify them. Nativist fear-mongering is not compatible with the comprehensive vision of security entailed by the gift of fearlessness.

Fearlessness and Sovereignty

Discussion of *abhayadāna* from the classic *Laws of Manu* (4.232) goes further than security, however; in Hibbets' translation, "a bestower of fearlessness receives [in turn] sovereignty."[34] In this legal tradition, a ruler's authority to govern follows from his or her capacity to grant fearlessness. Fearlessness may be a gift to refugees and outsiders but, directed toward one's own populace, it is a prerequisite for rulership. As Hibbets writes, "Whoever can ensure the protection of the people is entitled to rule [...].; since one of the primary functions of the king is protection of his subjects, he is, in fact, empowered by his 'gift' of security."[35] According to this logic, the greater the number of refugees who are welcomed, the more authority, power, and legitimacy accrue to the leader or state offering refuge. When the first Muslim migrants from Mecca sought refuge with the Christian king of Aksum, tradition holds that the king exulted in the honor of their choosing his protection above that of any other king; granting fearlessness to the migrants enhanced his power and prestige.

When Tibetan Buddhists buy animals to spare them from the butcher or save the lives of endangered creatures, as described by Patrul Rinpoché,[36] they display this same logic: that the protection of the vulnerable enhances the power or sovereignty of the protector. In the Tibetan practice of life release, in which animals are saved from slaughter and released into the wild as an expression of *abhayadāna*, the merit from these ceremonies is often dedicated to the long life of a Buddhist master. The act of saving vulnerable lives in a leader's name expands his or her life-force rather than diminishing it.[37] As in the English idiom, to perform an act of mercy or liberality makes one "the bigger person."

In *abhayadāna*, then, we find a productive divergence from the framework in which contemporary refugee policy debates tend to operate. Rather than amplify the fear inscribed in the identity of "refugee," in the logic of *abhayadāna*, the state bolsters both its security and its sovereignty when it grants refugees fearlessness. If national security were re-envisioned as fearlessness, extended to domestic subjects and to refugees alike, then the international refugee regime would function more effectively. Furthermore, refugees would enjoy greater security in their resettlement sites rather than facing the violence and intimidation that accompany xenophobia.

Fearlessness: Gift or Rightful Due?

Transposing the ethics of a gift economy onto a modern political economy defined by legal rights and responsibilities is not seamless. In contemporary states, the "gift" of fearlessness must sometimes be demanded and even seized when it has been withheld from the governed.

In the months following August of 2017, when the exodus of hundreds of thousands of Rohingya people from Myanmar unfolded, Aung San Suu Kyi's government was criticized for failing to prevent, properly acknowledge, and make restitution for atrocities against the Rohingya. Yet, in a more promising moment in Aung San Suu Kyi's career, she invoked *abhayadāna* in a 1990 essay entitled "Freedom from Fear," published as she battled against the military government in her homeland. Drawing upon traditional Buddhist ethical categories to describe the failure of the military administration, she writes:

> Within a system which denies the existence of basic human rights, fear tends to be the order of the day. Fear of imprisonment, fear of torture, fear of death, fear of losing friends, family, property or means of livelihood, fear of poverty, fear of isolation, fear of failure.[38]

When a state fails its basic function of providing fearlessness or security for its populace, Aung San Suu Kyi calls her compatriots to seize the gift of fearlessness for themselves. She writes, "Fearlessness may be a gift but perhaps more precious is the courage acquired through endeavor, courage that comes from cultivating the habit of refusing to let fear dictate one's actions [...]."[39] Here, Aung San Suu Kyi's understanding of *abhayadāna* challenges the modern construction of "refugee" as an object of fear rather than as a subject of courage, a victim rather than an agent. She offers hope that oppressed people can seize the gift of fearlessness for themselves, disrupting the politics of fear when the state fails to do its duty.

Conclusion

In applying the gift of fearlessness as a critical lens to the contemporary refugee crisis, my argument is that, as an ethical concept, *abhayadāna* is both capacious and expedient. It is capacious because it allows room for exploring more than one dimension of a moral problem, both upholding the moral good of refugee protection and recognizing the rightful duty of the state to provide security for its subjects. In this capacity, *abhayadāna* opens common avenues for authentic conversation across a political spectrum that may seem to be intractably polarized. Furthermore, the concept of the gift of fearlessness is expedient for our contemporary context because it shifts our critical focus from refugees to states. *Abhayadāna* charges governments to take moral responsibility for the ways in which they use refugee policy to instill and ignite fear in their own populations—through fear-mongering rhetoric, intimidating policies that threaten violence or seizure, and generalized instability or capricious action—thereby undermining security, both domestically and internationally. *Abhayadāna*'s more expansive vision of security demands ethical action not only at the border, but at the center of political power.[40]

Notes

1 This chapter is adapted from Kilby, Christina. "Global Refugee Crisis and the Gift of Fearlessness," *Journal of Buddhist Ethics* 26 (2019): 307–327. Accessed on 6 May 2026. https://blogs.dickinson.edu/buddhistethics/files/2019/12/Kilby_19_Final-1.pdf.

2 There is a distinction between the total number of registered refugees worldwide and the number identified as needing resettlement. Only a small proportion of refugees are identified as needing resettlement, depending on whether they have a foreseeable alternative durable solution, such as returning to their homes or remaining in their country of refuge. When recommending a refugee for resettlement, some of the factors considered include legal and/or physical protection needs, risk of domestic abuse, risk of minors lacking guardians, survival of violence and/or torture, medical needs, and the potential to reunite with family. Refer to UNHCR, *Resettlement Handbook*, chapter 3.2. Accessed on 5 December 2025 at www.unhcr.org/resettlement-handbook/3-resettlement-submission-categories/3-2-the-resettlement-submission-categories/.

3 United Nations High Commissioner for Refugees (UNHCR). "2026 Projected Global Resettlement Needs (PGRN)." 24 June 2025. Accessed on 5 December 2025. www.unhcr.org/publications/2026-projected-global-resettlement-needs-pgrn#:~:text=Global%20refugee%20resettlement%20needs%20are,different%20regions%20around%20the%20world.

4 "Migration and Migrants: A Global Overview." International Organization for Migration. Accessed on 5 December 2025. https://worldmigrationreport.iom.int/what-we-do/world-migration-report-2026/chapter-2/refugees-and-asylum-seekers.Refer to chapter 2, Table 3, "Number of refugees needing resettlement and number of refugees resettled globally, from 2005."

5 Wike, Richard, Bruce Stokes, and Katie Simmons. "Europeans Fear Wave of Refugees Will Mean More Terrorism, Fewer Jobs." Pew Research Forum, 11 July 2016. Accessed 18 November 2018. www.pewresearch.org/global/2016/07/11/europeans-fear-wave-of-refugees-will-mean-more-terrorism-fewer-jobs/.

6 "Refugee Cap to be Set at Record Low 7,500 in FY 2026." *Global Refuge,* 6 October 2025. Accessed on 6 December 2025 at www.globalrefuge.org/news/trump-administration-cuts-refugee-admissions-to-all-time-low-for-fy-2026/.

7 Moore, Matthew J. *Buddhism and Political Theory.* New York: Oxford University Press, 2016.

8 Betts, Alexander, Gil Loescher, and James Milner. *UNHCR: The Politics and Practice of Refugee Protection,* 2nd edition. New York: Routledge, 2011.

9 United Nations High Commissioner for Refugees. *Convention and Protocol Relating to the Status of Refugees.* [1951 and 1967.] Accessed 18 November 2018. www.unhcr.org/en-us/1951-refugee-convention.html.

10 For further discussion of how the roles of "refugee" and "terrorist" have become entangled in current political imaginaries, refer to Ahmed, Sara. *The Cultural Politics of Emotion.* New York: Routledge, 2013. p. 79 ff.

11 Ahmed, Sara. *The Cultural Politics of Emotion.* New York: Routledge, 2013. pp. 62–63.

12 Gonzalez-Barrera, Ana and Jens Manual Krogstad. "What We Know About Illegal Immigration from Mexico." Pew Research Forum, 28 June 2019. Accessed

3 November 2019. www.pewresearch.org/fact-tank/2019/06/28/what-we-know-about-illegal-immigration-from-mexico/.

13 Hibbets, Maria. "Saving Them from Yourself: An Inquiry into the South Asian Gift of Fearlessness," *Journal of Religious Ethics* 27, 3 (1999): 435–462. p. 441.

14 Hibbets, Maria. "Saving Them from Yourself: An Inquiry into the South Asian Gift of Fearlessness," *Journal of Religious Ethics* 27, 3 (1999): 435–462. p. 441. The concept of *abhayadāna* resonates in some ways with the "freedom from fear" articulated by Franklin D. Roosevelt. My thanks to Daniel Cozort for this observation.

15 Heim, Maria. *Theories of the Gift in South Asia: Hindu, Buddhist, and Jain Reflections on Dāna*. New York: Routledge, 2004. p. 122.

16 Hibbets, Maria. "Saving Them from Yourself: An Inquiry into the South Asian Gift of Fearlessness," *Journal of Religious Ethics* 27, 3 (1999): 435–462. p. 442.

17 Heim, Maria. *Theories of the Gift in South Asia: Hindu, Buddhist, and Jain Reflections on Dāna*. New York: Routledge, 2004. pp. 123–124.

18 Heim, Maria. *Theories of the Gift in South Asia: Hindu, Buddhist, and Jain Reflections on Dāna*. New York: Routledge, 2004. pp. 123–124.

19 For a Tibetan example, refer to Tsong-kha-pa, *The Great Treatise on the Stages of the Path (Lam Rim Chen Mo)*, Volume 2. Transl. Lamrim Chenmo Translation Committee, ed. Guy Newland and Joshua Cutler. Boston: Snow Lion, 2014. p. 122. For a Theravādin example, refer to the *Cariyāpiṭaka Aṭṭhakathā*, translated by Bhikkhu Bodhi in *The Discourse on the All-Embracing Net of Views: The Brahmajāla Sutta and Its Commentaries*. Kandy, Sri Lanka: Buddhist Publication Society, 1978. p. 276. Note that the gift of fearlessness is distinct from the four fearlessnesses of a Buddha, which pertain to transcendent realizations rather than to the visceral experience of fear for one's life. However, according to the *Cariyāpiṭaka Aṭṭhakathā*, the two types of fearlessness coincide in the power and virtue of a bodhisattva, who is both "fearless and a giver of fearlessness" (p. 260).

20 Refer to Reiko Ohnuma's discussion of the interrelation between these first two types of gifts in "The Gift of the Body and the Gift of Dharma," *History of Religions*, Vol. 37, 4 (1998): 323–359.

21 The lay bodhisattva, as both a lay person and a being who has undertaken a religious vow, sits at the boundary of these two groups. As Reiko Ohnuma has shown ("The Gift of the Body and the Gift of Dharma," *History of Religions* 37, 4 (1998): 323–359), in Mahāyāna narratives, the bodhisattva gives the gift of the body as a correlate to the gift of dharma that he or she will give as a fully realized being; the lay bodhisattva thus straddles the boundary between these two types of gifts and the two communities responsible for giving them.

22 Patrul Rinpoché. *Words of My Perfect Teacher: A Complete Translation of a Classic Introduction to Tibetan Buddhism*. Transl. by the Padmakara Translation Group. Boulder: Shambhala, 1998. p. 238.

23 Barstow, Geoff. *Food of Sinful Demons: Meat, Vegetarianism, and the Limits of Buddhism in Tibet*. New York: Columbia University Press, 2019.

24 tshul khrims blo gros (Tsultrim Lodrö). *Shes rab sgron me'i 'od snang* (*Luminosity of the Lamp of Insight*). 2013. Buddhist Digital Resource Center (BDRC), purl.bdrc.io/resource/W1AC345. [BDRC bdr:W1AC345]. pp. 80–81.

25 "A Brief Biography of Khenpo Tsultrim Lodrö." Luminous Wisdom. Accessed on 5 December 2025. www.luminouswisdom.org/index.php/biography/biography-2.

26 sum pa ye shes dpal 'byor (Sumpa Khenpo). *Expressing the Conduct of the Supreme Pandita Sumpa Yeshé Penjor: Alchemy for the Ear (paN+Di ta sum pa ye shes dpal 'byor mchog gi spyod tshul brjod pa sgra 'dzin bcud len)*. In *Collected Works,* vol. 8 (nya), 373–960. Beijing: Tibetan Civilization Publishing House of China, 2001. Buddhist Digital Resource Center work ID W25006. p. 471.

27 Buddhadasa Bhikkhu. "New Life of Peace." Transl. by Santikaro Bhikkhu. 11 February 1986. Published by the Dhammadana Foundation, copyright 1997 by *Evolution/Liberation.* Accessed on 8 December 2025 at www.dhammatalks.net/Books/Bhikkhu_Buddhadasa_Natural_Cure_for_Spiritual_Disease3.htm.

28 "Bhaya-bherava Sutta: Fear & Terror" (MN 4), translated from the Pāli by Thanissaro Bhikkhu. *Access to Insight (BCBS Edition)*, 30 November 2013. Accessed on 8 December 2025. www.accesstoinsight.org/tipitaka/mn/mn.004.than.html.

29 Nussbaum, Martha. *The New Religious Intolerance: Overcoming the Politics of Fear in an Anxious Age*. Cambridge: Harvard University Press, 2012. p. 25.

30 Thanissaro Bhikkhu. "Freedom From Fear." *Access to Insight (BCBS Edition)*, 5 June 2010. Accessed on 8 December 2025 at www.accesstoinsight.org/lib/authors/thanissaro/fear.html.

31 Hibbets, Maria. "Saving Them from Yourself: An Inquiry into the South Asian Gift of Fearlessness." *Journal of Religious Ethics* 27, 3 (1999): 435–462. p. 441.

32 Hibbets, Maria. "Saving Them from Yourself: An Inquiry into the South Asian Gift of Fearlessness." *Journal of Religious Ethics* 27, 3 (1999): 435–462. pp. 441–442.

33 *Upāsakaśīlasūtra* (*The Sutra on Upāsaka Precepts*). Translated by Shih, Heng-ching. Bukkhyo Dendo Kyokai, 1991. p. 107.

34 Hibbets, Maria. "Saving Them from Yourself: An Inquiry into the South Asian Gift of Fearlessness." *Journal of Religious Ethics* 27, no. 3 (1999): 435–462. p. 442.

35 Hibbets, Maria. "Saving Them from Yourself: An Inquiry into the South Asian Gift of Fearlessness." *Journal of Religious Ethics* 27, no. 3 (1999): 435–462. p.442.

36 Patrul Rinpoché. *Words of My Perfect Teacher: A Complete Translation of a Classic Introduction to Tibetan Buddhism.* Translated by the Padmakara Translation Group. Boulder: Shambhala, 1998. p. 238.

37 "On Rinpoche's Birthday: An Offering of Life." Mindrolling International, 26 August 2018. Accessed on 7 December 2025. www.khandrorinpoche.org/on-rinpoches-birthday-an-offering-of-life/.

38 Aung San Suu Kyi. *Freedom from Fear: and Other Writings*. London: Penguin, 2010. p. 184.

39 Aung San Suu Kyi. *Freedom from Fear: and Other Writings*. London: Penguin, 2010. p. 184.

40 For an analysis of state applications of *abhayadāna* in times of armed conflict, refer to Kilby, Christina. "The Gift of Fearlessness: A Buddhist Framework for the Protection of Vulnerable Populations Under International Humanitarian Law." In Andrew Bartles-Smith, Kate Crosby, Peter Harvey, Asanga Tilakaratne, Daniel Ratheiser, Noel Maurer Trew, Stefania Travagnin, Elizabeth J. Harris, Venerable Mahinda Deegalle, and Christina A. Kilby, eds. *Buddhism and International Humanitarian Law,* pp. 330–342. New York: Routledge, 2023.

6 Buddhist Visions of Security

Toward a Buddhist Discourse on Security and Insecurity

The remedy for displacement is not merely emplacement, but security. In this world where space is always political, "dwelling" requires more than mere physical habitat, which can only support "bare life" (*zoê*, after Giorgio Agamben).[1] "Security" pertains to the fuller sense of human life, in all its social and political dimensions, that those "without shelter, without protector" are also seeking to regain to make a dignified human life tenable. This means that in addition to resources within Buddhist traditions that address displacement and emplacement, we must also investigate Buddhist perspectives on the larger issue of insecurity and security, the root dialectic underlying the displacement crisis. In this context, "security" does not refer to the ultimate security Buddhism envisions as liberation from cyclic existence. Instead, this chapter explores several Buddhist discourses relating to human security that have implications for how our global community can understand and respond to the sufferings of displacement in our time.

Protection is a concern visible (and for that matter, audible) in many aspects of life in Buddhist societies.[2] For centuries, monarchs in Asia have built Buddhist temples and sponsored rituals in order to secure protection for the state. Buddhists chant mantras, prayers, and spells, or inscribe *yantra* tattoos on their bodies, in order to seek protection from harm. Monks and nuns perform rituals to protect their communities from drought or disease or to placate local landscape spirits or ghosts. In the Tibetan tradition, protector deities safeguard every monastery and every practice lineage. In Buddhism's textual tradition, scriptures and liturgies that appeal to worldly protection are manifold.[3]

Drawing on the gift of fearlessness explored in the previous chapter, the Tibetan tradition has inherited a map of human insecurity and a deity who responds to it. Tara Who Protects from the Eight Great Fears (*tArA 'jigs pa chen po brgyad las sgrol ba*) is a divinized bodhisattva who compassionately sees the plight of the suffering and intervenes to protect those in danger. Tara is widely propitiated among the tantric lineages of Tibet, Mongolia, and the Himalayas. As an enlightened embodiment of compassion, her masculine

DOI: 10.4324/9781003318149-6

counterpart is Avalokiteśvara (Tib. *spyan ras gzigs*). Although Tara takes many forms to accomplish various ends for her devotees, one of Tara's salvific roles is to protect beings from eight (sometimes sixteen or thirty-two) great fears or threats: lions, elephants, snakes, ghosts, fire, water, robbers, and wrongful imprisonment.[4] A map of human insecurity as imagined in the ancient world, many of these fears relate closely to the experiences of displaced people today.

The Tibetan tradition also interprets these fears psychologically as "the lion of pride, the elephant of ignorance, the fire of anger, the snakes of jealousy, the thieves of wrong views, the chains of miserliness, the flood of attachment, and the carnivorous demon of doubt."[5] These eight great fears or dangers are not spiritual allegories, but a multivalent set of external dangers to life and property on the one hand, and internal obstacles to spiritual development on the other. In this section, I address the external manifestations of these eight forms of danger because of their relevance to the experience of displacement. By exploring these fears and Tara's responses to them, especially as depicted in a visual collection of nine paintings from the nineteenth century, we learn something new about how Buddhists in one part of the world have imaginatively engaged with the realities of insecurity that are intertwined with displacement.

Eight Great Fears as a Map of Human Insecurity

The Rubin Museum in New York holds a set of Tibetan thangka paintings depicting Tara dispelling the eight fears, which are enumerated in *dhāraṇī* and tantric texts associated with Tara as well as Avalokiteśvara.[6] In this set, one central painting portrays Tara in her green form in *abhayamudrā* attitude (right hand raised with palm facing forward in a gesture of protection and assurance); she sits with one leg tucked under her, as in meditative equipoise, while the other leg extends from her seat in signal that she is ready to jump to one's aid at any moment. Flanking this central image are four paintings on each side that illustrate her compassionate responses to each of eight great fears.

Fear of Dangerous Animals

The first three fears in this list are of dangerous wild animals: lions, elephants, and snakes. While Buddhist texts refer to occasional snake bites or the rampages of elephants into human villages, wild animals are generally threats of the wilderness, not of the village; the dangers of wild animals are encountered outside the bounds of human community and village life. This means that such dangers, while stemming from the natural environment and never fully escapable, primarily threaten those who are traveling, exiled, or otherwise cast out from family and community. Only serious ascetics would venture into such wilderness spaces willingly, ready to confront the dangers these animals pose. Taking such dangers seriously, the *vinaya* literature instructs monks and nuns to choose residences that are likely to be free of animal threats such as poisonous snakes and scorpions.[7] One of the early applications of *mettā* meditation was for monastics trying to pacify dangerous animals in wilderness meditation settings.[8]

While dangerous wild animals were a common part of life in the ancient world, they also speak to fears that persist today for many, especially those who are displaced. In the painting of Tara protecting people from elephants,[9] overtones of sexual aggression are quite visible: the endangered people in the painting are two women, peacefully collecting foliage that they carry in large baskets on their backs. The elephants who threaten them (likely male elephants in musth, when they are most aggressive) are extending their trunks to touch the feet of one woman and the skirt of the other. Yet the women are serene and their bodies seem to sway with ease as they walk; they are not afraid of the elephants but enjoy the fearlessness of Tara's sovereignty over the animals. What would it look like for displaced women and girls to move in total safety and ease? Such security is almost unthinkable today in light of the gender-based violence that women and girls face in everyday life across cultures, which is further exacerbated in contexts of displacement. What kind of governance could realize such a vision of security and mobility for women? What is needed in the face of predators, whether animal or human, is to belong to a community that offers the collective power of protection and care.

Lions place humans in the precarious position of prey vulnerable to predators. The heartbreaking experience of the Lost Boys of Sudan being attacked by lions as they migrated to escape danger brings this ancient fear vividly to life in our recent history. Those on the move are rendered prey in more ways than one; the Lost Boys' conscription as child soldiers was yet another form of horrific predation they endured. In the painting of Tara protecting people from lions,[10] a white snow lion with a fiery orange mane claws at the heels of a frightened man. From her perch in the adjacent pagoda, Tara holds a lotus in one hand and offers the *abhayamudrā* with another; from her hand in *abhayamudrā*, a golden string descends to a magical guardian with a white body, wearing garments made of leaves. He pulls at the wrist of the helpless man, rescuing him from the pursuing lion. A subsequent image of the distressed man appears safely on the pagoda at Tara's feet, with hands folded. The lion enters the scene on the right side of the painting among stylized rocks and plants, grounded by a hazy horizon with clouds. He comes from the uncertainty and precarity of the wilderness. In contrast, on the lower left side of the painting is a park-like scene: two deer lie quietly beside a calm pond, where two ducks swim beside flowering lotuses. This left-hand scene represents a tamed wilderness under Tara's dominion. Tara brings those in fear of lions (or human predators) to a domesticated nature where humans have power over the wilderness and live in relative peace. The vision of security evoked by these images of Tara offering fearlessness from dangerous animals is one where people enjoy the collective protection of human civilization.

Fear of Ghosts and Demons

Ghosts, demons, and various forms of hostile spirits are part of the shared world of many Buddhists today, who undertake activities to circumvent or remedy the problems these beings pose. Ghost beliefs are culturally specific and can be complicated by the incongruence between local cultures and the typologies of spirits imagined in ancient India and outlined in the Buddhist canons.

The atrocities of the Khmer Rouge resulted in many Cambodians living in fear of the ghosts of loved ones who died violent deaths and therefore would haunt the living. The fact that many people could not locate and bury the bodies of their family members and offer the proper funerals and merit-making on their behalf compounded their suffering. There is a significant scholarly literature on the prevalence of ghost experiences among refugees from Cambodia.[11] In the Cambodian context, encounters with ghosts are not only terrifying in themselves, but are also thought to lead to a host of negative health consequences, such as being frightened to death or having one's soul called away, leading to severe physical and mental deterioration. Furthermore, encounters with ghosts tend to recall painful thoughts of the violent death the deceased person experienced, causing grief and anguish. What kind of security can keep humans safe from the ghosts of genocide? For Cambodians suffering ghost encounters for decades after the genocide, security might mean the ability to offer merit to those who have died and to begin healing their historical memory—perhaps even the ability to return to the site of violence and perform belated funerary rites.

Psychological safety can also benefit from the expertise of monks or nuns. In the Tibetan thangka portraying the fear of ghosts,[12] a monk is being attacked by two different beings, identified in the curator's item description as a ghost and a demon. In one corner of the painting, the monk is shown again reciting a scripture, while a placated ghost approaches him carrying a vessel of jewels. A depiction of the monk appears a third time at the pagoda of Tara, safe and sound. The jewels that the ghost was carrying to the monk are now being offered by the monk at Tara's feet. To the side, a goddess plays the flute. Her beautiful music enhances the peace of mind that the monk must be feeling now that he has been saved from the ghost and demon. Her music serves as a divine correlate to the human sound of scriptural recitation depicted below.

In this scene, it is not a golden thread that saves the monk from the malevolent spirits, but his recitation of scripture. In many Buddhist contexts, monastics play a major role in protecting families or communities from ghosts through the recitation of scriptures or blessings. When approaching the problem of psychological danger in Buddhist communities, security may be greatly enhanced by access to ritual practitioners like monks or nuns (or in some contexts, wizards, oracles, or other practitioners) in order for those ritual specialists to make merit and offer rituals of protection. Piyadassi Thera writes that protective recitations work because of the power of truth, the power of virtue, the power of love, and the power of sound.[13] The healing role of music and the sound of chanting as essential to these protective ceremonies should not be discounted. As one researcher has noted, the Cambodian healing ritual of *lieng arak* is disappearing in the United States among Cambodian refugees because, among other reasons, the musical specialists properly trained in the liturgy are too few in the diaspora: the healing is in the music, a claim that music therapists and neuroscientists continue to reiterate today.[14] When musical and ritual traditions are sustained in resettlement sites, memory and healing can be supported in ways that promote psychological protection.[15]

Fear of Fire and Water

The next two fears are elemental: fire and water. In the Tibetan thangka portraying protection from the danger of fire,[16] we see a burning two-storey house with one person fleeing and one person trapped upstairs. From her throne, Tara points a finger, from which issues a whelming gray cloud where a dragon waits. Tara appears to be summoning the dragon to produce rain, which quenches the flames that engulf the house directly below. Two red-crowned cranes also grace Tara's pagoda, one gazing at the sky and the other flying above with a flowering branch in its beak. In Tibetan art, cranes are often depicted in pairs because they are known for their strong mating bonds. The positions of the cranes in this Tibetan painting mirror the positions of the two people whose house is burning: one looking up toward their beloved above. The cranes can be read as embodying the wish not to be parted from loved ones. Tara's compassion for the people fleeing fire includes not only the danger to their lives and property, but also the pain and grief of separation that often accompanies disasters.

The depiction of Tara's protection from the fear of water[17] portrays a boat struggling on a swirling sea. A dark cloud hovers at the front of the boat where a sea monster awaits. The boat is laden with jewels, and the endangered passenger looks upward to Tara with hands folded in supplication. Further along in the scene, a boat appears to be safely docked at Tara's pagoda and jewels are being offloaded as gifts to Tara. The rendering of the water is subtle and detailed with swirls and eddies, punctuated by clusters of jewels in golden hue, delicately placed across the waves. The contrast in this painting between the riches of the sea (jewels) and the dangers of the sea (storms and monsters) is striking. One may observe that the wind changes direction in this visual narrative: the first boat encountering the dark storm cloud has its sails billowing backward, as if the storm is blowing it farther from the safety of Tara's pagoda. The second boat image, docked at the pagoda, has sails gently billowing forward as if the winds shifted and brought it quickly to Tara's safe harbor.

Fire and water are dangerous forces of nature that continue to threaten human security today, especially with the escalation of climate volatility. Natural disaster is one of the major causes of displacement. The destruction of one's home by fire or water causes other difficulties, such as loss of valuable property and animals, loss of important documents that grant access to government services or education, loss of photographs or family heirlooms, and loss of cultural objects. The threat of water conjures contemporary images of unsafe passage for migrants, whether the dangers of fleeing in crowded boats across the Mediterranean or the English Channel or the South China Sea. The Boat People—hundreds of thousands of people who fled Vietnam after the fall of Saigon—faced violence from pirates, dehydration and starvation, sexual assault, and drowning due to the capsizing of overcrowded vessels. General estimates claim that between 200,000 and 400,000 refugees died at sea during that mass exodus.

What vision of security from fire and water do these images of Tara offer? Besides a miracle of compassion that can change the direction of the winds or summon rain, what kind of security do these images promise? Both images illustrate the necessity of safe passage when escape is necessary, which is one of the provisions of international humanitarian law. The image of the two family members who are separated and longing for each other, like the cranes, speaks to the need for family reunification when loved ones are separated due to disaster. The image of boats delivering their freight of jewels to shore illustrates the economic opportunity that security actualizes, bringing to mind the vast number of displaced people who flee in order to seek sustaining livelihoods as well as the economic benefits they can bring in turn to their communities of reception. We will never achieve a world that is without fire or flood, but we can achieve a world where the risks and sufferings these disasters pose is greatly mitigated: through climate action, risk and disaster reduction policies, humanitarian access corridors, family reunification efforts, and labor migration policies that are informed and humane.

Fear of the Failure of Law

The final two paintings in the set depict the fear of robbers and wrongful imprisonment.[18] These two fears relate to the reach of the law: whether it is not sufficiently robust (in cases of robbery) or whether it is corrupt or overreaching (in cases of wrongful imprisonment). In the thangka set, the depiction of robbery portrays a small merchant caravan with elephants and horses laden with jewels. As the caravan is being attacked by thieves, Tara from her pagoda above holds a golden thread in her left hand that links to two guardian spirits below, in puppet-like fashion, as they successfully ward off the thieves with bow and arrows and sword. One thief is shown impaled on a stake while the others crouch in fear. Giving fearlessness to those in danger does not seem to preclude Tara, or any authority, from instilling appropriate fear in those who perpetrate harm.

Here, the fear of losing one's property and livelihood is vividly portrayed. For displaced people, such fears are well founded. The displaced are frequently separated from their property when they flee, exploited by smugglers who charge exorbitant fees, or robbed of their money or goods en route. When migrants return home, they may find that their homes have been destroyed or their property stolen. Through gazing upon Tara and her response to the attack of robbers, the viewer gains a vision of what law and justice might tangibly look like: the intervention of advocates who successfully mete out punishment and uphold justice.

In the painting of the fear of wrongful imprisonment, security looks like a bird being sent along Tara's golden thread to comfort and free the inmate, whose wife or mother is at the pagoda supplicating Tara for his release. Above the prison cell, a ruler appears to be handing down a document—perhaps a decree that the prisoner will be freed. Unjust rulers are the danger in this scene; just governance and "the right to have rights," as Hannah Arendt described it,[19] are the remedy. Displaced people, some of whom become stateless, are without fundamental legal security when they have no government to vouch for them, or when they are perceived as threats to the state where they live or to which they flee.

Fear Made Visible

What might it mean to the patrons and viewers of these thangkas to gaze upon illustrations of fear and insecurity? To see one's greatest fears come to life, in vivid color and empathetic detail, and then to gaze with hope upon the primal gazer Tara, who sees the sufferings of all and responds in saving ways, is a form of meditation. There is an important function served in bringing the psychological experience of fear into the material world of visual art. Fear tends to take vague and ever-expanding shapes in the mind; it is characterized more by invisibility than by visibility, by suspicion and speculation rather than by statistics and definitions. By materializing fear, fear becomes subject to material intervention: in this case, Tara's intervention. Yet the interventions portrayed in these images are visible as the proper role not only of a deity, but of anyone with the power to grant *abhayadāna*. The patrons of this elaborate painting set would likely have enjoyed the status and influence to promote either fear or fearlessness in their political orbits; the painter may have hoped that through this artistic offering, his patrons would be tangibly reminded of their obligations to shape society after the model of Tara's protective power.

The vision of security that Tara offers is not only ultimate or nirvanic security, but security in this world: safety from the threats to one's life (lions, elephants, fire), physical health (snake poison), mental health (ghosts), mobility (water), property (robbers), and liberty (wrongful imprisonment). These dimensions of security echo with surprising vividness the definition of human security proposed by the United Nations Development Programme (UNDP) in 1994:

> The concept of security has for too long been interpreted narrowly: as security of territory from external aggression, or as protection of national interests in foreign policy or as global security from the threat of a nuclear holocaust. It has been related more to nation-states than to people ... who sought security in their daily lives. For many of them, security symbolizes protection from the threat of disease, hunger, unemployment, crime, social conflict, political repression and environmental hazards.[20]

This early definition of human security from the UNDP echoes the eight great fears, which in this case are relatively consistent across significant historical and cultural difference. The UNDP report on security shows other striking resonances with Buddhist doctrine; it summarizes, "Human security is a *universal* concern; [...] The components of human security are *interdependent*; [...] Human security is *easier to ensure through early prevention* than later intervention; [...] and Human security is *people-centered*" (original emphasis).[21] Buddhist teachings on the universality of beings' desire to be happy and to avoid suffering, on interdependence as fundamental to existence, on the proper analysis of causes and conditions in order to effect transformation, and on the uniquely central position of humans in the cosmos are all relevant to this definition of human security that now enjoys global currency. These resonances suggest that deeper dialogue between Buddhist traditions and contemporary humanitarian policy will be mutually intelligible as well as beneficial.

The Limits of the Four Noble Truths and the Mandala as a Model for Human Security

Doctrinally, one of the major challenges in building an approach to human security drawn from Buddhism is the centrality of the four noble truths. If craving is the source of suffering, then the remedy for the sufferings of displacement is to uproot craving—which may help mitigate future displacement caused by bad actors' cravings for resources, territory, or ethnic superiority, but which does not sufficiently address displaced people's suffering in the present. Their suffering is not the proximal result of undeveloped spirituality or excessive attachment; their suffering is the result of not being "attached" or anchored securely enough to the structures and resources that meet their basic needs as dignified human beings. In this light, despite serving as the foundation of Buddhist doctrine, the four noble truths alone are inadequate for informing compassionate and effective responses to human suffering.

Dr. A.T. Ariyaratne, founder of the Sarvodaya Shramadana movement in Sri Lanka, addressed this problem by interpreting the Four Noble Truths as entailing both external/social and internal/individual struggles for liberation.[22]

While individuals work to uproot the causes of suffering (craving) within themselves, communities work to uproot the causes of suffering (economic depression, environmental problems, inequality, and so forth) that affect villages. The Four Noble Truths then become a model for analyzing cause and remedy that extends beyond the spiritual to address social and material causes of suffering.[23] The Sarvodaya movement even claims that "before people can realize the existential meaning of the four noble truths, they must see the social meaning of them."[24]

Ven. Dr. Pinnawala Sangasumana, also of Sri Lanka, has taken another novel approach to resolving the limits of the four noble truths for addressing sufferings like displacement.[25] Rather than attributing the sufferings of displaced people to attachment, Ven. Sangasumana attributes their sufferings to "inbetweenness" as a state of insecurity, and uses the mandala as a model for anchoring and centering the person within a secure socio-political structure. The "mandala of security" that he developed identifies the various modes of "in-betweenness" that plague internally displaced persons (IDPs): in between places, in between homes, in between communities, livelihoods, and futures. A mandala (Sanskrit *maṇḍala)* is not only a form, but a place, in both architectural and cosmic senses. It is an ancient Indic paradigm of shelter and order: to be in place, to be centered, to be secure. If we look for mandalas within Buddhist traditions, we find models of security and emplacement. Tara's protection from the eight fears can also assume the constructive, grounding symbolism of a mandala: when portrayed in a single image rather than as a painting set, the central deity (whether Tara or Avalokiteśvara) is encircled by eight smaller versions of the central deity with implements symbolizing each of the eight fears. The order and completeness conveyed by a mandala aesthetically conjure a sense of security, even when the content addresses fear.

The brilliance of Ven. Sangasumana's mandala model is that it circumvents the four noble truths with their focus on craving and detachment as the cause and remedy of suffering, respectively; instead, his model establishes a positive discourse of grounding, orienting, and structuring, which are also part of the Buddhist tradition. This critical shift in discourse opens important new ways for Buddhists to speak about displacement. Ven. Sangasumana writes,

> When forced to migrate people must leave behind them an array of physical, social and cultural assets and possessions, and it is these tangible and intangible realities that my research aims to highlight. The loss of these things eventually compel [sic] displaced [people] to fall into a status of perpetual fluctuation between perceptible and imperceptible realities as well as clinging and detaching. This state of uncertainty is here identified as "inbetweenness"[,] a situation full of remorse, incertitude, inconclusiveness, fear, anxiety and change. Therefore one of the arguments of my research is that if the lives of the displaced are to be restored then it is mandatory that their state of inbetweenness is ended. This means that

> the displaced people are in the state of inbetweenness until they either get back to their original village or resettle in another place where they can establish or recreate not only their lost assets and properties but also their social contacts, networks, and normal lifestyles. Hence, the aim of my research is to conceptualize the human displacement from a perspective of inbetweenness.[26]

Here Ven. Sangasumana uses "clinging," the English word often used to translate the Pāli *taṇhā* (clinging or craving, the source of suffering), in a positive sense: IDPs are in a state of fluctuation between clinging (emplacing) and detaching (being uprooted again). Elsewhere, Ven. Sangasumana does critique attachment, but not attachment to basic needs like home or family: he critiques the attachment to ideology, material resources, and territory that he believes has helped to drive conflict and displacement in Sri Lanka.[27]

Ven. Sangasumana identifies a series of "fix-points," which are the anchors of security that IDPs need to re-establish their lives, resulting in an eight-point mandala with "security" at its center and the fix-points of habitat, livelihood, family, services, identity, social status, relationship, and accessibility arrayed in the eight directions around it. Ven. Sangasumana emphasizes the interdependence of the fix-points, pointing out for example that "habitat" (place of residence) and "identity" strongly influence one another. Together, these fix-points interact to cumulatively strengthen or weaken the security of a person. Ven. Sangasumana's research also draws on the link between the gift of fearlessness and human security:

> [...] fear is invariably a strong indicator of insecurity. When someone is in fear of possible attack or looseness of fix points, elements of mental trauma such as anxiety, suspicion, feeling of insecurity etc. are inculcated in that person's mind and thereby a process of inbetweenness is gradually building-up.[28]

The gift of fearlessness complements the four noble truths in an important way. While the four noble truths relieve the suffering caused by craving what is not necessary or wholesome, the gift of fearlessness relieves the suffering caused by lacking the basic security necessary for a dignified life. The four noble truths show what an individual must do for oneself, while the gift of fearlessness shows what an individual must do on behalf of others within their orbit of power. Only when taken together do these teachings properly acknowledge the varied causes of suffering that people experience and show the path to relieving them.

A Relational Mandala of Security in the *Sigālovāda Sutta*

The *Sigālovāda Sutta* in the Pāli scriptures employs the image of a social mandala as a model for human security. According to the sutta, while the Buddha is walking on his morning alms rounds one day, he encounters a young householder named Sigāla, freshly bathed and with palms together, worshipping the six directions: eastern, southern, northern, western, lower, and upper. Sigāla's aim in performing the ritual of worshipping the six directions is that the directions may be "protected, made peaceful and secure." Sigāla is seeking security through this ritual that orients him in space and aspires toward peace and protection in every direction surrounding him. True to form, the Buddha engages young Sigāla in a conversation about his practice.

> And how, young man, does the noble disciple protect the six directions? These six directions should be known: mother and father as the east, teachers as the south, spouse and family as the west, friends and colleagues as the north, workers and servants as the lower direction, and ascetics and Brahmans as the upper direction.[29]

Rather than critique the ritual outright for its Brahmanical character, as the Buddha sometimes does in the Pāli scriptures, here he reinterprets the ritual through a lens of human relationality. The Buddha defines one's orientation in the world—one's place, in the most literal sense—in terms of relationships of mutual obligation and support. To be secure in place is not only to be secure within physical space, but to be secure within the web of social relationships.

In the lines that follow, the Buddha gives explanations for how each of these six relationships, centered around the family and household, can be "protected and made peaceful and secure." Bhikkhu Bodhi notes that

> Although the Buddha himself left the household life in order to adopt the life of a renunciant, he did not lose sight of the crucial role that the family plays in shaping a person's character and determining the general atmosphere of society as a whole.[30]

In this text, security and protection are not only enjoyments that await those who have reached spiritual liberation, but are worldly realities of a good and peaceful life in this web of human interdependence. If we read the sutta through the lens of contemporary discourse on human security, we see a six-part framework for understanding what gives humans a place in the social world that is "protected and made peaceful and secure."

The east, the mother and father, represents not only a person's relationship to her parents but also her relationship to her ancestors and her heritage. The Buddha instructs:

> In five ways should a mother and father as the eastern direction be respected by a child: "I will support them who supported me; I will do my duty to them; I will maintain the family lineage and tradition; I will be worthy of my inheritance; and I will make donations on behalf of dead ancestors."[31]

He then names the complementary duties of the parents, explaining,

> And, the mother and father so respected reciprocate with compassion in five ways: by restraining you from wrongdoing, guiding you towards good actions, training you in a profession, supporting the choice of a suitable spouse, and in due time, handing over the inheritance. In this way, the eastern direction is protected and made peaceful and secure.[32]

The relationships that individuals cultivate with their families of origin as well as their ancestral heritage constitute an important dimension of human security. Parents can usher their children securely into adulthood to establish their own families and inherit the family's property; children can care for their parents as they age, continue the family line, and honor family traditions. Yet family separation is a common occurrence in displacement contexts, and one of the most painful. Families often try to migrate together, even when the "children" are adults.[33] Family decisions to separate are often made because of financial desperation or dangerous border conditions; such decisions are often contingent on plans to pursue family reunification policies after reaching their destination, as observed in the Eastern Mediterranean route in 2015–2020.[34] In the contemporary displacement regime, securing the "eastern direction" can include enabling displaced people to bring their parents with them for resettlement; to send money to their parents, who might remain at home; or to retain travel access for return visits, especially for care-giving. Supporting this dimension of human security could also mean helping displaced people retain access to their language, cultural wisdom, traditional practices, family graves, or sacred sites that are particularly meaningful to them. "Inheritance" here can be understood literally as finances and property, but also figuratively; robust support of displaced people should involve a consideration of the inheritances, tangible and intangible, that they might benefit from accessing.

The southern direction represents one's teachers, who may be envisioned to include formal educators as well as the elders in one's community who impart wisdom. The Buddha explains, "In five ways should teachers as the southern direction be respected by a student: by rising for them, regularly attending lessons, eagerly desiring to learn, duly serving them, and receiving instruction."[35] Likewise,

> teachers so respected reciprocate with compassion in five ways: by training in self-discipline, ensuring the teachings are well-grasped, instructing in every branch of knowledge, introducing their friends and colleagues, and providing safeguards in every direction. In this way, the southern direction is protected and made peaceful and secure.[36]

Providing education for displaced populations is an invaluable service, and contemporary understandings of the benefits of education are remarkably similar to those listed here: not only knowledge and credentials, but self-discipline and a future orientation, connections and networks, and mitigation of further vulnerability. At a time when about half of the world's displaced children are out of school, and when a large proportion of teachers in displacement contexts are minimally qualified, there is an urgent need to implement global commitments to education for refugee and displaced children.[37] Education also supports time bindedness; education is an active investment in the future as well as a collective act of faith that there will be a future for the children that is worthy of investment.

The western direction represents one's wife (in Sigāla's case). According to the Buddha, "In five ways should a wife as the western direction be respected by a husband: by honoring, not disrespecting, being faithful, sharing authority, and by giving gifts."[38] In return,

> The wife so respected reciprocates with compassion in five ways: by being well-organized, being kindly disposed to the in-laws and household workers, being faithful, looking after the household goods, and being skillful and diligent in all duties. In this way, the western direction is protected and made peaceful and secure.

Cultural views about the proper role of women in the family vary, and in displacement contexts, the gendered norms that families bring with them sometimes clash with the norms of the host community. For this reason, attention to the changing dynamics of gendered authority in refugee families is a key component of the cultural orientation programs offered by the U.S. resettlement agency Church World Service in my community of Harrisonburg, Virginia. Yet this ancient text emphasizes what contemporary humanitarian actors do: that when women are secure, they are empowered to contribute more effectively to their entire family's security. In this passage, we read references to women's role in the family's economic security ("looking after the household goods" and "being skillful and diligent in all duties"), to their decision-making power ("sharing authority"), and to their establishment of constructive relationships within and beyond their family unit ("being kindly disposed to the in-laws and household workers"). Security for women enhances the security of the entire family by empowering them to cultivate a positive web of relationships, both internally and externally facing.

The northern direction represents friends and colleagues. The rupture of friendships during times of displacement is not as often highlighted in humanitarian reports as other relationships are, but the Buddha takes the social benefits that friends and colleagues offer very seriously. He says, "In five ways should friends and colleagues as the northern direction be respected: by generosity, kind words, acting for their welfare, impartiality, and honesty."[39] Furthermore,

> friends and colleagues so respected reciprocate with compassion in five ways: by protecting you when you are vulnerable, and likewise your wealth, being a refuge when you are afraid, not abandoning you in misfortunes, and honoring all your descendants. In this way, the northern direction is protected and made peaceful and secure.[40]

The northern direction appeals to the importance of an individual's network of support beyond the family unit. The mention of "colleagues" also gestures toward the importance of dignified work and relationships beyond the household in the wider community. The opportunity not only to earn a livelihood but also to enjoy networks of companionship and mutual support enhances the safety net for vulnerable populations and decreases their need to rely on ongoing support from host communities.

When economically and socially secure, a person may be able to benefit others with the same support of dignified work and community, as the Buddha envisions in the next verse. The lower direction represents employees:

> In five ways should workers and servants as the lower direction be respected by an employer: by allocating work according to aptitude, providing wages and food, looking after the sick, sharing special treats, and giving reasonable time off work. And, workers and servants so respected reciprocate with compassion in five ways: being willing to start early and finish late when necessary, taking only what is given, doing work well, and promoting a good reputation. In this way, the lower direction is protected and made peaceful and secure.[41]

Evident from this text is that Sigāla is a young man of means; references to inheritances, gifts, the protection of wealth, and the employment of household workers all indicate that Sigāla already enjoys a certain level of economic security. One challenge with applying this sutta to the question of security for displaced populations is the gap between Sigāla's position of wealth and the position of economic vulnerability in which displaced people often find themselves (even if they were wealthy before being displaced). Only after one's immediate security needs are met can one provide for the employment and welfare of others. Yet like the gift of fearlessness, the authority exercised through employment can be a blessing and a support to others, even in the humblest contexts. The economic interdependence illustrated in this verse also speaks to the critical role of trust in contemporary human security discourse: Leaning and Arie note that "Specialization and interdependence are important features of social and economic development and also can be seen as instances of human security in action—trust in constructive arrangements through time."[42]

The relational paradigm of security offered here demonstrates how the benefits of security extend into all directions, from the individual to the family, the household, colleagues, friends, employees, and finally, those practicing paths of religious discipline:

> In five ways should ascetics and Brahmans as the upper direction be respected: by kindly actions, speech, and thoughts, having an open door, and providing material needs. And, ascetics and Brahmans so respected reciprocate with compassion in six ways: by restraining you from wrongdoing, guiding you to good actions, thinking compassionately, telling you what you ought to know, clarifying what you already know, and showing you the path to heaven. In this way, the upper direction is protected and made peaceful and secure.[43]

The Buddha encourages Sigāla to heed the guidance of the community's religious experts and to offer them respect, hospitality, and material support. From a Buddhist perspective, making merit through acts of generosity to worthy recipients like renunciants provides security in one's future births. Yet the Buddha does not directly mention the importance of karma in this set of verses; instead, he emphasizes the teacherly role of "ascetics and Brahmans" and the benefits of restraint, guidance, instruction, and clarification that the listener receives from them. In other words, supporting ascetic practitioners grants the benefactor closer proximity to the teachings and rituals that can guide them in times of difficulty. Such emotional and cognitive support for navigating life's challenges bolsters one's resilience in the face of life's inevitable challenges.

Socially, the respect and support offered to ascetics also grant dignity and a good reputation to the giver, placing him or her in the company of the upright. Earlier in this sutta, the Buddha advises Sigāla on how to avoid socially disadvantageous states such as "disrepute" (verse 8), having "friends and colleagues display their contempt" (verse 11, in reference to the consequences of gambling), and "bad companionship" (verse 12).[44] The company one keeps makes a difference, preventing a person from going morally astray and keeping one "firmly grounded in this world and the next" (verse 3). The social benefits of listening to the wise and supporting the sangha provide security for one's life in the here-and-now as well as in one's journey of rebirths.

When considered within the web of interdependence that is human life, no aspect of human security affects one individual alone. Even the cultivation of friendships or acts of charity are critical dimensions of security that ripple out to benefit not only the individual at the center of the mandala, but all those to whom she is related. Dasho Karma Ura, analyzing the Gross National Happiness policy in Bhutan, writes that "By recognizing the true nature of interdependence, one can see that all Karma is collective, that all enlightenment is collective, and therefore that happiness and the policies required to promote it must be oriented toward collective achievement."[45] This is a radical statement for a Buddhist, but it speaks to the politically constructive possibilities of Buddhist philosophical understandings of identity and action.

Buddhism and Contemporary Human Security Discourse

The relationships that the Buddha explores in the *Sigālovāda Sutta* as sources of protection echo the findings of Leaning and Arie in their paper for USAID that undertook a bold redefinition of human security in the year 2000.[46] Leaning and Arie argued that up to that time, human security measures focused almost exclusively on material resources, but that the psycho-social dimensions of security are equally important. Leaning and Arie's work expounds on four primary psycho-social needs that humans share: these are identity, recognition, participation, and autonomy.

> Identity, at the level of the individual, means that a person knows who he is; knows where he came from socially and geographically; can lay adequate claim to a history and a set of possessions; and can prove or establish these facts without much fear of challenge from external groups or authorities. Recognition is the certainty that these facts of existence and history are acknowledged and accepted by others within a network of family and social relationships. Recognition confers dignity. Participation, for the individual, is the opportunity and capacity to engage with others in economic, political, or social relationships, networks, and enterprises. Autonomy, an attribute of empowered being and standing in the world, speaks to a person's ability to determine his own path, independently think about and shape his own future, and resist confinement in subject, victim, or passive modes.[47]

The *Sigālovāda Sutta*'s mandala of social relationships establishes identity by naming the key social roles the worshipper inhabits; recognition, by defining those roles within relationships of reciprocity; participation, by prescribing actions to be performed by each party; and autonomy, by cultivating the social conditions enabling people to discern wisely and act effectively as their lives unfold. The Buddha envisioned reciprocal modes of human relatedness within this mandala of interdependence as the way leading to protection, peace, and security in this world. While echoing the spirit behind many of Leaning and Arie's insights, this sutta also pushes the contemporary psycho-social security model in new directions by highlighting the importance of friendship, employment, and almsgiving to the development of a secure and actualized human life. The sutta emphasizes reciprocity rather than rights, offering a model that can speak more directly to cultural contexts where human rights discourse and individualistic conceptions of the self do not find firm footing.

To draw this chapter to a close, let us reflect on what these mandala models from Buddhism's artistic and ritual traditions contribute to the constructive aims of this book: to help build a more informed, effective, and compassionate displacement regime. Leaning and Arie's work ultimately revolves around the argument that human security depends upon strong connections to "home, community, and the future."[48] These three pillars of human security resonate strongly with the emphasis on protection, social relationships of meaning and support, and time bindedness that we have explored in this book. In the Buddhist sources we have examined, "home" encompasses both physical and political dimensions of shelter and protection; these dimensions are explored through sacred texts and negotiated through discipline and law. "Community" encompasses the living and the dead, monastics and lay people, spirit beings and animals, as well as many layers of individual and collective responsibility. Finally, "future" encompasses the psychological, ritual, and economic activities through which humans exercise agency over the world they are always creating, for this and future lifetimes.

Leaning and Arie's framework for human security not only clarifies these Buddhist insights, but demonstrates their critical relevance for reimagining how global communities conceptualize and pursue security. We have seen that Buddhist traditions and histories around displacement provide psychological depth, ethical complexity, ritual pragmatism, legal sophistication, artistic sense-making, and political constructivism. These contributions are all legible within contemporary humanitarian discourse, yet just different enough to challenge some of the entrenched assumptions that structure the displacement regime. As a religious tradition, Buddhism contributes philosophical depth and nuance to questions of identity, community, morality, and responsibility. Yet perhaps Buddhism's greatest value in the struggle for human security is its focus on practice: healing, belonging, and emplacement are not mere concepts in this tradition, but are narrated, embodied, painted, and ritualized. Like the future itself, security is something we make real through *action.*

Notes

1 Agamben, Giorgio. *The Omnibus Homo Sacer.* Translated by Daniel Heller-Roazen. United Kingdom: Stanford, CA: Stanford University Press, 2017.

2 Frydenlund, Iselin. "The Protection of Dharma and Dharma as Protection: Buddhism and Security across Asia." In Chris Seiple, Dennis R. Hoover, and Pauletta Otispp, eds., *The Routledge Handbook of Religion and Security*, pp. 102–112. New York: Routledge, 2012.

3 For example, in the Pāli canon, refer to "The Book of Protection: Paritta." Translated from the original Pāli, with introductory essay and explanatory notes by Piyadassi Thera, with a foreword by V.F. Gunaratna. *Access to Insight (BCBS Edition)*, 30 November 2013. Accessed on 1 January 2026 at www.accesstoinsight.org/lib/authors/piyadassi/protection.html.

4 Occasionally, this list varies, with infectious disease replacing the fear of wrongful imprisonment, for example.

5 Chodron, Thubten. *How to Free Your Mind: The Practice of Tara the Liberator*. Boulder, CO: Shambhala Publications, 2013. Refer to chapter 3.

6 Himalayan Art Resources. "Buddhist Deity: Tara, Eight Fears (set 1)." Rubin Museum of Art images. Photographed Image Copyright © 2004. Accessed on 12 December 2025. https://www.himalayanart.org/search/set.cfm?setID=70. Item 832 and the accompanying set. For a brief video commentary on the painting set by Jeff Watts, see Himalayan Art Resources. "Tara & Eight Fears: Painting Set 1." Accessed on 29 December 2025. www.youtube.com/watch?v=REavkoZU-BM.

7 Heirman, Ann. "How to Deal with Dangerous and Annoying Animals: A *Vinaya* Perspective." *Religions* 10, no. 2 (2019): 1–17. p. 9.

8 "Ahi Sutta: A Snake" (AN 4.67), translated from the Pāli by Piyadassi Thera. *Access to Insight (BCBS Edition)*, 30 November 2013. Accessed on 12 December 2025. www.accesstoinsight.org/tipitaka/an/an04/an04.067.piya.html.

9 Himalayan Art Resources. "Buddhist Deity: Tara, Eight Fears (set 1)." Rubin Museum of Art images. Photographed Image Copyright © 2004. Accessed on 12 December 2025. https://www.himalayanart.org/search/set.cfm?setID=70. Item 833.

10 Himalayan Art Resources. "Buddhist Deity: Tara, Eight Fears (set 1)." Rubin Museum of Art images. Photographed Image Copyright © 2004. Accessed on 12 December 2025. https://www.himalayanart.org/search/set.cfm?setID=70. Item 831.

11 For an introduction to clinical applications of this issue, refer to Hinton D.E., Pich V., Chhean D., Pollack M.H. "'The Ghost Pushes You Down': Sleep Paralysis-Type Panic Attacks in a Khmer Refugee Population." *Transcultural Psychiatry* 42, 1 (2005): 46–77; and Hinton, D.E. "Auditory Hallucination Among Traumatized Cambodian Refugees: PTSD Association and Biocultural Shaping." *Culture, Medicine and Psychiatry* 45 (2021): 727–750; and Hinton, D.E., R. Reis, and J. de Jong. "Ghost Encounters Among Traumatized Cambodian Refugees: Severity, Relationship to PTSD, and Phenomenology." *Culture, Medicine and Psychiatry* 44 (2020): 333–359.

12 Himalayan Art Resources. "Buddhist Deity: Tara, Eight Fears (set 1)." Rubin Museum of Art images. Photographed Image Copyright © 2004. Accessed on 12 December 2025. https://www.himalayanart.org/search/set.cfm?setID=70. Item 827.

13 "The Book of Protection: Paritta." Translated from the original Pāli, with introductory essay and explanatory notes by Piyadassi Thera, with a foreword by V.F. Gunaratna. *Access to Insight (BCBS Edition)*, 30 November 2013. Accessed on 1 January 2026 at www.accesstoinsight.org/lib/authors/piyadassi/protection.html.

14 Men, Chean Rithy. "The Changing Religious Beliefs and Ritual Practices Among Cambodians in Diaspora." *Journal of Refugee Studies* 15, no. 2 (June 2002): 222–233. https://doi.org/10.1093/jrs/15.2.222.

15 Jahnke, Art. "How Cambodian Music Recalls Ancestors and Brings Comfort." *The Brink: Pioneering Research from Boston University*. 25 November 2019. Accessed on 12 December 2025. www.bu.edu/articles/2019/cambodian-ritual-music-and-dance/.

16 Himalayan Art Resources. "Buddhist Deity: Tara, Eight Fears (set 1)." Rubin Museum of Art images. Photographed Image Copyright © 2004. Accessed on 12 December 2025. https://www.himalayanart.org/search/set.cfm?setID=70. Item 834.

17 Himalayan Art Resources. "Buddhist Deity: Tara, Eight Fears (set 1)." Rubin Museum of Art images. Photographed Image Copyright © 2004. Accessed on 12 December 2025. https://www.himalayanart.org/search/set.cfm?setID=70. Item 829.

18 Himalayan Art Resources. "Buddhist Deity: Tara, Eight Fears (set 1)." Rubin Museum of Art images. Photographed Image Copyright © 2004. Accessed on 12 December 2025. https://www.himalayanart.org/search/set.cfm?setID=70. Items 828 and 830.

19 Arendt, Hannah. *The Origins of Totalitarianism*. New York: Houghton Mifflin Harcourt, 1973. p. 296.

20 United Nations Development Programme. *Human Development Report 1994*. New York: Oxford University Press, 1994. Accessed on 12 December 2025 at https://hdr.undp.org/content/human-development-report-1994. p. 22.

21 United Nations Development Programme. *Human Development Report 1994*. New York: Oxford University Press, 1994. Accessed on 12 December 2025 at https://hdr.undp.org/content/human-development-report-1994. pp. 22–23.

22 Bond, George D. "The Good Life as Envisioned by A.T. Ariyaratne and the Sarvodaya Movement." In Sallie King, ed., *Buddhist Visions of the Good Life for All*, pp. 82–94. New York: Routledge, 2021. p. 86.

23 Sid Brown makes a similar interpretive move when she describes ignorance as the cause of suffering for young women and education as the solution. Refer to Brown, Sid. *The Journey of One Buddhist Nun: Even Against the Wind*. Albany, NY: State University of New York Press, 2001. p. 94.

24 Bond, George D. "The Good Life as Envisioned by A.T. Ariyaratne and the Sarvodaya Movement." In Sallie King, ed., *Buddhist Visions of the Good Life for All*, pp. 82–94. New York: Routledge, 2021. p. 86.

25 Sangasumana, Ven. Pinnawala. "Mapping Inbetweenness: A Conceptual Model for War-Induced Resettlement in Sri Lanka." *Social Science Research Network*, 26 November 2012. http://doi.org/10.2139/ssrn.3455629.

26 Sangasumana, Ven. Pinnawala. "Mapping Inbetweenness: A Conceptual Model for War-Induced Resettlement in Sri Lanka." *Social Science Research Network*, 26 November 2012. http://doi.org/10.2139/ssrn.3455629. pp. 1–2.

27 Sangasumana, Ven. Pinnawala. "Buddhist Perspective on Addressing War-Displacement." In *Buddhist Approach to Political Conflict and Peace Development*. UNDV Conference Volume (The International Buddhist Conference on the United Nations Day of Vesak Celebrations), pp. 85-101. Bangkok: Mahachulalongkornrajavidyalaya University, 2009. p. 89.

28 Sangasumana, Ven. Pinnawala. "Mapping Inbetweenness: A Conceptual Model for War-Induced Resettlement in Sri Lanka." *Social Science Research Network*, 26 November 2012. http://doi.org/10.2139/ssrn.3455629. p. 12.

29 "Sigalovada Sutta: The Buddha's Advice to Sigala" (DN 31). Translated from the Pāli by John Kelly, Sue Sawyer, and Victoria Yareham. *Access to Insight (BCBS Edition)*, 30 November 2013. Accessed on 29 December 2025. www.accesstoinsight.org/tipitaka/dn/dn.31.0.ksw0.html. Refer to verse 27.

30 Bhikku Bodhi. "A Map of the Good Life: The 38 Blessings of the Maṅgala Sutta." In Sallie King, ed., *Buddhist Visions of the Good Life for All*, pp. 9–35. Routledge, 2021. https://doi.org/10.4324/9781003100454-3.

31 "Sigalovada Sutta: The Buddha's Advice to Sigala" (DN 31). Translated from the Pāli by John Kelly, Sue Sawyer, and Victoria Yareham. *Access to Insight (BCBS*

Edition), 30 November 2013. Accessed on 29 December 2025. www.accesstoinsight.org/tipitaka/dn/dn.31.0.ksw0.html. Verse 28.

32 "Sigalovada Sutta: The Buddha's Advice to Sigala" (DN 31). Translated from the Pāli by John Kelly, Sue Sawyer, and Victoria Yareham. *Access to Insight (BCBS Edition)*, 30 November 2013. Accessed on 29 December 2025. www.accesstoinsight.org/tipitaka/dn/dn.31.0.ksw0.html. Verse 28.

33 Bastaki, Jinan. "'Not Without My Daughter': EU Asylum Law, Gender, and the Separation of Refugee Families." *Refugee Survey Quarterly* 38, no. 3 (2019): 266–289.

34 Dubow, Talitha, and Katie Kuschminder. "Family Strategies in Refugee Journeys to Europe." *Journal of Refugee Studies* 34, no. 4 (2021): 4262–4278.

35 "Sigalovada Sutta: The Buddha's Advice to Sigala" (DN 31). Translated from the Pāli by John Kelly, Sue Sawyer, and Victoria Yareham. *Access to Insight (BCBS Edition)*, 30 November 2013. Accessed on 29 December 2025. www.accesstoinsight.org/tipitaka/dn/dn.31.0.ksw0.html. Verse 29.

36 "Sigalovada Sutta: The Buddha's Advice to Sigala" (DN 31). Translated from the Pāli by John Kelly, Sue Sawyer, and Victoria Yareham. *Access to Insight (BCBS Edition)*, 30 November 2013. Accessed on 29 December 2025. www.accesstoinsight.org/tipitaka/dn/dn.31.0.ksw0.html. Verse 29.

37 Geneva Global Hub for Education in Emergencies. *Education in Emergencies & Children on the Move*. Accessed on 29 December 2025 at https://eiehub.org/education-in-emergencies-and-displacement.

38 "Sigalovada Sutta: The Buddha's Advice to Sigala" (DN 31). Translated from the Pāli by John Kelly, Sue Sawyer, and Victoria Yareham. *Access to Insight (BCBS Edition)*, 30 November 2013. Accessed on 29 December 2025. www.accesstoinsight.org/tipitaka/dn/dn.31.0.ksw0.html. Verse 30.

39 "Sigalovada Sutta: The Buddha's Advice to Sigala" (DN 31). Translated from the Pāli by John Kelly, Sue Sawyer, and Victoria Yareham. *Access to Insight (BCBS Edition)*, 30 November 2013. Accessed on 29 December 2025. www.accesstoinsight.org/tipitaka/dn/dn.31.0.ksw0.html. Verse 31.

40 "Sigalovada Sutta: The Buddha's Advice to Sigala" (DN 31). Translated from the Pāli by John Kelly, Sue Sawyer, and Victoria Yareham. *Access to Insight (BCBS Edition)*, 30 November 2013. Accessed on 29 December 2025. www.accesstoinsight.org/tipitaka/dn/dn.31.0.ksw0.html. Verse 31.

41 "Sigalovada Sutta: The Buddha's Advice to Sigala" (DN 31). Translated from the Pāli by John Kelly, Sue Sawyer, and Victoria Yareham. *Access to Insight (BCBS Edition)*, 30 November 2013. Accessed on 29 December 2025. www.accesstoinsight.org/tipitaka/dn/dn.31.0.ksw0.html. Verse 32.

42 Leaning, Jennifer, and Sam Arie. *Human Security: A Framework for Assessment in Conflict and Transition*. USAID Complex Emergency Response and Transition Initiative, December 2000. p. 58.

43 "Sigalovada Sutta: The Buddha's Advice to Sigala" (DN 31). Translated from the Pāli by John Kelly, Sue Sawyer, and Victoria Yareham. *Access to Insight (BCBS Edition)*, 30 November 2013. Accessed on 29 December 2025. www.accesstoinsight.org/tipitaka/dn/dn.31.0.ksw0.html. Verse 33.

44 "Sigalovada Sutta: The Buddha's Advice to Sigala" (DN 31). Translated from the Pāli by John Kelly, Sue Sawyer, and Victoria Yareham. *Access to Insight (BCBS Edition)*, 30 November 2013. Accessed on 29 December 2025. www.accesstoinsight.org/tipitaka/dn/dn.31.0.ksw0.html.

45 Dasho Karma Ura. "Gross National Happiness and Buddhism." *Dharma World* 34 (Oct–Dec 2007): 28–30. This source was quoted in Michael Givel, "Mahayana Buddhism and Gross National Happiness in Bhutan," *International Journal of Wellbeing* 5 (2):14–27. p. 16, which was in turn cited in Clayton, Barbra, "The Development of Well-Being: Gross National Happiness and Bhutan's Vision for the Ideal Society." In Sallie King, ed., *Buddhist Visions of the Good Life for All*, pp. 95–120. New York: Routledge, 2021. https://doi.org/10.4324/9781003100454-3. I was unable to access the original source.

46 Leaning, Jennifer and Sam Arie. *Human Security: A Framework for Assessment in Conflict and Transition.* December 2000. USAID Complex Emergency Response and Transition Initiative, directed by Tulane University.

47 Leaning, Jennifer, and Sam Arie. *Human Security: A Framework for Assessment in Conflict and Transition.* USAID Complex Emergency Response and Transition Initiative, December 2000. p. 16. While Leaning and Arie specify here that their definitions pertain to the individual, the original source (Amoo, Sam. *The Challenge of Ethnicity and Conflicts in Africa: The Need for a New Paradigm.* New York: United Nations Development Programme Emergency Response Division, 1997) names these four as group needs rather than individual needs.

48 Leaning, Jennifer, and Sam Arie. *Human Security: A Framework for Assessment in Conflict and Transition.* USAID Complex Emergency Response and Transition Initiative, December 2000. p. 4.

Conclusion

Despite its emphasis on renunciation and detachment, Buddhism is a tradition strongly oriented toward placemaking and security. This means that Buddhists have immense resources to contribute to our global understanding of displacement and effective responses to it. They bring rich historical experiences, ethical and legal frameworks, and literary and artistic traditions that engage with questions of displacement and security in distinctive ways, echoing universal human concerns but also opening new avenues for inquiry and practice. Buddhist traditions illustrate the fundamental importance of human relationships to place, to power, and to time; they challenge governance models that rely on fear, and they empower ordinary people to build better futures for themselves and others. Attending to Buddhist voices in the contemporary displacement crisis also enriches academic perspectives on Buddhism, revealing the tradition's deep and persistent concerns with home, protection, and human security that have not been sufficiently emphasized in western scholarship.

In this work, my goal has been not only to make critical contributions to displacement studies and to Buddhist studies, but also to inform constructive responses to our current displacement crisis. I close with a summary of this book's findings that I believe can be applied to the work of several key groups active in the displacement regime today.

For Buddhist Community Leaders

Buddhist monastics and lay leaders guide their communities in understanding the Buddha's teachings and putting them into practice. They serve on the front lines of disaster and provide essential support to their communities, as well as to people with religions and nationalities different from their own. They are witnesses and advocates for the needs of displaced people when governing authorities ignore their plight. For them, I offer the following support for their work:

Sacred stories are powerful ways to engage communities in reflection on the ethics of displacement and hospitality. Central narratives, like the *Vessantara jātaka*, have the power to open new modes of questioning and

DOI: 10.4324/9781003318149-7

perspective-taking on otherwise contentious topics. I encourage Buddhist community leaders to think creatively about how the sacred narratives they have inherited could motivate their communities toward greater openness and service toward displaced people.

As they bring their concerns and petitions to governing authorities on behalf of displaced people and the communities supporting them, they should remember that connecting with other Buddhists across geographies and lineages can strengthen their voice. They can also strengthen their voice by uplifting the perspectives of women, especially when women are excluded from official leadership roles such as higher ordination. The gift of fearlessness is just as relevant today as it was thousands of years ago; may they have the courage to keep its call alive.

For Humanitarian Actors

There are tens of thousands of professionals serving humanitarian organizations that respond to displacement and support conditions for security and development. These organizations rely on countless volunteers, motivated by religion or humanistic goodwill to aid those in distress. Humanitarian workers are often serving people in cultures and communities beyond their familiarity, trying to meet universal human needs while humbly attending to the sensitivities of difference. For them, I offer the following support for their work in Buddhist contexts:

Memorials and funerary rituals can help create peaceful relations between the living and the dead, the present and the past. Survivors of traumatic loss may need these services as much as they need food and shelter. Likewise, merit-making opportunities can promote psychological safety and a healthy grasp of the future for Buddhists grappling with displacement. I encourage humanitarian actors to draw on Buddhism's rich resources for understanding personal agency and time bindedness as they assist displaced people in moving forward with their lives.

As they provide clinical care for the displaced, I urge humanitarian actors to evaluate with local specialists whether meditation should be advised for those experiencing trauma. Not all meditation is the same and not all meditation promotes inner peace. As they seek to offer culturally responsive forms of care in Buddhist communities, they should remember to look beyond canonical Buddhism to discern a group's spiritual conceptions of wellness and healing; these conceptions are often strongly intertwined with cultural traditions, such as beliefs in ghosts or souls, that enrich Buddhists' understandings of self and community.

Human dignity encompasses a dialectic between the universal and the particular. May humanitarian actors have the creativity to meet the varied needs of global communities experiencing displacement.

For Governing Authorities and Policy Makers

Political leaders hold the authority to change law, policy, and culture. They face immensely challenging issues, many of which may seem to have no solution. Leaders and policy makers should remember that they have the power and the responsibility to prevent displacement, to mitigate its sufferings, and to create future pathways to peace and security.

Addressing displacement must include resolving statelessness. A person's right to state protection is fundamental to human security, and protection is the sign of a strong and sovereign state. Dehumanizing rhetoric and unmerciful acts of exclusion do not make a state safer, but make it less secure. A great leader takes responsibility for their role in causing harm or well-being, understanding that political structures directly impact the dignity of ordinary people. Leaders must not discount the impact that even small acts of virtue can make.

As governing authorities seek ways to create just structures and improve state responses to displacement, they should prioritize family unity and reunification. Family relationships constitute the most foundational security a person has. Authorities should also protect monastic communities' work in disaster relief and hospitality. The monastic sangha depends on the government for support; the government should empower them to continue the selfless work of assistance and sheltering that they are inspired to do for those in need.

State leaders are not alone in addressing displacement and its cascading challenges. Regional partners and international organizations are fighting the same battle and are stronger when working together.[1] Buddhist organizations across the globe have been serving in humanitarian roles for many decades, and they bring a wealth of experience and volunteer power to serve communities in distress.

May governing authorities and policy makers have the conviction and humanity to build a future of security for all people, and may that future begin here.

Note

1 Kilby, Christina. "Call For a Buddhism-Inspired Asian Regional Compact on Internal Displacement." *International Relations,* 25 January 2024. Accessed on 3 January 2026. www.e-ir.info/2024/01/25/call-for-a-buddhism-inspired-asian-regional-compact-on-internal-displacement/.

Bibliography

Abrahamian, Andray. "Myanmar's Ma Ba Tha Fades with Barely a Whimper." *The Interpreter*, 2 August 2016. Accessed on 6 December 2025. www.lowyinstitute.org/the-interpreter/myanmar-s-ma-ba-tha-fades-barely-whimper.

Agamben, Giorgio. *The Omnibus Homo Sacer*. Translated by Daniel Heller-Roazen. United Kingdom: Stanford, CA: Stanford University Press, 2017.

Agger, Inger. "Calming the Mind: Healing after Mass Atrocity in Cambodia." *Transcultural Psychiatry* 52, no. 4 (2015): 543–560. DOI: 10.1177/1363461514568336.

Agger, Inger. "Testimony Ceremonies in Asia: Integrating Spirituality in Testimonial Therapy for Torture Survivors in India, Sri Lanka, Cambodia, and the Philippines." *Transcultural Psychiatry* 49 (2012): 568–589.

"Ahi Sutta: A Snake" (AN 4.67), translated from the Pāli by Piyadassi Thera. *Access to Insight (BCBS Edition)*, 30 November 2013. Accessed on 12 December 2025. www.accesstoinsight.org/tipitaka/an/an04/an04.067.piya.html.

Ahmed, Sara. *The Cultural Politics of Emotion*. New York: Routledge, 2013.

"Alīnacitta-Jātaka." *The Jataka, Vol. II*, translated by W.H.D. Rouse, 1895. No. 156, pp. 13–17. Accessed on 3 January 2026. https://sacred-texts.com/bud/j2/j2009.htm

Al-Issa, Ihsan, and Michel Tousignant, eds. *Ethnicity, Immigration, and Psychopathology*. Dordrecht, Netherlands: Springer, 1997.

Alvarez Ortega, Miguel. "Buddhism and Law." In Courtney Bruntz, ed. *Oxford Bibliographies in Buddhism*. Oxford: Oxford University Press, 2016. Accessed on 11 June 2024.

Amnesty International. "Myanmar: Four Years after Coup, World Must Demand Accountability for Atrocity Crimes." 31 January 2025. Accessed on 26 November 2025. www.amnesty.org/en/latest/news/2025/01/myanmar-four-years-after-coup-world-must-demand-accountability-for-atrocity-crimes/.

Amnesty International. "Myanmar: Scrap 'Race and Religion' Laws that Could Fuel Discrimination and Violence." 3 March 2015. Accessed on 6 December 2025. www.amnesty.org/en/latest/news/2015/03/myanmar-race-and-religion-laws/.

Amnesty International and the International Commission of Jurists. "Myanmar: Parliament Must Reject Discriminatory 'Race and Religion' Laws." 3 March 2015. Accessed on 7 May 2026. https://www.amnesty.org/en/documents/asa16/1107/2015/en/.

Amoo, Sam. *The Challenge of Ethnicity and Conflicts in Africa: The Need for a New Paradigm.* New York: United Nations Development Programme Emergency Response Division, 1997.

"Anuradha Sutta: To Anuradha" (SN 22.86). Translated from the Pāli by Thanissaro Bhikkhu. *Access to Insight (BCBS Edition)*, 30 November 2013. Accessed on 11 June 2024. www.accesstoinsight.org/tipitaka/sn/sn22/sn22.086.than.html.

"Anusota Sutta: With the Flow" (AN 4.5). Translated from the Pāli by Thanissaro Bhikkhu. *Access to Insight (BCBS Edition)*, 3 July 2010. Accessed on 10 May 2024. www.accesstoinsight.org/tipitaka/an/an04/an04.005.than.html.

Arendt, Hannah. *The Origins of Totalitarianism.* New York: Houghton Mifflin Harcourt, 1973.

Aung San Suu Kyi. *Freedom from Fear: and Other Writings.* London: Penguin, 2010.

Barstow, Geoff. *Food of Sinful Demons: Meat, Vegetarianism, and the Limits of Buddhism in Tibet.* New York: Columbia University Press, 2019.

Bartles-Smith, Andrew, Kate Crosby, Peter Harvey, Asanga Tilakaratne, Daniel Ratheiser, Noel Maurer Trew, Stefania Travagnin, Elizabeth J. Harris, Mahinda Deegalle, and Christina A. Kilby, eds. *Buddhism and International Humanitarian Law.* Special Issue of *Contemporary Buddhism* 22, nos. 1–2 (2021).

Bartles-Smith, Andrew, Kate Crosby, Peter Harvey, Asanga Tilakaratne, Daniel Ratheiser, Noel Maurer Trew, Stefania Travagnin, Elizabeth J. Harris, Venerable Mahinda Deegalle, and Christina A. Kilby, eds. *Buddhism and International Humanitarian Law.* New York: Routledge, 2023.

Bastaki, Jinan. "'Not Without My Daughter': EU Asylum Law, Gender, and the Separation of Refugee Families." *Refugee Survey Quarterly* 38, no. 3 (2019): 266–289.

Beckford, James A., ed. *Migration and Religion.* London: Edward Elgar Publishing, 2016.

Beiser, Morton. "Changing Time Perspective and Mental Health Among Southeast Asian Refugees." *Culture, Medicine and Psychiatry* 11 (1987): 437–464.

Beiser, Morton, and Ilene Hyman. "Southeast Asian Refugees in Canada." In Ihsan Al-Issa and Michel Tousignant, eds., *Ethnicity, Immigration, and Psychopathology*, pp. 35–41. Dordrecht: Springer, 1997.

Beiser, Morton, and K.A.S. Wickrama. "Trauma, Time and Mental Health: A Study of Temporal Reintegration and Depressive Disorder Among Southeast Asian Refugees." *Psychological Medicine* 34, no. 5 (2004): 899–910.

Benedict, Adriana Lee, Linda Mancini, and Michael A. Grodin. "Struggling to Meditate: Contextualising Integrated Treatment of Traumatised Tibetan Refugee Monks." *Mental Health, Religion and Culture* 12, no. 5 (2009): 485–499. DOI: 10.1080/13674670902788908.

Betts, Alexander, Gil Loescher, and James Milner. *UNHCR: The Politics and Practice of Refugee Protection*, 2nd edition. New York: Routledge, 2011.

"Bhaya-Bherava Sutta: Fear & Terror" (MN 4). Translated from the Pāli by Thanissaro Bhikkhu. *Access to Insight (BCBS Edition)*, 30 November 2013. Accessed on 8 December 2025. www.accesstoinsight.org/tipitaka/mn/mn.004.than.html.

Bhikkhu Bodhi. "A Map of the Good Life: The 38 Blessings of the Maṅgala Sutta." In Sallie King, ed., *Buddhist Visions of the Good Life for All*, pp. 9–35. Routledge, 2021. https://doi.org/10.4324/9781003100454-3.

"Bhikkhu Pāṭimokkha: The Bhikkhus' Code of Discipline." Translated by Thānissaro Bhikkhu. *Access to Insight (BCBS Edition)*, 17 December 2013. Accessed on 20 June 2023. www.accesstoinsight.org/tipitaka/vin/sv/bhikkhu-pati.html.

"Bhikkhunī Pāṭimokkha: The Bhikkhunīs' Code of Discipline." Translated by Thānissaro Bhikkhu. *Access to Insight (BCBS Edition)*, 17 December 2013. Accessed on 20 June 2023. www.accesstoinsight.org/tipitaka/vin/sv/Bhikkhunī-pati.html.

Bond, George D. "The Good Life as Envisioned by A.T. Ariyaratne and the Sarvodaya Movement." In Sallie King, ed., *Buddhist Visions of the Good Life for All*, pp. 82–94. New York: Routledge, 2021.

Brown, Sid. *The Journey of One Buddhist Nun: Even Against the Wind*. Albany, NY: State University of New York Press, 2001.

Buddhadasa Bhikkhu. "New Life of Peace." Translated by Santikaro Bhikkhu. 11 February 1986. Published by the Dhammadana Foundation, copyright 1997 by *Evolution/Liberation*. Accessed on 8 December 2025. www.dhammatalks.net/Books/Bhikkhu_Buddhadasa_Natural_Cure_for_Spiritual_Disease3.htm.

"Buddhist Community Hall Destroyed and Four Khmer Krom Monks Arrested in Crackdown." *CSW*, 3 April 2024. Accessed on 20 June 2024. www.csw.org.uk/2024/04/03/press/6201/article.htm.

"Cariyāpiṭaka Aṭṭhakathā." Translated by Bhikkhu Bodhi in *The Discourse on the All-Embracing Net of Views: The Brahmajāla Sutta and Its Commentaries*, pp. 243-316. Kandy, Sri Lanka: Buddhist Publication Society, 1978.

Centre for Law and Democracy. "Myanmar: Analysis of the Military's Changes to the Penal Code." 10 May 2021. Accessed on 26 November 2026. www.law-democracy.org/live/myanmar-analysis-of-the-militarys-changes-to-the-penal-code/.

Cheah, Joseph. *Race and Religion in American Buddhism: White Supremacy and Immigrant Adaptation*. Oxford: Oxford University Press, 2011.

Chhim, S. "Baksbat (Broken Courage): A Trauma-Based Cultural Syndrome in Cambodia." *Medical Anthropology* 32, no. 2 (2013): 160–173.

Clayton, Barbra. "The Development of Well-Being: Gross National Happiness and Bhutan's Vision for the Ideal Society." In Sallie King, ed., *Buddhist Visions of the Good Life for All*, pp. 95–120. New York: Routledge, 2021. https://doi.org/10.4324/9781003100454-3.

Cohen, Amichai, and David Zlotogorski. *Proportionality in International Humanitarian Law: Consequences, Precautions, and Procedures*. Oxford: Oxford University Press, 2021.

Collins, Steven, ed. *Readings of the Vessantara Jātaka*. New York: Columbia University Press, 2016.

Cotter, Cédric. "The Religious Convictions of Henri Dunant, Founder of the ICRC." 11 August 2021. Accessed on 29 August 2025. https://blogs.icrc.org/religion-humanitarianprinciples/the-religious-convictions-of-henri-dunant-founder-of-the-icrc/.

Csoma Körösi, Alexander. "An Analysis of the Dulva, A Portion of the Tibetan Work Entitled the Kah-gyur." *Asiatic Researches* 20 (1836): 41–93.

Dasho Karma Ura. "Gross National Happiness and Buddhism." *Dharma World* 34 (Oct–Dec 2007): 28–30.

Denis, Diane. "From Metaphors to Life in Tibetan Settlements and Back Again: Space, an Important Factor for Resilient Response to the Suffering Caused by Armed Conflict." *Journal of Buddhist Ethics* 31 (2024): 51–80.

Denis, Diane. "Fundamental Intelligence, a Buddhist Justification for the Universal Principles Underlying IHL." In Andrew Bartles-Smith, Kate Crosby, Peter Harvey, Asanga Tilakaratne, Daniel Ratheiser, Noel Maurer Trew, Stefania Travagnin, Elizabeth J. Harris, Venerable Mahinda Deegalle and Christina A. Kilby, eds., *Buddhism and International Humanitarian Law,* pp. 167–192. New York: Routledge, 2023.

Dubow, Talitha and Katie Kuschminder. "Family Strategies in Refugee Journeys to Europe." *Journal of Refugee Studies* 34, no. 4 (2021): 4262–4278.

Feeny, Thomas. "Caught Between a Crocodile and a Snake: Childhood in a Rohingya Refugee Camp, Bangladesh." In *Childhood in South Asia: A Critical Look at Issues, Policies, and Programs*, ed. Jyotsna Pattnaik, pp. 1–18. Greenwich, CT: Information Age Publishing, 2005.

Free Expression Myanmar. "New Report: 505A Act of Revenge." 31 January 2022. Accessed on 26 November 2025. https://freeexpressionmyanmar.org/505a-act-of-revenge/.

French, Rebecca R. "What is Buddhist Law?" *Buffalo Law Review* 63 (2015): 833–872.

Frydenlund, Iselin. "The Protection of Dharma and Dharma as Protection: Buddhism and Security across Asia." In Chris Seiple, Dennis R. Hoover, and Pauletta Otispp, eds., *The Routledge Handbook of Religion and Security*, pp. 102–112. New York: Routledge, 2012.

Geneva Global Hub for Education in Emergencies. *Education in Emergencies & Children on the Move*. Accessed on 29 December 2025. https://eiehub.org/education-in-emergencies-and-displacement.

Givel, Michael. "Mahayana Buddhism and Gross National Happiness in Bhutan." *International Journal of Wellbeing* 5, no. 2 (2015): 14–27.

Global Refuge. "Refugee Cap to be Set at Record Low 7,500 in FY 2026." 6 October 2025. Accessed on 6 December 2025. www.globalrefuge.org/news/trump-administration-cuts-refugee-admissions-to-all-time-low-for-fy-2026/.

Goers, M., K. Hunersen, L.S. Karim, A. Jeffery, A. Zedan, C. Robinson, J. Metzler. "Child Marriage Among Displaced Populations – A 2019 Study in Kurdistan Region of Iraq." *BMC Public Health* 22 (2022): 796. DOI: 10.1186/s12889-022-13220-x.

Gonzalez-Barrera, Ana and Jens Manual Krogstad. "What We Know About Illegal Immigration from Mexico." Pew Research Forum, 28 June 2019. Accessed on 3 November 2019. www.pewresearch.org/fact-tank/2019/06/28/what-we-know-about-illegal-immigration-from-mexico/.

Gould, Rebecca Ruth. "The Obligation to Migrate and the Impulse to Narrate: Soviet Narratives of Forced Migration in the Nineteenth Century Caucasus." In Ray Jureidini, Hamad Bin and Said Fares Hassan, eds. *Migration and Islamic Ethics*, pp. 154–173. Leiden: Brill, 2019.

Gravers, Mikael. "Religious Imaginary as an Alternative Social and Moral Order—Karen Buddhism Across the Thai-Burma Border." In Alexander Horstmann and Jin-Heon Jung, eds., *Building Noah's Ark for Migrants, Refugees, and Religious Communities*, pp. 45–76. New York: Palgrave Macmillan, 2015.

Hallisey, Charles, translator. *Poems of the First Buddhist Women: A Translation of the Therigatha*. Cambridge, MA: Harvard University Press, 2021.

Hallisey, Charles and Anne Hansen. "Narrative, Sub-Ethics, and the Moral Life: Some Evidence from Theravāda Buddhism." *Journal of Religious Ethics* 24, no. 2 (1996): 305–327.

Harrington, Laura. "Exorcising the Mandala: Kālacakra and the Neo-Pentecostal Response." *Journal of Global Buddhism* 13 (2012): 147–171. DOI: 10.5281/zenodo.1306642.

Harris, Elizabeth J. "Buddhism and International Aid: A Case Study from Post-Tsunami Sri Lanka." In Hiroko Kawanami and Geoffrey Samuel, eds., *Buddhism, International Relief Work, and Civil Society*, pp. 1–26. New York: Palgrave Macmillan, 2013.

Harris, Elizabeth J. "Buddhist Empirical Realism and the Conduct of Armed Conflict." In Andrew Bartles-Smith, Kate Crosby, Peter Harvey, Asanga Tilakaratne, Daniel Ratheiser, Noel Maurer Trew, Stefania Travagnin, Elizabeth J. Harris, Venerable Mahinda Deegalle and Christina A. Kilby, eds., *Buddhism and International Humanitarian Law*, pp. 147–166. New York: Routledge, 2023.

Harvey, Peter. "'Freedom of the Will' in the Light of Theravada Buddhist Teachings." *Journal of Buddhist Ethics* 14, no. 1 (2007): 35–98.

Heim, Maria. *Theories of the Gift in South Asia: Hindu, Buddhist, and Jain Reflections on Dāna*. New York: Routledge, 2004.

Heim, Maria. *Voice of the Buddha: Buddhaghosa on the Immeasurable Words*. New York: Oxford University Press, 2018.

Hein, Jeremy and Tarique Niazi. "The Primordial Refugees: Religious Traditions, Global Forced Migration, and State-Society Relations." *International Sociology* 31, no. 6 (2016): 726–741. DOI: 10.1177/0268580916662388.

Heirman, Ann. "How to Deal with Dangerous and Annoying Animals: A *Vinaya* Perspective." *Religions* 10, no. 2 (2019): 1–17.

Hibbets, Maria. "Saving Them from Yourself: An Inquiry into the South Asian Gift of Fearlessness." *Journal of Religious Ethics* 27, no. 3 (1999): 435–462.

Hills, David. "Metaphor." In Edward N. Zalta and Uri Nodelman, eds., *The Stanford Encyclopedia of Philosophy*. Stanford, CA: The Metaphysics Research Lab, 2022. Entry last revised 12 August 2022. Accessed on 25 November 2025. https://plato.stanford.edu/archives/fall2024/entries/metaphor/.

Himalayan Art Resources. "Buddhist Deity: Tara, Eight Fears (set 1)." Rubin Museum of Art images. Photographed Image Copyright © 2004. Accessed on 12 December 2025. https://www.himalayanart.org/search/set.cfm?setID=70.

Himalayan Art Resources. "Tara & Eight Fears: Painting Set 1." Accessed on 29 December 2025. www.youtube.com/watch?v=REavkoZU-BM.

Hinton, D.E. "Auditory Hallucination Among Traumatized Cambodian Refugees: PTSD Association and Biocultural Shaping." *Culture, Medicine and Psychiatry* 45 (2021): 727–750.

Hinton, D.E., A. Hinton, K.-T. Eng, and S. Choung. "PTSD Severity and Key Idioms of Distress Among Rural Cambodians: The Results of a Needs Assessment Survey." In B. van Schaack, D. Reicherter and Y. Chhang, eds., *Cambodia's Hidden Scars: Trauma Psychology in the Wake of the Khmer Rouge*, pp. 47–68. Phnom Penh: Documentation Center of Cambodia (DC-Cam), 2011.

Hinton, D.E., A.L. Hinton, K.-T. Eng, and S. Choung. "PTSD and Key Somatic Complaints and Cultural Syndromes Among Rural Cambodians: The Results of a Needs Assessment Survey." *Medical Anthropology Quarterly* 26, no. 3 (2012): 383–407.

Hinton, D.E., A.L. Hinton, V. Pich, J.R. Loeum, and M.H. Pollack. "Nightmares Among Cambodian Refugees: The Breaching of Concentric Ontological

Security." *Culture, Medicine and Psychiatry* 33 (2009): 219–265. DOI: 10.1007/s11013-009-9131-9.

Hinton, D.E., M.A. Kredlow, V. Pich, E. Bui, and S.G. Hofmann. "The Relationship of PTSD to Key Somatic Complaints and Cultural Syndromes Among Cambodian Refugees Attending a Psychiatric Clinic: The Cambodian Somatic Symptom and Syndrome Inventory (CSSI)." *Transcultural Psychiatry* 50, no. 3 (2013): 347–370.

Hinton D.E., V. Pich, D. Chhean, and M.H. Pollack. "'The Ghost Pushes You Down': Sleep Paralysis-Type Panic Attacks in a Khmer Refugee Population." *Transcultural Psychiatry* 42, 1 (2005): 46–77.

Hinton, D.E., R. Reis, and J. de Jong. "Ghost Encounters Among Traumatized Cambodian Refugees: Severity, Relationship to PTSD, and Phenomenology." *Culture, Medicine and Psychiatry* 44 (2020): 333–359.

Hinton, Devon E., Rebecca A. Ojserkis, Baland Jalal, Sonith Peou, and Stefan G. Hofmann. "Loving-Kindness in the Treatment of Traumatized Refugees and Minority Groups: A Typology of Mindfulness and the Nodal Network Model of Affect and Affect Regulation." *Journal of Clinical Psychology* 69 (2013): 817–828.

Holy Bible, New Revised Standard Version, Anglicised. Accessed on 20 May 2026. www.biblegateway.com/versions/New-Revised-Standard-Version-Anglicised-NRSVA-Bible/.

Horstmann, Alexander. "Secular and Religious Sanctuaries: Interfaces of Humanitarianism and Self-Government of Karen Refugee-Migrants in Thai-Burmese Border Spaces." In Alexander Horstmann and Jin-Heon Jung, eds., *Building Noah's Ark for Migrants, Refugees, and Religious Communities*, pp. 129–156. New York: Palgrave Macmillan, 2015.

Horstmann, Alexander, and Jin-Heon Jung, eds. *Building Noah's Ark for Migrants, Refugees, and Religious Communities*. New York: Palgrave Macmillan, 2015.

Huntington, Samuel. "The Clash of Civilizations." *Foreign Affairs* 72, no. 3 (1993): 22–49.

International Committee of the Red Cross. "Faith-Based Organizations and Religious Leaders: Essential Partners in Humanitarian Action." Last modified 22 July 2015. Accessed on 12 September 2025. www.icrc.org/en/document/faith-based-organizations-and-religious-leaders-essential-partners-humanitarian-action.

International Committee of the Red Cross. *Gendered Impacts of Armed Conflict and Implications for the Application of International Humanitarian Law*. Geneva, 2022.

International Committee of the Red Cross. "Internally Displaced Persons and International Humanitarian Law (Factsheet)." 6 April 2022. Accessed on 25 July 2023. www.icrc.org/en/document/internally-displaced-persons-and-international-humanitarian-law-factsheet.

International Committee of the Red Cross. "Number of Missing People Registered with the Red Cross and Red Crescent Movement up Nearly 70% in Five Years." 29 August 2025. Accessed on 25 November 2025. www.icrc.org/en/statement/tragedy-of-missing-persons-urgently-requires-more-determined-international-response.

International Committee of the Red Cross. "Project on the Interface Between Buddhism and IHL." *Religion and Humanitarian Principles*. 2 March 2020. Accessed on 20 June 2023. https://blogs.icrc.org/religion-humanitarianprinciples/project-on-the-interface-between-buddhism-and-ihl/.

International Committee of the Red Cross. "Religion and Humanitarian Principles—About." Accessed on 12 September 2025. https://blogs.icrc.org/religion-humanitarianprinciples/about/.

International Committee of the Red Cross. "Rules." International Humanitarian Law Database. Accessed on 20 June 2023. https://ihl-databases.icrc.org/en/customary-ihl/v1.

International Committee of the Red Cross. "What is IHL?" 18 September 2015. Accessed on 20 June 2023. www.icrc.org/en/document/what-ihl.

International Rescue Committee. "Is it Legal to Cross the U.S. Border to Seek Asylum?" July 1, 2022. Accessed on 8 May 2024. www.rescue.org/article/it-legal-cross-us-border-seek-asylum.

Jahnke, Art. "How Cambodian Music Recalls Ancestors and Brings Comfort." *The Brink: Pioneering Research from Boston University*. 25 November 2019. Accessed on 12 December 2025. www.bu.edu/articles/2019/cambodian-ritual-music-and-dance/.

"Kacchapa-Jātaka" (The Tortoise That Loved His Home Too Much). In *The Jataka; or, Stories of the Buddha's Former Births,* edited by E.B. Cowell, vol. 2. no. 178, pp. 55–56. Translated from the Pāli by W.H.D. Rouse. Cambridge: Cambridge University Press, 1895. Accessed on 10 May 2024. www.pitt.edu/~dash/jataka.html#tortoiserefused.

Kent, Alexandra. "Reconfiguring Security: Buddhism and Moral Legitimacy in Cambodia." *Security Dialogue* 37, no. 3 (2006): 343–361. DOI: 10.1177/0967010606069179.

Khin Khin Ei. (trans. Khet Mar, English version by Joshua Lipes). "Myanmar Monk Rejects Terrorist Label Following Communal Clashes." *Radio Free Asia*. 21 June 2013. Accessed on 6 December 2025. www.rfa.org/english/news/myanmar/monk-06212013182954.html.

Kilby, Christina. "A Humanitarian Reading of the Vessantara Jataka." International Committee of the Red Cross, *Religion and Humanitarian Principles*. 7 October 2022. Accessed on 8 May 2024. https://blogs.icrc.org/religion-humanitarianprinciples/humanitarian-reading-vessantara-jataka/.

Kilby, Christina. "Buddhism and Migration." In Anna Rowlands and Elena Fiddian-Qasmiyeh, eds., *Oxford Handbook of Religion and Contemporary Migration*. New York: Oxford University Press, 2027, forthcoming.

Kilby, Christina. "Buddhism, Immigrants and Refugees." In Courtney Bruntz, ed., *Oxford Bibliographies in Buddhism*. New York: Oxford University Press, 2022.

Kilby, Christina. "Call For a Buddhism-Inspired Asian Regional Compact on Internal Displacement." *International Relations,* 25 January 2024. www.e-ir.info/2024/01/25/call-for-a-buddhism-inspired-asian-regional-compact-on-internal-displacement/

Kilby, Christina. "Global Refugee Crisis and the Gift of Fearlessness." *Journal of Buddhist Ethics* 26 (2019): 307–327. Accessed on 20 May 2026. https://blogs.dickinson.edu/buddhistethics/files/2019/12/Kilby_19_Final-1.pdf.

Kilby, Christina. "Legal Reasoning About Displacement and Responsibility: A Dialogue Between the Buddhist Monastic Discipline and IHL." *Journal of Buddhist Ethics* 30 (2023): 231–254. Accessed on 8 October 2023. https://blogs.dickinson.edu/buddhistethics/files/2023/10/Kilby_23_FD-final.pdf.

Kilby, Christina. "The Gift of Fearlessness: A Buddhist Framework for the Protection of Vulnerable Populations Under International Humanitarian Law." In Andrew Bartles-Smith, Kate Crosby, Peter Harvey, Asanga Tilakaratne, Daniel Ratheiser, Noel Maurer Trew, Stefania Travagnin and Elizabeth J. Harris, Venerable Mahinda Deegalle, and Christina A. Kilby. eds., *Buddhism and International Humanitarian Law*, pp. 330–342. New York: Routledge, 2023.

Kilby, Christina. "'The World is Without Shelter, Without Protector': Buddhism, the Protection of Displaced People, and International Humanitarian Law." In Deniz Coşan Eke and Eric M. Trinka, eds., *Religion, Religious Groups and Migration*, pp. 9–28. London: Transnational Press, 2023.

King, Sallie, ed. *Buddhist Visions of the Good Life for All*. New York: Routledge, 2021.

King, Sallie. "The Problems and Promise of Karma from an Engaged Buddhist Perspective." In Jake Davis, ed., *A Mirror is for Reflection: Understanding Buddhist Ethics*, pp. 166–183. Oxford: Oxford University Press, 2017.

Ladwig, Patrice. "Emotions and Narrative: Excessive Giving and Ethical Ambivalence in the Lao Vessantara Jātaka." In Steven Collins, ed., *Readings of the Vessantara Jātaka*, pp. 57–76. New York: Columbia University Press, 2016.

Langer, Rita. *Buddhist Rituals of Death and Rebirth: Contemporary Sri Lankan Practice and Its Origins*. London: Routledge, 2007.

Leaning, Jennifer, and Sam Arie. *Human Security: A Framework for Assessment in Conflict and Transition*. USAID Complex Emergency Response and Transition Initiative, December 2000.

Lopes, Ana C. *Tibetan Buddhism in Diaspora: Cultural Re-signification in Practice and Institutions*. London: Routledge, 2015.

Lopez, Donald. "Buddhism in the Real World." *Tricycle: The Buddhist Review* (Summer 2021). Accessed on 25 November 2025. https://tricycle.org/magazine/history-of-buddhism-and-activism/.

Luminous Wisdom. "A Brief Biography of Khenpo Tsultrim Lodrö." 28 February 2017. Accessed on 5 December 2025. www.luminouswisdom.org/index.php/biography/biography-2.

Makidono, Tomoko. "The Vessantara Jātaka in the Maṇi bka' 'bum and the Fifth Dalai Lama's 'Khrung rab." *The Indian International Journal of Buddhist Studies* 21 (2021), article 5. Accessed on 1 May 2024. https://digitalcommons.linfield.edu/iijbs/vol21/iss1/5.

Mavelli, Luca, and Erin K. Wilson, eds. *The Refugee Crisis and Religion: Secularism, Security and Hospitality in Question*. New York: Rowman and Littlefield, 2017.

McAra, S.A. "Indigenizing or Adapting? Importing Buddhism into a Settler-Colonial Society." *Journal of Global Buddhism* 8 (2007): 132–156.

McLellan, Janet. "Religious Responses to Bereavement, Grief, and Loss Among Refugees." *Journal of Loss and Trauma* 20, no. 2 (2014): 131–138. DOI: 10.1080/15325024.2013.833807.

"Measures on the Management of the Reincarnation of Living Buddhas in Tibetan Buddhism" (State Religious Affairs Bureau Order Number 5). Translated by the International Campaign for Tibet. Congressional-Executive Commission on China. 18 July 2007. Accessed on 26 November 2025. www.cecc.gov/resources/legal-provisions/measures-on-the-management-of-the-reincarnation-of-living-buddhas-in-0.

Men, Chean Rithy. "The Changing Religious Beliefs and Ritual Practices Among Cambodians in Diaspora." *Journal of Refugee Studies* 15, no. 2 (June 2002): 222–233. https://doi.org/10.1093/jrs/15.2.222.

Meyer, Birgit, and Peter van der Veer, eds. *Refugees and Religion: Ethnographic Studies of Global Trajectories*. London: Bloomsbury Academic, 2021.

"Migration and Migrants: A Global Overview." In *World Migration Report 2026*, chapter 2. International Organization for Migration. Accessed on 5 December 2025. https://worldmigrationreport.iom.int/what-we-do/world-migration-report-2026/chapter-2/refugees-and-asylum-seekers.

Mindrolling International. "On Rinpoche's Birthday: An Offering of Life." 26 August 2018. Accessed on 7 December 2025. www.khandrorinpoche.org/on-rinpoches-birthday-an-offering-of-life/.

mkhan po tshul khrims blo gros (Khenpo Tsultrim Lodrö). *shes rab sgron me'i 'od snang (Luminosity of the Lamp of Insight)*. 2013. Buddhist Digital Resource Center, bdr:W1AC345.

Monier-Williams, M. *Sanskrit-English Dictionary,* entry for 'saṃsāra.' Oxford: Clarendon Press, 1899. Accessed on 10 May 2024. www.sanskrit-lexicon.uni-koeln.de/scans/MWScan/2020/web/webtc/indexcaller.php.

Moore, Matthew J. *Buddhism and Political Theory*. New York: Oxford University Press, 2016.

Mørch, Maximillian. "Bhutan's Dark Secret: The Lhotsampa Expulsion: The Mass Deportation of Bhutanese-Nepalis in the 1990s Remains Unresolved 20 Years Later." *The Diplomat*. September 21, 2016. Accessed on 12 September 2025. https://thediplomat.com/2016/09/bhutans-dark-secret-the-lhotshampa-expulsion/.

"More than 100 Rohingya Refugees Jailed for Trying to Flee Myanmar Camps." *The Guardian*. 11 January 2023. Accessed on 28 November 2025. www.theguardian.com/world/2023/jan/11/more-than-100-rohingya-refugees-jailed-for-trying-to-flee-myanmar-camps.

"Myanmar Passes 'Anti-Polygamy' Law." *Deutsche Welle*, 31 August 2015. Accessed on 3 December 2025. www.dw.com/en/myanmar-passes-controversial-anti-polygamy-law/a-18684571.

Nāgārjuna. "bShes pa'i spring yig (Letter to a Friend)." *bsTan 'gyur* (sde dge), edited by zhu chen tshul khrims rin chen, translated from the Sanskrit by sKa ba dpal brtsegs, vol. 173, Delhi Karmapae Choedhey, Gyalwae Sungrab Partun Khang, 1982–1985, pp. 82–94. Buddhist Digital Resource Center (BDRC), purl.bdrc.io/resource/MW23703_4182.

Naidu, Maheshvari. "Displaced Sense: Displacement, Religion and Sense-Making." *Journal for the Study of Religion* 29, no. 1 (2016): 104–126.

Ngo, Tam T.T. and Nga T. Mai. "In Search of a Vietnamese Buddhist Space in Germany." In Birgit Meyer and Peter van der Veer, eds., *Refugees and Religion: Ethnographic Studies of Global Trajectories*, pp. 105–122. London: Bloomsbury Academic, 2021.

Nu Nu Lusan. "In Myanmar, A Monk Takes on the Junta." *The New Humanitarian,* 20 October 2022. Accessed on 26 November 2025. www.thenewhumanitarian.org/feature/2022/10/20/Myanmar-protests-monks-junta-Buddhist.

Nussbaum, Martha. *The New Religious Intolerance: Overcoming the Politics of Fear in an Anxious Age*. Cambridge, MA: Harvard University Press, 2012.

Ohnuma, Reiko. "The Gift of the Body and the Gift of Dharma." *History of Religions* 37, no. 4 (1998): 323–359.

Patrul Rinpoche. *Words of My Perfect Teacher: A Complete Translation of a Classic Introduction to Tibetan Buddhism*. Translated by the Padmakara Translation Group. New Haven: Yale University Press, 2011.

Philpott, Daniel. "The Challenge of September 11 to Secularism in International Relations." *World Politics* 55 (October 2002): 66–95.

Quran. Translation by M.A.S. Abdel Haleem. Accessed on 20 May 2026. https://quran.com/an-nisa/97?translations=85.

Rangkla, Prasert. "Refuge and Emplacement through Buddhism: Karen Refugees and Religious Practices in a Northwestern Border Town of Thailand." *Asia Pacific Journal of Anthropology* 14, no. 1 (2013): 8–22.

"Ratthapala Sutta: About Ratthapala" (MN 82), translated from the Pāli by Thanissaro Bhikkhu. *Access to Insight (BCBS Edition)*, 30 November 2013. Accessed on 20 May 2026. www.accesstoinsight.org/tipitaka/mn/mn.082.than.html.

Religions for Peace. "UNHCR-Religions for Peace Multi-Religious Council of Leaders." 13 April 2021. Accessed on 12 July 2024. www.rfp.org/unhcr-religions-for-peace-multi-religious-council-of-leaders/.

Richman, Paula, ed. *Questioning Ramayanas: A South Asian Tradition.* Berkeley: University of California Press, 2001.

Samarakoon, Bhagya. "Restraint in Warfare and Appamāda: the Concept of Collateral Damage in International Humanitarian Law in Light of the Buddha's Last Words." In Andrew Bartles-Smith, Kate Crosby, Peter Harvey, Asanga Tilakaratne, Daniel Ratheiser, Noel Maurer Trew, Stefania Travagnin, Elizabeth J. Harris, Venerable Mahinda Deegalle and Christina A. Kilby, eds., *Buddhism and International Humanitarian Law*, pp. 307–329. New York: Routledge, 2023.

Sangasumana, Ven. Pinnawala. "Buddhist Perspective on Addressing War-Displacement." In *Buddhist Approach to Political Conflict and Peace Development.* UNDV Conference Volume (The International Buddhist Conference on the United Nations Day of Vesak Celebrations), pp. 85-101. Bangkok: Mahachulalongkornrajavidyalaya University, 2009.

Sangasumana, Ven. Pinnawala. "The Role of Buddhist Monks in Disaster Management: A Case Study from Sri Lanka." United Nations Day of Vesak Conference. *Social Science Research Network*, 6 May 2011. https://papers.ssrn.com/sol3/papers.cfm?abstract_id=3455602.

Sangasumana, Ven. Pinnawala. "Mapping Inbetweenness: A Conceptual Model for War-Induced Resettlement in Sri Lanka." *Social Science Research Network*, 26 November 2012. http://doi.org/10.2139/ssrn.3455629.

Schonthal, Benjamin. "Buddhist Legal Pluralism: Looking Again at Monastic Governance in Modern South and Southeast Asia." *Buddhism, Law & Society* 3 (2017–18): vii–xxxvii.

Schopen, Gregory. "Counting the Buddha and the Local Spirits in: A Monastic Ritual of Inclusion for the Rain Retreat." *Journal of Indian Philosophy* 30, no. 4 (2002): 359–88.

Schopen, Gregory. "Hierarchy and Housing in a Buddhist Monastic Code: A Translation of the Sanskrit Text of the *Śayanāsanavastu* of the *Mūlasarvāstivāda -vinaya*—Part 1." *Buddhist Literature* 2 (2000): 92–196.

Shah, S.A. "Ethnomedical Best Practices for International Psychosocial Efforts in Disaster and Trauma." In J.P. Wilson and C.S. Tang, eds., *Cross-Cultural Assessment of Psychological Trauma and PTSD*, pp. 51–64. New York: Springer, 2007.

Sharma, Ursula. "Theodicy and the Doctrine of Karma." *Man, New Series* 8, no. 3 (1973): 347–364.

Shire, Warsan. "'No One Puts their Children in a Boat Unless the Water is Safer than the Land': A Poem about Seeking Asylum." Republished by *Global Citizen* on 7 September 2015. Accessed on 29 August 2025. www.globalcitizen.org/en/content/no-one-puts-their-children-in-a-boat-unless-the-wa/.

"Sigalovada Sutta: The Buddha's Advice to Sigala" (DN 31). Translated from the Pāli by John Kelly, Sue Sawyer, and Victoria Yareham. *Access to Insight (BCBS Edition)*, 30 November 2013. Accessed on 29 December 2025. www.accesstoinsight.org/tipitaka/dn/dn.31.0.ksw0.html.

"Skinny Gotami & the Mustard Seed" (Commentary to the Therīgāthā 10.1). Translated by Andrew Olendzki. *Access to Insight (BCBS Edition)*, 30 November 2013. Accessed on 25 November 2025. www.accesstoinsight.org/noncanon/comy/thiga-10-01-ao0.html.

Smart, Ninian. *The World's Religions*. Cambridge: Cambridge University Press, 1998.

sum pa mkhan po ye shes dpal 'byor (Sumpa Khenpo Yeshé Penjor). *Expressing the Conduct of the Supreme Pandita Sumpa Yeshé Penjor: Alchemy for the Ear (paN+Di ta sum pa ye shes dpal 'byor mchog gi spyod tshul brjod pa sgra 'dzin bcud len)*. In *Collected Works* 8 (nya), 373–960. Beijing: Tibetan Civilization Publishing House of China, 2001. Buddhist Digital Resource Center work ID W25006. Accessed on 6 May 2026. Buddhist Digital Resource Center (BDRC), purl.bdrc.io/resource/MW25006.

Thānissaro Bhikkhu. "Freedom from Fear." *Access to Insight (BCBS Edition)*, 5 June 2010. Accessed on 8 December 2025. www.accesstoinsight.org/lib/authors/thanissaro/fear.html.

Thānissaro Bhikkhu. "Refuge: An Introduction to the Buddha, Dhamma, & Sangha." *Access to Insight (BCBS Edition)*, 30 November 2013. Accessed on 25 November 2025. www.accesstoinsight.org/lib/authors/thanissaro/refuge.html.

Thānissaro Bhikkhu. *The Buddhist Monastic Code I: The Pāṭimokkha Rules Translated and Explained*. Valley Center, CA: Metta Forest Monastery, 1994.

Thānissaro Bhikkhu. *The Buddhist Monastic Code II: The Khandhaka Rules Translated and Explained*. Valley Center, CA: Metta Forest Monastery, 2001.

"The Book of Protection: Paritta." Translated from the original Pāli, with introductory essay and explanatory notes by Piyadassi Thera, with a foreword by V.F. Gunaratna. *Access to Insight (BCBS Edition*), 30 November 2013. Accessed on 1 January 2026. www.accesstoinsight.org/lib/authors/piyadassi/protection.html.

Thubten Chodron. *How to Free Your Mind: The Practice of Tara the Liberator*. Boulder, CO: Shambhala Publications, 2013.

Trew, Noel Maurer. "'Not Knowing is Most Intimate'; Koan Practice and the Fog of War." In Andrew Bartles-Smith, Kate Crosby, Peter Harvey, Asanga Tilakaratne, Daniel Ratheiser, Noel Maurer Trew, Stefania Travagnin, Elizabeth J. Harris, Venerable Mahinda Deegalle and Christina A. Kilby, eds., *Buddhism and International Humanitarian Law*, pp. 228–256. New York: Routledge, 2023.

Trinka, Eric M. "Migration and Internal Religious Pluralism: A Review of Present Findings." *The Journal of Interreligious Studies* 28 (2019): 20–37.

Tsong-kha-pa. *The Great Treatise on the Stages of the Path (Lam Rim Chen Mo)*, volume 2. Translated by the Lamrim Chenmo Translation Committee, ed. Guy Newland and Joshua Cutler. Boston: Snow Lion, 2014.

Tuan, Yi-fu with Martha A. Strawn, ed. *Religion: From Place to Placelessness*. Chicago, IL: University of Chicago Press, 2009.

Tweed, Thomas. *Crossing and Dwelling: A Theory of Religion*. Cambridge, MA: Harvard University Press, 2006.

"UN Human Rights Chief Points to 'Textbook Example of Ethnic Cleansing' in Myanmar." *UN News*, 11 September 2017. Accessed on 28 November 2025. https://news.un.org/en/story/2017/09/564622-un-human-rights-chief-points-textbook-example-ethnic-cleansing-myanmar.

United Nations. *United Nations Charter (full text)*. [26 June 1945]. Accessed on 12 September 2025. www.un.org/en/about-us/un-charter/full-text.

United Nations Development Programme. *Human Development Report 1994*. New York: Oxford University Press, 1994. Accessed on 12 December 2025. https://hdr.undp.org/content/human-development-report-1994.

United Nations High Commissioner for Refugees. "2026 Projected Global Resettlement Needs (PGRN)." 24 June 2025. Accessed on 5 December 2025. www.unhcr.org/media/projected-global-resettlement-needs-2026.

United Nations High Commissioner for Refugees. "Acute Food Insecurity and Malnutrition Rise for Sixth Consecutive Year in World's Most Fragile Regions – New Report." 16 May 2025. Accessed on 29 August 2025. www.unhcr.org/news/announcements/acute-food-insecurity-and-malnutrition-rise-sixth-consecutive-year-world-s-most.

United Nations High Commissioner for Refugees. "Figures at a Glance." Accessed on 29 August 2025. www.unhcr.org/us/about-unhcr/overview/figures-glance.

United Nations High Commissioner for Refugees. *Principles and Standards for Settlement Planning*. Updated 26 June 2025. Accessed on 26 November 2025. https://emergency.unhcr.org/emergency-assistance/settlement-and-shelter/guidance-settlements/principles-standards-settlement-planning.

United Nations High Commissioner for Refugees. *Resettlement Handbook*. Accessed on 5 December 2025 at www.unhcr.org/resettlement-handbook/3-resettlement-submission-categories/3-2-the-resettlement-submission-categories/

United Nations High Commissioner for Refugees. "Rohingya Refugee Crisis Explained." 22 August 2024. Accessed on 26 November 2025. www.unrefugees.org/news/rohingya-refugee-crisis-explained/.

United Nations High Commissioner for Refugees. *Convention and Protocol Relating to the Status of Refugees*. [1951 and 1967.] Accessed 18 November 2018. www.unhcr.org/en-us/1951-refugee-convention.html.

United Nations Office of the High Commissioner for Human Rights. "Faith for Rights." Accessed on 12 September 2025. www.ohchr.org/en/faith-for-rights.

Upāsakaśilasūtra (*The Sutra on Upāsaka Precepts*). Translated by Shih, Heng-ching. Berkeley: Bukkhyō Dendō Kyōkai and Numata Center for Buddhist Translation and Research, 1991.

Usarski, Frank. "'The Last Missionary to Leave the Temple Should Turn Off the Light': Sociological Remarks on the Decline of Japanese 'Immigrant' Buddhism in Brazil." *Japanese Journal of Religious Studies* 35, no. 1 (2008): 39–59.

van den Assum, Laetitia. "Out of the Spotlight, Myanmar's Rohingya Face Worst Violence in 7 Years." United States Institute of Peace, 2024. Accessed on 28 November 2025. www.usip.org/publications/2024/09/out-spotlight-myanmars-rohingya-face-worst-violence-7-years.

"Varṣa Skandhaka." *Dharmaguptaka Vinaya,* fascicle 37. Translated by Christie Chang, ed. Thubten Chodron and Thubten Damcho. *Taishō Tripiṭaka (*CBETA edition*)*, vol. 22. Taipei: Bodhi Foundation for Culture and Education, 2014. Accessed on 20 May 2026. https://dharmaguptakavinaya.wordpress.com/wp-content/uploads/2014/06/varsa-skandhaka-2014-06-22-bilingual.pdf.

"Vessantara-Jātaka." *The Jataka, Vol. VI*, translated by E.B. Cowell and W.H.D. Rouse, 1907. No. 547, pp. 246–306. Accessed on 3 January 2026. https://sacred-texts.com/bud/j6/j6013.htm.

Vu, A, A. Adam, A. Wirtz, K. Pham, L. Rubenstein, N. Glass, C. Beyrer, and S. Singh. "The Prevalence of Sexual Violence among Female Refugees in Complex

Humanitarian Emergencies: A Systematic Review and Meta-analysis." *PLoS Currents* 6 (18 March 2014). PMID: 24818066.

Wakefield, Alex. "The Missing and Their Families: Buddhism and the Role of Ritual in Processing Grief and Ambiguous Loss." *Journal of Buddhist Ethics* 30 (2023): 255–283.

Weick, Karl E. "The Collapse of Sensemaking in Organizations: The Mann Gulch Disaster." *Administrative Science Quarterly* 38 (1993): 628–652.

Werth, Paul. *Text Worlds: Representing Conceptual Space in Discourse*. Harlow, UK: Longman, 1999.

Wike, Richard, Bruce Stokes, and Katie Simmons. "Europeans Fear Wave of Refugees Will Mean More Terrorism, Fewer Jobs." *Pew Research Forum* (11 July 2016). Accessed on 18 November 2018. www.pewglobal.org/2016/07/11/europeans-fear-wave-of-refugees-will-mean-more-terrorism-fewer-jobs/.

Williams, Duncan Ryūken. *American Sutra: A Story of Faith and Freedom in the Second World War*. Cambridge, MA: Harvard University Press, 2019.

Yifa. *The Origins of Buddhist Monastic Codes in China: An Annotated Translation and Study of the Chanyuan Qinggui*. Honolulu: University of Hawai'i Press, 2002.

Zornberg, Avivah Gottlieb. *The Particulars of Rapture: Reflections on Exodus*. New York: Doubleday, 2011.

Index

Note: Endnotes are indicated by the page number followed by 'n' and the endnote number (e.g., 20n1 refers to endnote 1 on page 20.)

www.ingramcontent.com/pod-product-compliance
Lightning Source LLC
LaVergne TN
LVHW010547300926
849162LV00002B/255